The Pedagogies of Cultural Studies

Pedagogy is foundational to cultural studies. At the very outset cultural studies positioned pedagogy as significantly more than just formalised and institutionally-centred activations of teaching and learning. For cultural studies, pedagogy is witnessed in the social practices, relationships, routines and life-ways that people engage in the living of lives.

This collection presents accounts that move beyond simple (and simplistic) articulations of pedagogy as occurring solely within the classroom. Taking the Self, the disciplinary formations and institutional settings of cultural studies as its sites of activation, The Pedagogies of Cultural Studies seeks to look again at the implications presented by pedagogy and the foundation that pedagogy provides for doing cultural studies. Evident not only in the objects of study prefigured by cultural studies but also in the practice of the discipline itself, pedagogy mediates cultural studies' disciplinary terrain and the signatures that shape its conduct.

Andrew Hickey is Associate Professor in Communications in the School of Arts and Communication, University of Southern Queensland, and President of the Cultural Studies Association of Australasia.

Routledge Research in Cultural and Media Studies

For a full list of titles in this series, please visit www.routledge.com.

55 **Transnational Horror Across Visual Media**
Fragmented Bodies
Edited by Dana Och and Kirsten Strayer

56 **International Perspectives on Chicana/o Studies**
"This World is My Place"
Edited by Catherine Leen and Niamh Thornton

57 **Comics and the Senses**
A Multisensory Approach to Comics and Graphic Novels
Ian Hague

58 **Popular Culture in Africa**
The Episteme of the Everyday
Edited by Stephanie Newell and Onookome Okome

59 **Transgender Experience**
Place, Ethnicity, and Visibility
Edited by Chantal Zabus and David Coad

60 **Radio's Digital Dilemma**
Broadcasting in the Twenty-First Century
John Nathan Anderson

61 **Documentary's Awkward Turn**
Cringe Comedy and Media Spectatorship
Jason Middleton

62 **Serialization in Popular Culture**
Edited by Rob Allen and Thijs van den Berg

63 **Gender and Humor**
Interdisciplinary and International Perspectives
Edited by Delia Chiaro and Raffaella Baccolini

64 **Studies of Video Practices**
Video at Work
Edited by Mathias Broth, Eric Laurier, and Lorenza Mondada

65 **The Memory of Sound**
Preserving the Sonic Past
Seán Street

66 **American Representations of Post-Communism**
Television, Travel Sites, and Post-Cold War Narratives
Andaluna Borcila

67 **Media and the Ecological Crisis**
Edited by Richard Maxwell, Jon Raundalen, and Nina Lager Vestberg

68 **Representing Multiculturalism in Comics and Graphic Novels**
Edited by Carolene Ayaka and Ian Hague

69 **Media Independence**
Working with Freedom or Working for Free?
Edited by James Bennett and Niki Strange

70 Neuroscience and Media
New Understandings and Representations
Edited by Michael Grabowski

71 American Media and the Memory of World War II
Debra Ramsay

72 International Perspectives on Shojo and Shojo Manga
The Influence of Girl Culture
Edited by Masami Toku

73 The Borders of Subculture
Resistance and the Mainstream
Edited by Alexander Dhoest, Steven Malliet, Barbara Segaert, and Jacques Haers

74 Media Education for a Digital Generation
Edited by Julie Frechette and Rob Williams

75 Spanish-Language Television in the United States
Fifty Years of Development
Kenton T. Wilkinson

76 Embodied Metaphors in Film, Television, and Video Games
Cognitive Approaches
Edited by Kathrin Fahlenbrach

77 Critical Animal and Media Studies
Communication for Nonhuman Animal Advocacy
Edited by Núria Almiron, Matthew Cole, and Carrie P. Freeman

78 The Middle Class in Emerging Societies
Consumers, Lifestyles and Markets
Edited by Leslie L. Marsh and Hongmei Li

79 A Cultural Approach to Emotional Disorders
Psychological and Aesthetic Interpretations
E. Deidre Pribram

80 Biopolitical Media
Catastrophe, Immunity and Bare Life
Allen Meek

81 The Emotional Life of Postmodern Film
Affect Theory's Other
Pansy Duncan

82 Social Memory Technology
Theory, Practice, Action
Karen Worcman and Joanne Garde-Hansen

83 Reviving Gramsci
Crisis, Communication, and Change
Marco Briziarelli and Susana Martínez Guillem

84 Motherhood in the Media
Infanticide, Journalism, and the Digital Age
Barbara Barnett

85 The Pedagogies of Cultural Studies
Edited by Andrew Hickey

The Pedagogies of Cultural Studies

Edited by
Andrew Hickey

NEW YORK AND LONDON

First published 2016
by Routledge
711 Third Avenue, New York, NY 10017

and by Routledge
2 Park Square, Milton Park, Abingdon, Oxon OX14 4RN

First issued in paperback 2018

Routledge is an imprint of the Taylor & Francis Group, an informa business

© 2016 Taylor & Francis

The right of the editor to be identified as the author of the editorial material, and of the authors for their individual chapters, has been asserted in accordance with sections 77 and 78 of the Copyright, Designs and Patents Act 1988.

All rights reserved. No part of this book may be reprinted or reproduced or utilised in any form or by any electronic, mechanical, or other means, now known or hereafter invented, including photocopying and recording, or in any information storage or retrieval system, without permission in writing from the publishers.

Trademark notice: Product or corporate names may be trademarks or registered trademarks, and are used only for identification and explanation without intent to infringe.

Library of Congress Cataloging-in-Publication Data

Names: Hickey, Andrew T., 1977– editor.
Title: The pedagogies of cultural studies / edited by Andrew Hickey.
Description: New York: Routledge, [2016] |
Series: Routledge research in cultural and media studies; 85 | Includes bibliographical references and index.
Identifiers: LCCN 2015044962
Subjects: LCSH: Culture—Study and teaching. | Pedagogical content knowledge.
Classification: LCC HM623 .P43 2016 | DDC 306—dc23LC record available at http://lccn.loc.gov/2015044962

ISBN 13: 978-1-138-59808-9 (pbk)
ISBN 13: 978-1-138-91631-9 (hbk)

Typeset in Sabon
by codeMantra

For Chris, my brother, my teacher

Contents

List of Figures   xi
Acknowledgments   xiii
Foreword   xv
GRAEME TURNER

SECTION I
The Embodiment of Cultural Studies/ The Embodiment of Pedagogy

1 The Pedagogies of Cultural Studies: A Short Account of the Current State of Cultural Studies   3
ANDREW HICKEY

2 Cultural Studies and the Pedagogy of Community-Engaged Research   24
ROB GARBUTT

3 Learning to be Men: Masculinities, Pedagogy, and Science Fiction   39
LINDA WIGHT

4 Ramping Up Cultural Studies: Pedagogy and the Activation of Knowledge   51
BADEN OFFORD

SECTION II
Alterity, the Other and the Pedagogical Exchange

5 Creative Practice as Pedagogy: An Ecology of Experimentation   71
KIM SATCHELL

6 The Tactical Researcher: Cultural Studies Research as Pedagogy   93
AMANDA THIRD

7 Questioning Care   116
    LISA SLATER

SECTION III
The Sites of Cultural Studies Pedagogy

 8 Cultural Studies, Pedagogy and Reimagining
    Multicultural Education: Working with Teachers
    to Effect Change in Schools   133
    MEGAN WATKINS

 9 Cultural Studies, DIY Pedagogies, and Storytelling   149
    GREGORY MARTIN AND ANDREW HICKEY

10 Lessons from the Site: Catastrophe and Cultural Studies   165
    KATRINA SCHLUNKE

11 Women Who Surf: Female Difference, Intersecting
    Subjectivities and Cultural Pedagogies   179
    REBECCA OLIVE

12 Notes Toward a *Signature Pedagogy* for Cultural Studies:
    Looking Again at Cultural Studies' Disciplinary Boundaries   196
    ANDREW HICKEY

    Contributors   215
    Index   219

List of Figures

5.1	Look at me now: Headland and South Solitary Island. Photograph Kim Satchell.	73
5.2	Eagle ancestor totem. Artwork Kim Satchell. Photograph Shekinah Satchell.	75
5.3	Kim Satchell on a finless surfboard design, gliding in the barrel. Photograph Nicky Schmidenberg.	78
5.4	Strange handmade surfboard designs for auto-choreography and body English. Photograph Shekinah Satchell.	81
5.5	Fish ancestor totem. Artwork Kim Satchell. Photograph Shekinah Satchell.	83
5.6	Catch of the day. Artwork Kim Satchell. Photograph Shekinah Satchell.	85
5.7	Self-formation: a practice of soul-making. Artwork Kim Satchell. Photograph Shekinah Satchell.	87
10.1	Writing on. Photograph Katrina Schlunke.	169

Acknowledgments

This volume represents the outcome of a collective project that grew from the symposium *Cultural Studies on the Divide: the Pedagogies of Cultural Studies*, a gathering of cultural studies scholars hosted by the University of Southern Queensland in February 2014. The symposium became possible because of the coalescence of several avenues of opportunity. Funding provided through an Australian Government *Collaborative Research Network* initiative enabled the symposium to be convened. To Mark Harvey in particular, thank you for having faith in this project.

Just as importantly, the conceptual provocation for this event drew from earlier discussions developed through, what its participants have called, the *Cavanbah Collective*. This group of cultural studies scholars and fellow travelers, of whom I am humbled to be a part, consists of several of the contributors to this volume—Baden Offord, Rob Garbutt, Kim Satchell, and Rebecca Olive—as well as scholars including Soenke Biermann, Nigel Hayes, and Elizabeth Stephens. Cavanbah meets regularly, although informally, to talk all things cultural studies. The group functions as part think-tank, peer network, critical complex, and collegial support system. I am deeply grateful for the opportunity to be a part of Cavanbah and the chance it provides to talk through ideas such as those presented in this volume.

A special thanks is due to each of the contributors. In a higher education landscape of upheaval and change, where decreasing time to devote to such activities as dialogue and discussion is ever present, it would have been far easier for each contributor to simply decline the invitation to write for this volume. It is with significant appreciation for their imaginative consideration of pedagogy and cultural studies that I thank the authors presented here. For the contribution of the *Foreword*, Graeme Turner deserves special mention for his willingness to undertake the task of providing the opening provocation. What an honor it is to have his words open this volume.

Appreciation is extended to Nigel Hayes and Soenke Biermann whose active participation, good humor, and company made *Cultural Studies on the Divide* the symposium it was. While it may not be apparent in name, their presence is nonetheless marked throughout this volume.

At the University of Southern Queensland, many current and former colleagues should be recognized for their work in assisting both the conduct of

Cultural Studies on the Divide and this book. Louise Patching and Marissa Parker in particular were always on hand for advice and assistance with the practical elements of dealing with university processes. Carly Smith's sagely reviews of my own contributions were readily undertaken and offered with constructive rigor. Chris Lee, Pat Danaher, Lorelle Burton, Thiru Aravinthan, and Karen Trimmer provided the impetus for the symposium and subsequently this volume.

Finally, the team at Routledge, in particular Andrew Weckenmann, Felisa Salvago-Keyes, and Allie Simmons enabled the smooth development and production of this volume. Your guidance and patience as this work came together was also much appreciated.

To you all, thank you for allowing this volume to materialize.

Andrew Hickey

Foreword

Graeme Turner

In many locations today, maybe even in most, the professional life of those who teach in the university is getting harder. Employment is becoming more precarious as casual and short-term appointments become the default first choice for underfunded teaching departments, while the burgeoning culture of monitoring and assessment is there to continually remind those who *do* have jobs of the benchmarks of performance they are meant to meet. All the while, funding declines as the policy settings for higher education increasingly privilege the maintenance of the science, technology, engineering, and mathematics (STEM) disciplines in research, and an instrumentalist training agenda in teaching. These are policy orientations which do not serve disciplines in the humanities well. Cultural studies, while not experiencing the kinds of pressures felt in, say, classics, has found it more challenging to prosper in the 2000s than it did during the 1980s and 1990s. It also faces significant competition; cultural studies' success in developing fields of teaching and research around the media and popular culture has shown the way to emerging fields from within the humanities and social sciences. In such a context, then, it is not surprising to be told that the heyday of cultural studies is over, that students are no longer interested in ideas such as those animated by cultural studies, and that those employed to teach cultural studies need to shift their focus toward more applied or vocational programs.

There is enough to such suggestions to give them some traction; unfortunately, in some universities now, cultural studies is losing some of its appeal to undergraduates and thus attraction for university administrators. Among the many factors implicated in this, admittedly uneven, tendency is, paradoxically, cultural studies' outstanding success as a research discipline. Many of those who once led the teaching of cultural studies in Australia now devote most of their energies to research, leaving the prosecution of the teaching of cultural studies to junior colleagues employed on sessional contracts, separated from the development of curricula, and facing an uncertain professional future. In Australia, at least, teaching is in danger of becoming a consolation prize for those who are unable to secure research funding. The long-term structural effect of this on the sector is corrosive, but it also has consequences on the development and renovation of teaching programs, the mentoring of staff members new to teaching, and the vitality and responsiveness the discipline demonstrates in its teaching practices. Consequently, while our research is looking good, we need to look carefully at what now constitutes the dominant patterns of the teaching of cultural studies.

I have suggested this in a number of locations before, accusing cultural studies in Australia, but also elsewhere, of having lost its interest in pedagogy and in danger of becoming complacent in its mission and theoreticist in its approaches to the teaching of undergraduates. The simple version of this position argues that the original novelty of cultural studies as a teaching program—that is, its acceptance of the popular as a site of cultural production and consumption, its provision of new modes of analysis for the understanding of everyday life, and its interest in taking seriously the role that popular media forms play in our lives—was of considerable assistance to us at the beginning. There was an implied pedagogy in the very fact that we took our students' everyday experiences seriously, and the dominance of textual analysis of these experiences as a major strategy for both the practice and the pedagogy of cultural studies was helpful in demonstrating what we might learn from using cultural studies methods. There was a genuine excitement at being able to approach our topics, and mobilize tools of analysis, in new and productive ways. Cultural studies is no longer novel, however, and it hasn't been so for quite a long time. Many of its insights and assumptions have become part of the common sense of the culture and some of its favorite tools of analysis are now being taught to students in high school, let alone elsewhere in the university. The problem is that just as this was starting to become clear, cultural studies had moved on. With some important exceptions, for much of cultural studies, teaching was no longer where its heart was. It had made the transition from being a critical, to a research, discipline (and that is another story I won't go into here). What Stuart Hall had famously described as the work of 'theoretical clarification' had begun to take on a life of its own, a life that was not necessarily directed toward taking us to the 'somewhere more important' he had nominated as the goal of theory. Instead, in my view, as a gradual tendency, it took us away from our students' interests in favor of following our own. There is nothing wrong with that, in principle, but it was not partnered with an equivalent interest in tailoring our pedagogic practices in the classroom and the content of our curricula to the changing contexts into which we were teaching. I don't think it is unfair to argue that the history of the teaching of cultural studies in the West over the last decade has tended toward the complacent rather than the adventurous. For a long time, with notable exceptions such as Henry Giroux, very few people talked in print about their teaching at all. Somehow, despite reminders from figures such as Larry Grossberg, we seemed to forget that teaching was one of the fundamental ways of 'doing cultural studies'.

It is pleasing, then, to see the pedagogies of cultural studies take their place as the subject of this collection. It includes essays which engage directly and explicitly with the practice of teaching cultural studies in the university today—and provides examples of how that might be most usefully done, as well as evidence of how well they have worked for their students. These are very much discussions that need to be had within cultural studies if it is to revitalize not only its teaching curriculum, but also its relations with its students. There are also essays here which broaden the notion of pedagogy to claim it as among the core capacities of the project of cultural studies. Several essays present accounts of cultural studies practices and events serving as a form of public pedagogy, teaching communities about their political and social possibilities; in other essays, cultural studies research is situated as a mode of public pedagogic 'engagement'. Along the way, we encounter repeated demonstrations of the continuing political salience of cultural studies within the university and within the community as a whole. Significantly, there is no sense, in these accounts, of the field winding down or of its teaching programs losing their relevance or their power to inspire students; indeed, several contributors present persuasive alternative accounts. In the current environment, it is certainly welcome to read such strong demonstrations of the resilience of the field and the commitment of those who teach it.

Hopefully, this volume is a sign of an emerging and more diverse conversation within cultural studies about how we go about teaching our programs today in a manner that is more responsive to current conditions as well as to the interests and needs of our students. As a significant provocation to such a conversation, the volume concludes with Andrew Hickey's discussion of the possibility of developing what he calls 'signature cultural studies pedagogies'. He resists the temptation to proceed straight to nominating what these might be, but he does argue for a connection between such pedagogies and a cultural studies epistemology. This is a brave note to end on, and a good platform for the discussion of the pedagogies of cultural studies for the future.

Section I
The Embodiment of Cultural Studies/The Embodiment of Pedagogy

1 The Pedagogies of Cultural Studies

A Short Account of the Current State of Cultural Studies

Andrew Hickey

From February 3 to 5, 2014, a group of scholars broadly connected to cultural studies convened at the University of Southern Queensland, Australia, to consider the place of pedagogy within current cultural studies scholarship. Working from the provocation that the title of the symposium provided, *Cultural Studies on the Divide: the Pedagogies of Cultural Studies*, the participants gave attention to the serious treatment of pedagogy as both a practice *and* conceptual motif through which cultural studies might be (re)imagined. The participants convened to consider what the enactment of cultural studies suggests in this moment, and how the place that cultural studies has carved out within the humanities (and higher education more generally) might continue to be imagined, pedagogically.

The place of pedagogy *within* cultural studies provided the point of focus for the discussion, but importantly, pedagogy came to be mobilized somewhat loosely in an attempt to move beyond stock definitions that delimit pedagogy (and the pedagogical) to little more than codified sets of practice deployed in formal 'classroom' settings. We sought to open for consideration pedagogy as something far larger—as something also situated within the research act, as demonstrated in academic public engagement, as something writ through scholarly social activism, and indeed as evidenced in the *coming-to-be* a cultural studies scholar. In this sense pedagogy presented as far more than that which occurs as an expression of formal education and provided for our discussions "a defining principle of a wide ranging set of cultural apparatuses" (Hammer and Kellner 2009: 91) useful for charting and understanding *practice*.

In charting the ways that the pedagogic infiltrates, enables, frames, and situates cultural studies in these multiple ways, the dialogue that developed during *Cultural Studies on the Divide* provoked a theorization of pedagogy as foundational to the 'doing' of cultural studies. It also allowed for an explication of what pedagogy might provide for the reimagining of cultural studies as a discipline. Our attention was focused specifically on what cultural studies' pedagogy might be, and how such formations might find activation within the practice spaces of the discipline. In digging into the pedagogies of cultural studies, we opened the opportunity to look again at what constitutes the discipline and how the discipline comes to be enacted.

Specific attention was given during the dialogues to what the pedagogies of cultural studies might reveal about the deepest held and most carefully guarded assumptions that carry through the discipline. Pedagogy in this sense became a means of *diagnosis* as much as a point of practice. This volume continues this concern from *Cultural Studies on the Divide* and presents an articulation of pedagogy that moves beyond well-worn (and incomplete) formulations of pedagogy as the 'art and science' of teaching and learning to consider pedagogy as a mode of explication for understanding the workings of the discipline itself. It is a mistake to reduce pedagogy to narrow definitions of formalized teaching and learning alone, aimed as these are toward *externally* positioned subjects. In taking a far wider consideration of pedagogy as that which includes the explication of the ways cultural studies is engaged with and expressed by its practitioners—through the ways its practitioners *come to* and enact the discipline—this volume presents pedagogy as crucial to the very workings of the discipline.

To recast one of the foundational assertions of cultural studies as a point of reference, we argue here that pedagogy is identifiable within:

> the whole environment, its institutions and relationships ... the field in which our ideas of the world, of ourselves and of our possibilities, are most widely and often most powerfully formed and disseminated.
> (Williams 1967: 15–16)

Pedagogy is also inherent in the workings of these relationships as they come to be practiced under the name of 'cultural studies'. When considered as itself an institution and set of relationships, the 'whole environment' of the discipline presents as a multidimensional formation of practices that are conveyed pedagogically, defined by the ways these come to be learned and enacted as expressions of the discipline.

The project core to this book sets out this application of pedagogy as a *mobilizing* concept. In taking this approach, this volume asks for the (re)consideration of pedagogy as an opportunity for inquiry, a conceptual apparatus made visible in practice and through which the disposition core to cultural studies might come to be understood and interrogated. This view of pedagogy suggests that it is something *performed*, with pedagogy taken throughout this volume as being suggestive of action. Hammer and Kellner (2009) put it nicely when noting that "cultural studies must be grounded in an act of doing" (93), with the realization of the discipline carried through the enactment that its practice provides. In doing cultural studies, the pedagogical is manifest, and with this realization of the pedagogic apparent, insight into the inner workings of the discipline is revealed. It is with that which comes to be taught and learned through the disciplinary formulations of cultural studies that our attention is given in this volume.

The arguments contained within the chapters that follow position pedagogy as a lens—a point of diagnosis—through which a deep interrogation of cultural studies might be made. Importantly, the contributions to this volume seek not only to offer a prescription for the continued practice of cultural studies, as indicated through the explication of the authors' own idiosyncratic applications of what each see as 'cultural studies', but concomitantly to open for scrutiny some of the more problematic aspects of *coming-to* cultural studies and the act of *being* a cultural studies scholar that this suggests. It is with the attendant assumptions that drive contemporary cultural studies as a discipline and the risks that doing cultural studies in this moment rouse, that this volume draws its impetus. In setting out to consider these aspects of cultural studies, we suggest that it is with pedagogy that a sense of what cultural studies *is* and what it should continue to be might be exposed. Pedagogy is the point at which the deepest assumptions of the discipline find articulation in practice, but it is also with pedagogy that the discipline might be interrogated.

Context and Self

It was with attention to the *contexts* (multiple as these are) within which the practice of cultural studies is set that a feature theme for the symposium emerged. Although the explicit focus of the symposium was with pedagogy and the place pedagogy holds according to the practice of the discipline, attention to context provided a sense of how it was that the 'doing' of cultural studies gained form. Several speakers discussed the contexts extant within what has come to be called the 'corporate university' (Aronowitz and Giroux 2000; Giroux and Myrsiades 2001) and how it is that the dramatic changes that have occurred within higher education systems in recent decades have affected what comes to be done under the name of cultural studies. Others highlighted pressures within cultural studies itself and the formative disciplinary contexts that prescribe certain recognizable practices as suitably (or not) 'cultural studies'. A number of participants gave attention to the context closest in—the *Self*—and described how coming-to-learn the scholarly Self was (*is*) a principally important, and ongoing, pedagogical project. In all, these iterations of our practice as necessarily contextual (and indeed, *contextualized*) provided a sense of the ways that cultural studies comes to be done.

In thinking about these contexts pedagogically, the participants spoke of their accounts of a discipline they identified with (and through) in diverse and peculiar, but always contextualized ways. As seemingly obvious as this might have been, the consideration of the contexts from which cultural studies is practiced offered a touchstone in our discussions. Thought of in these terms—as manifest in *institutional*, *disciplinary*, and *personal* formulations—we considered context as central to the understanding of pedagogy, much in the way that Henry Giroux (2004) suggests, where context provides a necessary component of the pedagogical exchange, shaping the ways that experience and knowledge form and how pedagogy itself comes to be enacted:

> Pedagogy is not simply about the social construction of knowledge, values and experiences; it is also a performative practice embodied in the lived interactions among educators, audiences, texts and institutional formations. (61)

To engage pedagogically is to be contextualized. Coming to terms with the Self as scholar, negotiating the demands of the university in this moment, and understanding intimately the dimensions of the discipline *as a discipline* requires a pedagogical engagement writ-through the learning of the Self, the learning of the field, and the learning of the terrain of higher education. These are the contexts from which the pedagogies of cultural studies operate. These contexts are what we sought to explore.

The connection of the 'personal *to* the professional' as it is sometimes called in the literature of reflective practice also carried as an undercurrent throughout the symposium. Especially in this moment, for a discipline that is (now) regularly cited as being in 'a precipitous decline' (Hesmondalgh 2013: 2) or worse still, 'crisis' (Sini 2011), the personal dimensions of practicing cultural studies presented as an important point for contemplating what the doing of cultural studies means. Of course, we didn't set out to suggest that there was agreement around what counts as cultural studies, but we did work from the position that cultural studies is recognizable and distinct from other (sometimes similar) disciplines and that these practices were worth articulating. If ours *is* a discipline in decline, it would seem a very good idea to give some attention to what now counts, what doesn't, and how the articulation of this might continue to frame the nature of the discipline. To do this we drew from the exploration of personal practice as the site at which the doing of cultural studies commences.

We cast these considerations pedagogically in terms of the points of disciplinary learning they represent and spent time thinking about what it means to come to cultural studies and how an awareness—as a cognizance—of this discipline and its requirements is acquired. A couple of assumptions were prefaced here: first, in coming-to the discipline something is required of its practitioners. This is manifest not just in the disciplinary formulations that specify cultural studies as a discipline, but also in the coming-to-learn the 'rules' of cultural studies and the ways that its practitioners are positioned. This drew attention to the *formality* attached to the expression of the discipline. We saw the expression of cultural studies in this sense being enacted according to recognized ways of doing things as formally prescribed expressions of what *counts* as cultural studies.

In the first sense, the practices attached to these disciplinary ways of doing things, mediated through prescribed methods and theory, discursive structures, and the prevailing politics the discipline adheres to provide the terrain upon which the act of 'doing' cultural studies is framed. But importantly, there are ways of thinking about a discipline and how it is that one should *be* as a cultural studies scholar that also give shape to the discipline. In these two senses the form of a discipline becomes apparent and an expression of its explicit and implicit rules find activation; that is, through the formulations that demark a discipline as *a* discipline, and through the practices enacted by those who come to practice it, the shape of a discipline materializes.

In charting a sense of what it meant to do cultural studies, we spent time discussing how we each came to learn and enact the rules of the discipline. Each of us had undertaken to *understand* cultural studies, even if the application of this learning of the discipline remained partial and idiosyncratic. Attempting to come to terms with the practice of cultural studies through its enactment, via the Self, drew us to recognize the interface that sits between the discipline and its practitioners. What did it mean to come to the discipline, to understand its shape and form, and ultimately, to take on the practice of cultural studies? How did one *declare one's Self as a cultural studies scholar and set about enacting defined sets of practice in the name of 'cultural studies'*?

To open this *aporia* for scrutiny, we set out exploring the second assumption implied within our discussion by arguing that this was a pedagogical space—a space in which exchange and learning occurred. This was where the learning-to-be a cultural studies scholar happened and where the transmission of the rules of cultural studies found activation. In short, coming to *know* not only the terrain of the discipline but also 'the rules of the game' constituted an important pedagogical encounter in the formation of the cultural studies scholar. This was more than a process of enculturation. This was where the discipline gained its form, but also where its practitioners gained their sense of Self. Via the production of practitioners who go on to enact the discipline, cultural studies finds meaning according to the pedagogical engagement its practitioners have in learning-to-be a cultural studies scholar.

Pedagogy indicates action in this sense—an agency witnessed in a 'doing'. In giving attention to pedagogy as a point of action, we considered how the will of the Self came to be enacted through this doing of cultural studies. This enabled a generative lens for our discussions and moved us beyond more somber recollections of "the complex ways in which individuals are formed by the institutions to which they belong, and in which, by reaction, the institutions took on the color of individuals thus formed" (Williams 1977: 14). We resisted positioning cultural studies as *disciplining* in this regard and sought to open for discussion the generative and productive capacity that the pedagogic suggests.

Although we were each keenly aware that certain formations of cultural studies counted more than others (according to the contexts in which these are enacted) and that the vagaries of fashionable theory, applications of certain methods and novelties in teaching and learning come and go but gain currency and relevance at different times and in different places, we worked through our deliberations to claim a possibility for invention and creativity. Accordingly, the contributions contained in this volume suggest that as a pedagogical endeavor (and by virtue of this, a *constructive* practice), cultural studies is as much about writing the world as it is the reporting of it. Engaging the full capacity of pedagogy as generative means:

> recognising that where and how the psyche locates itself in public discourse, visions, and passions provides the groundwork for agents to enunciate, act, and reflect on themselves and their relations to others and the wider social order.
> (Hammer and Kellner 2009: 92)

This carries implications for pedagogy on two counts: in how it is that the Self-as-scholar comes to cultural studies, and in what it is that cultural studies enables. The possibility within cultural studies sits with the cultural studies scholar, via the imaginative agency of the Self-as-scholar exerted according to the negotiation performed with/in disciplinary formulations. While recognizable in terms of the disciplinary formulations it prescribes as a discipline, the generative capacities of cultural studies are enacted through imaginative responses to the "radical contextualisation" (Hammer and Kellner 2009: 93) performed by cultural studies scholars. Pedagogy functions as a "referent for understanding the conditions" (Hammer and Kellner 2009: 92) at play in this radical contextualization, shaping the action of the cultural studies scholar, but also enabling imaginative responses from within the formulations the discipline prescribes.

This is not however to suggest that a pedagogical engagement with cultural studies, through the recognition and learning of its modes and practices (and indeed, the possibility for resisting these in imaginative and creative ways) automatically stands as a high water-mark of liberatory practice. As indicated throughout this volume, the disciplinary requirements of cultural studies have the capacity to constrain and limit action and creativity just as effectively. To engage with cultural studies means to engage with those characteristic forms that define its practice, to commit to the "professional attitudes, values and dispositions" (Beck and Eno 2012: 76) that shape its articulation. This engagement with the discipline requires acts of agency— engagement *with* the discipline—as the active mediation of disciplinary (and *disciplined*) practice. While we assert that the possibility for imaginative creativity is always present in the actions of the scholar-as-Self, the expression of agency can also be performed in the name of orthodoxy just as convincingly.

Cultural studies is not "the supreme abstraction, the perfect mental construct" (Mattelart and Mattelart 1998: 82), but an engagement with the world undertaken in certain ways and against certain formulations, set as it is according to the binds of contexts both within and beyond the discipline. Cultural studies, as a discipline, undertakes this engagement according to (often vehemently guarded) sets of practice.

At this point in time, there would seem to be quite a bit of orthodoxy in cultural studies, which given the resistant and critical foundations cultural studies initially grew from, is somewhat ironic. In coming-to cultural studies as pedagogical and in seeking some insight into what *makes* both the discipline and its practitioners, an opportunity to think again about the discipline is presented. The point made here resonates with Turner's (2012) suggestion that cultural studies is currently in the precarious position of possessing "the negative aspects of a discipline—its sense of boundaries—without enough of the positives, that is, a fully developed epistemology that can be taught as method" (8). Looking at cultural studies pedagogically offers the chance to take to task the uninterrogated and *sacred*, and to ask why cultural studies has taken the form it has. Taking a pedagogical account of cultural studies also offers an opportunity to look again at how the practice of its practitioners might be reimagined, creatively. In understanding cultural studies pedagogically, an insight into the workings of the discipline (and those who connect with it) can be revealed.

Configurations

In attempting to understand how it is that cultural studies comes to be configured *as* pedagogical, we took as a first step the consideration of what it meant to be cultural studies scholars and how this translated into recognizable forms of practice. This was not simply an attempt to indulge the tale-telling of individual practice or, more blandly, the exaltation of individual practices as innovative, cutting edge, or something similarly extraordinary. Our interest was not the show-and-tell of the 'products' of our personal practice.

In fact, this was anathema to the focus *Cultural Studies on the Divide* sought to take. At stake was a far larger concern interested in mapping a sense of the discipline through how it is we came to negotiate our scholarly *Selves*; an attempt to make sense of the (cap)abilities of cultural studies at this moment, through the people who do it. To achieve this, we sought everyday iterations of doing cultural studies and in keeping with cultural studies' prevailing object of scrutiny—the *everyday* as a site of practice and object of study—set about turning the gaze back inward to consider again the ways that we as its practitioners came to be formulated in the enactment of practice in ordinary, everyday ways. This was an attempt to make sense of what the contemporary practice of cultural studies meant when read from the personal, quotidian encounters its practitioners experienced.

From this, concerns around the scholar-as-Self, the places and climates in which cultural studies is done, and perhaps most importantly, what calling something *cultural studies* requires from its practitioners emerged as important themes from *Cultural Studies on the Divide*. It occurred that in two words, *context* and *Self*, the pedagogical implications of cultural studies could be defined. David Trend (1992) pointed long ago to these indicators when identifying that questions of pedagogy are contemplated:

> not just at the researcher's desk nor at the lectern but in the consciousness, through the process of thought, discussion, writing, debate, exchange; in the social and internal, collective and isolated struggle for control of understanding. (4)

It is with how we come to see ourselves as scholars, situated as we (typically) are in university settings,[1] undertaking our work in the wilds of community with (variously constituted) publics and functioning according to the terms that doing things under the name of 'cultural studies' require, that exchanges between Self and the discipline occur. This engagement with the consciousness of practice stands as pedagogical; an act of realization of the Self, a poiesis mediated by the coming-to cultural studies and its attendant ways of doing things. As an exchange, this dialogue between Self and the discipline surfaces in the cultivation of a sense of what counts as 'cultural studies' and what it means to be a cultural studies scholar. This "struggle for control of understanding" as Trend eloquently puts it, and the never quite accomplished mastery of the discipline, opens for view the requirements of the discipline and the ways these requirements then come to be met.

But there is more to this than just the recounting of individual practice. Personal practice is never performed in isolation, and the prevailing values that attach to cultural studies provide a fundamental context upon which the practice of it is deployed. Through the lengthy training that an academic career requires and the ongoing engagement with the discipline when 'in practice', the conception of the discipline *as a discipline* is in constant rehearsal. This too came to present as a theme within the dialogue of *Cultural Studies on the Divide*. We had each in our own way "signed on" to the tradition of cultural studies, as Ciccone (2009: xv) would put it, and in doing so came to recognize that there are specific ways of doing cultural studies that stand *for* the discipline.

In the case of some of the participants, these disciplinary requirements didn't present much of an issue, and a comfortable home was found within cultural studies according to its requisite practices. For others however, the connection was a little more fraught. To do cultural studies meant to align with certain sets of practices—"habits of mind" (Gurung, Chick and Haynie 2009: 2)—and perhaps even more markedly, certain expectations that specified the ways one might be a cultural studies scholar. This *condition* (and I do intentionally seek to conjure euphemistic suggestions of this being an ailment) of being a cultural studies scholar required something from its practitioners: the demonstration of recognizable practice and ways of *being*. Identifiable as expressions of the "signature pedagogies" (Gurung,

Chick and Haynie 2009; Schulman 2005) of cultural studies, these "signatures [or] defining characteristics that, when explicated, reveal the deepest beliefs" (Ciccone 2009: xv) of the discipline render as meaningful the coded ways of doing things that identify cultural studies *as a discipline* and its practitioners as cultural studies scholars.

Ciccone (2009) makes the point that "nothing uncovers hidden assumptions about desired knowledge, skills, and dispositions better than a careful examination of our most cherished practices" (xiv), and it was from this perspective that we sought to look again at what it means to do cultural studies. Whether with students in the classroom, in the field with research participants, or engaged with publics or 'industry', as a personal project mediated through disciplinary formations of what counts, cultural studies prescribes its own set of "signature pedagogies", albeit sometimes implicitly. These ways of dealing with Others, with ideas, with language, and what counts as knowledge stand as identifiable as the formulations of the discipline. This is where the discipline takes shape, according to its enactment.

At a fundamental level, there are ways of doing cultural studies that relate to questions of method. Certain forms of training, conducted in places like the university, covering the core content and methodological approaches for *doing* cultural studies, translate into the formation of scholars capable of then conducting these practices appropriately as cultural studies scholars. Gurung, Chick and Haynie (2009) see this as the process of settling the "habits of the discipline" (8) or as the confirmation of the "implicit structure" as Beck and Eno (2012) refer to it. This implicit structure establishes the boundary by which the discipline comes to be known. This structure sets the "moral dimensions that comprise a set of beliefs" of the discipline (Beck and Eno 2012: 55) as acts of reproduction handed down through the traditions of the discipline in order to maintain the discipline according to its recognized practices, attendant beliefs, and core values.

During *Cultural Studies on the Divide* we came to discuss the experiences we had each had when encountering the implicit structures of cultural studies and the requirements its signature pedagogies specify. While we were each aware of the more *explicit* articulations of cultural studies' signature pedagogies—the disciplinary formations that took shape in the ways that degree programs were formulated, the requirements inherent in the preparation of research programs, and the ways that specific assemblages of theory and method defined the discipline—it was with its implicit articulations particularly that our attention was focused. We had each experienced moments of not being so sure about the appropriateness of our work, and whether it qualified as 'cultural studies'. We discussed the everyday vulnerabilities we felt when having our writing and ideas adjudicated by grant review panels, or scrutinized by peers at conferences. We spoke about the anxieties experienced during the quieter, isolated moments when preparing manuscripts and how agonizing over the significance of what it was we had to say sometimes overwhelmed our practice. We discussed the encounters we had each had in the classroom teaching cultural studies, and how it was we each sought to engage our students with theory and method—to declare our mastery of the discipline, as the discipline required. We considered how we came to craft our claim to *speak* so that the artifice of our practice would fit with what was expected of us as cultural studies scholars. We added to this discussion by considering accounts of the pressures we felt from outside of the discipline, resident within publics who are increasingly quick to hold for explanation the value derived from the sorts of scholarly labors we had undertaken in the name of the discipline (and the humanities generally). These implicit measures of our practice stood as fundamentally important to what we felt we could say and do in the name of cultural studies.

Again, the three iterations of pedagogy alluded to above gained currency in these discussions. In recounting our experiences, we spoke of the *pedagogies of Self* (the personal), the *pedagogies of the field* (the disciplinary), and the *pedagogies of the institution* (the institutional). These iterations of pedagogy told us everything we needed to know about the nature and formulation of cultural studies, of what could be done in its name, and how we came to it as its practitioners. Here the Self collided full on with the discipline, and more problematically still, the world at large. What we were required to do as cultural studies scholars drew from the tasking of several masters: corporatized university structures that increasingly seek a return on the investment of time and salaries (via the full weight of bureaucratic systems geared to the scrutinizing evaluation of academic labor); publics who sometimes look upon what it is we have to say with combinations of fear, confusion, and derision; and colleagues, who with sharply tuned senses for what counts in this discipline, are quick to point out that which doesn't. These concerns cut to the very nature of how the disciplinary boundary is protected and maintained.

Our discussions were summed up nicely by Ruth Barcan's (2015) eloquently posed question: quite simply, were we "*good enough?*" (130). For Barcan (2015) becoming 'good enough' to speak for and from cultural studies is an intimately pedagogical process of learning to be within the profession and to practice one's scholarly craft according to recognized markers of what counts. Core to this is the placing of the Self within the discipline, and of positioning a sense of one's place against the markers the discipline prescribes, as set within broader higher education and public contexts.

We struggled with this. Underpinning *Cultural Studies on the Divide* was an intention to open for scrutiny those practices we engaged in order to think again about what counts—to the Self, for the discipline, for the institution—and how it is that those disciplinary measures, public expectations, and collegial scrutiny come to constrain the discipline and its creativity through this monitoring of personal practice. We had each witnessed displays of the 'right' (and 'wrong') ways of presenting papers at conferences, the 'right' (or 'wrong') deployments of the language of the discipline, demonstrations of knowledge about who was fashionably 'in' (or 'out') as the theorists of the moment and how with astute appropriateness in conversation one's *bona fides* as a scholar might be displayed through the deft mentioning of affiliation with the 'right' research center, colleague, or funding agency. We spoke of the informality, but vital significance, of establishing one's credentials and authority to speak according to one's 'rank' in the field, of the symbolic power of a title and a reputation. We gave attention to how we had developed strategies for engaging with media outlets, how we came to conduct research with 'industry partners', and what it meant to relay in 'plain language' what it was we did (as if our standard practice, and its language, was always going to be impenetrable). The pedagogy at work in these instances suggested practices of self-surveillance mobilized according to (perceived) assessments of the field and its requirements.

It was in these moments that the practice of cultural studies was reinforced and where, under the scrutiny that this practice provoked, recognizable traits of the discipline found currency. More importantly, it was also in these moments that aspects of being a cultural studies scholar were *learned* and the signature pedagogies of this discipline mobilized. In this sense we echoed Watkins, Noble, and Driscoll's (2015) suggestion that "these modalities either externally-derived or self-produced, involve subject formation" (5). Pedagogy provided our lens for considering the gamut of techniques, habits, orientations, and dispositions that constituted our practice. We determined that what was central to these concerns of practice, action, and agency were questions of pedagogy, whether this related to the act of coming-to cultural studies (within the deployment of an outwardly technical mastery of the discipline) or as a far more personal act of *becoming* the cultural studies scholar, of "learning to be an academic" as Barcan (2015) puts it. Pedagogy provided conceptual scope for considering these angles. By considering cultural studies in this way, we opened an opportunity to contemplate not only what cultural studies requires from us, but also where the opportunities to *mess up* the assumptions that attach to the discipline reside—a chance to think again about what it might mean to *do* cultural studies.

Pedagogy as Cultural Practice/Cultural Studies as Pedagogical Practice

As a slippery term, easily deployed, but far harder to pin down with meaningful accuracy, pedagogy carries its own stigma and disciplinary attachments, to education and studies of curriculum principally. Trend (1992) highlights the 'imprecision' inherent within definitions of the term and the problem of seeing pedagogy as "coterminous with teaching, merely describing a central activity in an education system" (2). This connection to education (as itself a discipline, but also an undertaking) as an activity residing in places like schools obscures the full range of possibility pedagogy provides.

Grossberg (1994) identifies an important conceptualization of pedagogy when noting that "cultural studies requires us to consider, not only pedagogy as a cultural practice, but the pedagogy of cultural practices" (16). In responding to the predominance of views that consider pedagogy in the former, we seek in this volume to give consideration to pedagogies of cultural practice as evidenced through the enactment of cultural studies. But in extending this beyond recent and comprehensive accounts of the ways that a pedagogy of cultural practices might be considered under the banner of "public" and "cultural pedagogies" (Burdick, Sandlin and O'Malley 2014; Sandlin, Schultz and Burdick 2010; Watkins, Noble, and Driscoll 2015), we seek to offer here consideration of the *pedagogy of cultural studies* as itself a cultural practice.

It is in this light that this volume presents a case for what constitutes pedagogy. In short, we see pedagogy as defined (and defining) sets of practices that come to be codified in recognizable ways—a "signature pedagogy" that specifies the parameters of the discipline (Schulman 2005)—but also as the prompt for a personal project of becoming.

In positioning pedagogy this way, we sought to unsettle the assumptions that attach to cultural studies and to think around where the pedagogies of cultural studies happen. In short, we sought to use, as Ciccone (2009: xiv) suggests, personal experience to develop a "spatial cognition" of our discipline and at the same time attempted to reorient some of its hidden assumptions and cherished practices; assumptions and practices that might be overdue for (re)consideration. While Grossberg's (1997) suggestion that the "enunciative positions" of cultural studies frame the "social relations ... and places of authority we construct" (385) within the discipline, it is according to the ways that these positions find articulation in practice that ultimately matters. The view taken in the chapters that follow positions practice as the point of articulation through which pedagogy is made apparent. As enacted through practice, pedagogy is witnessed *in the doing of cultural studies*. Cultural studies finds articulation through the work of its practitioners, in how it comes to be mobilized accordingly, and how this enactment of practice is subsequently recognized as 'cultural studies'. We follow Grossberg's (2010) lead in making this claim, in that "cultural studies is a way of inhabiting the position of scholar, teacher, artist, and intellectual, one way (among many) of politicizing theory and theorizing politics" (9). This is both the awareness of being the scholar—a practitioner of cultural studies—and what the disciplinary requirements suggest for the becoming of the Self. The contention presented in this volume follows as something like this: *the practice of cultural studies is necessarily pedagogical, but to seek an understanding of how this pedagogical foundation finds activation, it is with the cultural studies scholar engaged in coming-to cultural studies that attention should be turned.*

Heidegger's conceptualization of *Dasein* has some resonance here. It is with the notion of 'being there' as suggested in Heidegger's phenomenology that we found connection to the approach we had in mind for this volume. As Heidegger (1962) notes:

> In determining itself as an entity, *Dasein* always does so in light of a possibility which *is* itself and which, in its very Being, it somehow *understands*. (69, emphasis added)

It is with the doing of cultural studies that a sense of what cultural studies *is* emerges most clearly. In understanding the Self as the point at which practice emanates, insight into the nature of that practice takes form. It was in this sense—that is, with the exploration of cultural studies as a personal project—that a starting point for this volume developed. *This was an effort to draw attention to the recognition of ourSelves as cultural studies scholars within and through the practice that we each deployed in the name of cultural studies.* It was in particular with the positioning of pedagogy as that which acts on the Self and manifests through the formulations of the discipline of cultural studies, that our dialogue commenced. We suggest here, simply enough, that it is with its practitioners that a pedagogy of cultural studies might be extrapolated and that a sense of cultural studies' futures might find demarcation.

This was not the search for a set of fail-safe approaches or 'methods' for doing cultural studies (although, many of the contributions here do draw attention to the consequences of practice), but the *coming-to* of cultural studies. The narratives contained here preface the position of the cultural studies scholar as *Self*—an agentic, self-realized entity, the site upon which and from whom practice emanates as the awareness of Self in relation to other Selves and the practices cultural studies prescribes: *Dasein*. Configurations of the practice of cultural studies are always done according to the Self, set as they are among larger considerations of a field and its "intellectual moves and values" (Gurung, Chick and Haynie 2009: 3). This is the front line of the experience of being a cultural studies scholar—of not only doing cultural studies, but of also being aware that what it is that one is indeed doing *is* cultural studies.

Who Speaks? A Troubled Reading of Contemporary Cultural Studies

We had each our own take on what the discipline meant, but significantly a resonant theme within the conversation from *Cultural Studies on the Divide* circulated around the notion of *legitimacy*. For some participants, legitimacy was questioned in terms of not fully identifying with cultural studies, due in part to the location of employment these participants had in distinct discipline areas outside of 'cultural studies', or indeed from not having come through a bona fide cultural studies program of study. Even though the contributions to this volume speak to clear connections to the disciplinary concerns of cultural studies, this sense of a lack-of-legitimacy to speak in the name of cultural studies was significant.

More troubling, however, were acknowledgements by participants of a (perceived) hierarchy at work in contemporary cultural studies.[2] *Who* could speak, as the logic of these perceptions suggested, related to who one was and claims made over provenance of 'connection' within the discipline. This is a complex argument, and speaks to something larger than the nature of interpersonal civility or deference within cultural studies alone. Aside from questions of the (f)actual basis that these perceptions may well have, legitimacy again surfaces here, pointing to a not always openly discussed problem in cultural studies; that is, *who is authorized to speak?*

Firm expressions of this phenomenon are not that easily found, but it does seem to be recognized widely enough.[3] One recent example includes Gilbert Rodman's (2015) somewhat lengthy admissions at the commencement of his *Why Cultural Studies?* as to why the reader should take the time to consider his authority to speak on, and about, cultural studies. In establishing the legitimacy of his position to speak for cultural studies, Rodman notes:

> In the course of working on this book over the past several years, one of the most frequent questions I've been asked is about my 'right' to speak with any real authority about what cultural studies should (and shouldn't) do. (2015: xii)

He goes on, but at the nub of this admission is the suggestion that there is indeed not only a 'right' way to speak about cultural studies, but that this should be performed by the 'right' type of individual.

Should this be a worry to cultural studies? Should it be a concern that the explicit declaration of one's capacity to speak for cultural studies must be prefaced at the outset of the claim? Should it be a concern that postgraduate candidates quietly, but with genuine concern, note that it is important not to upset the order of cultural studies by speaking out-of-turn, or too boldly, for fear of jeopardizing any chance of employment they might otherwise have? Should it be a concern that an unwillingness to speak openly, justifiable as this may well be, is resulting in the production of (what I would see as) an orthodoxy in cultural studies practice? Should it be a worry that this is becoming a feature of cultural studies, written into the fabric of the discipline as a signature pedagogy in itself—a learned component of how to be a cultural studies scholar?

From another, but equally significant perspective, how should we contend with the *crisis narratives* (again, as I see them) that have begun to take hold in the retelling of our discipline? There is not the space here to chart the intricacies of these arguments, and the reader might refer to the following surveys of the field as indicative examples of what I see as the prevailing views contained within these narratives (Hesmondalgh 2013; O'Connor

2012; Rodman 2015: 3–17; Turner 2012). But how is it that these narratives have become so prominent? Why is it that "the Sigh" as Rodman (2015) observes, provoked when "yet another bit of meta-discourse about cultural studies" (8) is produced, rates so prominently in writing about the discipline? This state of affairs brings to mind McEwan's (2002) unabashed observations that "numerous arguments in the field of cultural studies ... tend to be meta-discourses on what cultural studies should be rather what it is" (428). Should it be a concern that the accounting of the state of cultural studies (and its broader setting within the field of the humanities) has become a project in itself, that the production of the meta-discourses that McEwan identifies constitute in themselves a reasonable focus of scholarly attention? It seems more than a little ironic that even within these crisis narratives the gaze hasn't quite fixed on how it is that cultural studies is (and might be) positioned in broader contexts, as McEwan goes on to note when suggesting that "[f]or all the self-analysis, cultural studies as a discipline often seems unaware of its own characteristics" (430).

This state of things brings to mind the regularly retold exclamation by Stuart Hall that cultural studies contains a "lot of rubbish" (in Rodman 2015: 15; cited also in Turner 2012: 2). This is further nuanced by Grossberg's (1994) warning that there is "no guarantee ... that every appearance of cultural studies is valuable or even progressive" (1). Is this perhaps why; that either we in cultural studies have become a bit too comfortable in our reluctant institutionalization and have not really stopped to take stock of what it is we do within these settings and in publics that have changed markedly since cultural studies first commenced? Or is it indeed just too risky to step beyond the orthodox and authorized ways of doing things?[4] In coming to argue for and protect the space that has been carved out, has cultural studies become insular and too protective of the gains it has made? In institutional contexts where cultural studies has spent (too) much time arguing a point that has largely become irrelevant (that is, whether it *is* disciplinary *or* not), the cost has been the creation of the sort of discipline (and a set of commensurate capacities for critical appraisal, reflexivity, and political activation) that the world could desperately use right at the moment, but which has been sidetracked with (perhaps justifiable) self-interest. If these assertions have any basis, and it seems that they might, then what a great shame for a discipline that holds as core to its guiding principles the invention of creative, imaginative, irreverent, and most of all, critical appraisals of *how things are*.

It is a central argument within this volume that it is time to look again at cultural studies and that this might be best mediated by explicating the pedagogies that underpin cultural studies' practice. To reinforce the points made earlier, it is through pedagogy as the enactment of agency and the point at which the realization of the habits of the discipline find articulation that the contributions to this volume draw attention. In coming to expose the signature pedagogies that define the discipline (and demarcate its boundaries), this volume sets out to provoke the reconsideration of what counts as cultural studies and how this act of looking again at the practice of its practitioners might reorient the discipline.

The Structure of this Volume

This volume is organized into three parts, corresponding broadly to themes that emerged from the dialogue during *Cultural Studies on the Divide*. Inherent within these three sections are concerns for the prevailing concepts broached earlier in this chapter—*context* and *Self*—but organized in such a way that these concepts surface at different points of conjuncture to provide a sense of the multiple ways context frames the practice of the cultural studies scholar-as-Self.

"Section 1—The Embodiment of Cultural Studies/The Embodiment of Pedagogy", takes as its focus the idea that pedagogy is embodied and lived through the cultural studies practitioner. But in building on existing accounts of embodiment in the literature of teaching and learning, the notion of embodiment positioned in these opening chapters comes to be realized *within* the pedagogical encounters of cultural studies. In particular, this section explores what it means to *experience* cultural studies *as* a pedagogical exchange.

Rob Garbutt launches the discussion by detailing what it means to 'do' cultural studies when 'in' community. Drawing on experiences gained from community engagement initiatives in which Garbutt was positioned as academic, author, and community member simultaneously, a consideration of *thinking through* the Self is presented in context of his engagements with community. Garbutt's inquiry focuses on what was uncovered in the 'pedagogical' encounter with Self, with Other, with place. He asks what can be learned about the Self when a cultural studies inquiry into community commences. Here, new ethics of encounter emerged and made for 'messy' texts and reportings, and more particularly, provoked even 'messier' contemplations of the Self in relation to Other—a key moment of learning.

Linda Wight conjures ideas of embodiment by asking what it means to critically translate readings of masculinity identified within science fiction film and literature into the classroom. In asking how these critical readings of masculinity form as part of a formal university coursework exploration of gender and sexuality, Wight provides insight into the always-incomplete nature of pedagogy—that pedagogy is an approximation, an uneasy combination of formal techniques of instruction and informal negotiations between Self and Other. From the realization of the limits of Self experienced by Wight, the chapter charts what it might mean to take from science fiction and how this content might morph into the classroom—into something that might be taught, but that also itself *teaches*.

Baden Offord draws attention to how the pedagogic comes to be *activated* through the Self. In conjuring the idea of 'activation', Offord brings to mind the point of the pedagogical exchange—the activation of new understandings, encounters, and relationships. The pedagogical encounter is a generative one in this sense, one that *activates* the participants involved. But importantly, Offord notes that within this dynamic of activation, concern for the ethics of the encounter are also vital, which is a topic that Kim Satchell (*Chapter 5*) revisits in his chapter.

With "Section 2: Alterity, the Other and the Pedagogical Exchange" the discussion shifts to consider the ways that Self and Other come to be recognized within the pedagogical exchange. How might we learn through others? How might the exchange take account of what comes to be known by the Other?

In making his case for the pedagogue who can see beyond and through the ordinary and everyday with sage-like dexterity and insight, Kim Satchell discusses how his own 'activations' via such disparate sources as a finless surfboard and assemblages of found objects encountered during meanderings along a beach inculcate a pedagogical exchange with natural ecologies and the other-than-human. This encounter with the everyday through a 'practice' of the everyday articulates a key foundation of cultural studies—the nature of the ordinary and its pedagogical influence. This chapter provides an important case-in-point for the book—that the pedagogical exchange happens in multiple ways and in everyday encounters, encounters that may also occur with nonhuman participants.

Amanda Third draws attention to the interpersonal and institutional dynamics of engagement in the act of doing cultural studies. This important consideration brings into sharp focus the multiple, sometimes competing, knowledge ecologies that cultural studies scholars work within and through. In particular, Third in drawing on Michel deCerteau (1984) notes how 'tactical' applications of knowledge and knowing, ontology, and epistemology circulate in certain ways and in certain spaces, arbitrating what can be known and who the knower must become as part of this exchange. As a site of pedagogy, the knowledge ecology within which these acts are played out primes the pedagogical exchange and, for the explicit purposes of this chapter, how it is that academics and cultural studies scholars might go about translating familiar 'knowledge' in wider engagements with community.

Lisa Slater frames her discussion around the notion of 'care' and how caring in contemporary cultures is learned. Slater highlights the central thematic of her chapter as being the *concern of what it might mean to 'care'* and how this application of care finds resolution in the Other. With this Slater identifies one of the key terms to emerge within the chapters of this volume: *interest*. While functioning as an *activation* as Baden Offord suggests (*Chapter 4*), the pedagogical exchange is also one of interest—interest in the Other, interest in the Self. However, this learning of the Other will always remain an incomplete project as the convergence of Self and Other can never be complete. What then does it mean to care, or to show interest in the care of the Other when doing cultural studies?

"Section 3: The Sites of Cultural Studies Pedagogy" explores the role that space plays in determining the pedagogical exchange. Drawing variously on critical pedagogy, public pedagogy, and broader theorizations of space and place, these chapters highlight the effects of place and spatiality on the pedagogy of cultural studies.

Megan Watkins delivers a striking account of how 'multicultural' policy applications in New South Wales' schools have been shaped by multiple influences (the clashing of "knowledge ecologies" to draw on Amanda Third's examples, *Chapter 6*). The way difference and culture came to be understood and enacted by teachers within the edicts of "multicultural policy" in schools provides a case example of the fluidity of knowledge constructs; the act of interpretation will always be dynamic, unpredictable, and messy. This important point highlights the ways that what comes to be intended within the pedagogical exchange may not necessarily translate *as intended*, with any sense of how the pedagogic does its work always requiring some account of what gets done by actual people functioning within multifarious sites of encounter.

Gregory Martin and Andrew Hickey continue this section with an exploration of *do-it-yourself* (DIY) pedagogies. Highlighting how the politics of space and being-in-place influence what can be known, this chapter considers the ways that new understandings might form through the engagement of *new* spaces—learning from the "border" territory as Henry Giroux (1992) might suggest—and the possibilities DIY might hold for renaming and appropriating existing understandings of the world. This is an important theme for considering how cultural studies might enact itself pedagogically in the usual haunts it has been associated with (pop culture, the 'ordinary', marginalized/marginalizing spaces).

Katrina Schlunke's chapter focuses on space, and importantly, encounters with the nonhuman, the role of Self within the pedagogical exchange, and the maintenance of prescribed knowledge ecologies for dealing with and surviving the 'crisis' that natural disasters bring. Schlunke draws on the way we learn from space and locatedness and in particular what the profound experience of dealing with a major natural disaster—a bush fire—might mean when considered pedagogically. In dealing with relocation following the destruction of her home, Schlunke works through such experiences as becoming the recipient of various forms of charity and public "interest" (to reapply Slater's term, *Chapter 7*). The encounters she faced postevent brought into stark focus how prescribed ways of knowing, being, and doing are reinforced and maintained at (and because of) the site of disruption.

Rebecca Olive's sojourn to the beach highlights the codified processes of embodiment she has experienced as a (female) surfer. In drawing attention to the protocols, behaviors, and mores of the surf-break, Olive explores the roles available to women and the ways that learned gender roles come to be assumed and resisted by (both) women (and men). This is simultaneously a cognitive and corporeal pedagogy, bound intimately with what the space of the surf-break requires and the ways dominant visionings of gender coalesce at the moment of the 'line-out'. Who you are/who you *learn to be* at the beach is borne of those perspectives encountered during the moment of the line-out and the protocols enacted by the human co-inhabitants of this space.

The final chapter draws together the threads contained within the volume by broaching the question: *what are the pedagogies of cultural studies?* In revisiting the themes from *Chapter 1*, this chapter takes the quotidian, everyday encounters discussed throughout the volume to pose a consideration of cultural studies' "signature pedagogies" (Schulman 2005). What might cultural studies declare as being central to its mission? What signature pedagogies stand as indicative of this? Connecting to concerns around where pedagogy happens, what it materializes as, who comes to be involved, and how the pedagogical engagement functions, this concluding chapter poses questions around what might continue to be considered in (and as) 'cultural studies'.

The intention underpinning *The Pedagogies of Cultural Studies* was to create a volume that opened for further inquiry and discussion the central role that pedagogy plays in cultural studies practice. At this moment for cultural studies it would seem a productive move to turn attention to how cultural studies is done, what drives its practice, and how this comes to be enacted in the world. A purpose underpinning this orientation was to capture quotidian expressions of cultural studies, enacted by a group of scholars who practice (with varying levels of connection) this discipline.

The Pedagogies of Cultural Studies wasn't interested in repeating arguments of the past, although reference to cultural studies' guiding practices, its central theoretical constructs, and principal methods is made throughout. Similarly, a spectrum of experience in and with cultural studies is drawn upon by the authors whose views are captured here.

We hope above all else that this volume prompts discussion around what counts as cultural studies, and perhaps more urgently, what cultural studies might continue to do. Although wanting to resist becoming another "meta-discourse" (McEwan 2002), we are aware that what presents here may appear as yet more chastising around what *should* happen in cultural studies. This is not our intention. This volume, we hope, declares a clear orientation toward practice, and it is intended that the examples and scenarios relayed throughout the volume offer a provocation for the wider consideration of the pedagogies of cultural studies. In this regard, this volume is necessarily incomplete. It cannot hope to capture every nuance and application of cultural studies, but what it does intend to do, in its own small way, is make a case for why the consideration of pedagogy in cultural studies should be a central concern—one that may continue to be problematized and critiqued as an ongoing discussion into cultural studies' continuing relevance.

Notes

1. It is acknowledged that important expressions of cultural studies are done 'outside' of the university, and it is not the case here that an assumption is taken that only cultural studies done 'within' the university counts. But it did so happen that each of the participants called upon for *Cultural Studies on the Divide* practiced within university settings.
2. It is interesting to note that something of a debate emerged via the Cultural Studies Association of Australasia's list-serv in early 2015, where among other themes it was noted by a protagonist that "In Australian [cultural studies], at least, it seems that hierarchy has become entrenched, certainly in the understanding of postgrads and ECRs".
3. The murmurings and quiet discussions at conferences of this phenomenon are a reasonable expression of this point. It seems that this is a phenomenon that is recognized but remains taboo and something that is not at all polite to talk about.
4. This also causes me to recall a moment I experienced at a prominent cultural studies symposium at which I was 'shushed' and told to wait my turn in a roundtable discussion. Perhaps I wasn't aware of my demeanor; at least I didn't think I was being disrespectful in adding my two cents during this discussion, only to be told that I should wait my turn to speak! At a cultural studies symposium! It was intriguing to note that the speaker I was being 'shushed' for was a 'big-name' in cultural studies, and for me, this signified the way that the authorization of speaking functioned. I stress that this wasn't the fault of the 'big name', but an indication of how deference operated in this particular instance, at least as I understood this.

References

Aronowitz, S., and Giroux, H.A. (2000). The corporate university and the politics of education. *The Educational Forum*, 64 (4): 332–39.

Barcan, R. (2015). Learning to be an academic: tacit and explicit pedagogies. In Watkins, M., Noble, G., and Driscoll, C. (eds). *Cultural pedagogies and human conduct* (pp. 129–43). London, Routledge.

Beck, D., and Eno, J. (2012). Signature pedagogy: a literature review of social studies and technology research. *Computers in the Schools*, 29 (1–2): 70–94.

Burdick, J., Sandlin, J.A., and O'Malley, M.P. (eds). (2014). *Problematizing public pedagogy*. New York, Routledge.

Certeau, M. de (1984). *The practice of everyday life*. Berkeley, University of California Press.

Ciccone, A.A. (2009). Foreword. In Gurung, R.A.R., Chick, N.L., and Haynie, A. (eds). *Exploring signature pedagogies: approaches to teaching disciplinary habits of mind* (pp. xi–xvi). Sterling, Stylus.

Giroux, H.A. (1992). *Border crossings: cultural workers and the politics of education*. New York, Psychology Press.

Giroux, H.A. (2004). Public pedagogy and the politics of neo-liberalism: making the political more pedagogical. *Policy Futures in Education*, 2 (3–4): 494–503.

Giroux, H.A., and Myrsiades, K. (2001). *Beyond the corporate university: culture and pedagogy in the new millennium*. Oxford, Rowman and Littlefield.

Grossberg, L. (1994). Introduction: bringin' it all back home—pedagogy and cultural studies. In Giroux, H.A., and McLaren, P. (eds). *Between borders: pedagogy and the politics of cultural studies* (pp. 1–25). New York, Routledge.

Grossberg, L. (1997). *Bringing it all back home: Essays on Cultural Studies*. Durham, Duke University Press.

Grossberg, L. (2010). *Cultural studies in a future tense*. Durham, Duke University Press.

Gurung, R.A.R., Chick, N.L., and Haynie, A. (2009). From generic to signature pedagogies: teaching disciplinary understandings. In Gurung, R.A.R., Chick, N.L., and Haynie, A. (eds). *Exploring signature pedagogies: approaches to teaching disciplinary habits of mind* (pp. 1–16). Sterling, Stylus.

Hammer, R., and Kellner, D. (2009). *Media/cultural studies: critical approaches*. New York, Peter Lang.

Heidegger, M. (1962). *Being and time*. New York, Harper Perennial.

Hesmondalgh, D. (2013). What cultural, critical and communication might mean—and why cultural studies is a bit like rave culture. *Communication and Critical/Cultural Studies*, 10 (2–3): 280–84.

Mattelart, A., and Mattelart, M. (1998). *Theories of communication: a short introduction*. London, Sage.

McEwan, P. (2002). Cultural studies as a hidden discipline. *International Journal of Cultural Studies*, 5 (4): 427–37.

O'Connor, J. (2012). We need to talk about cultural studies. *Cultural Studies Review*, 18 (2): 330–40.

Rodman, G. (2015). *Why cultural studies?* Malden, John Wiley and Sons.

Sandlin, J.A., Schultz, B.D., and Burdick, J. (eds). (2010). *Handbook of public pedagogy: education and learning beyond schooling*. New York, Routledge.

Schulman, L.S. (2005). Signature pedagogies in the professions. *Daedalus*, 134 (3): 52–59.

Sini, M. (2011). 'Oh the humanities!' (or: a critique of crisis). *Overland*, February.

Trend, D. (1992). *Cultural pedagogy: art/education/politics*. New York, Bergin and Garvey.

Turner, G. (2012). *What's become of cultural studies*. London, Sage.

Watkins, M., Noble, G., and Driscoll, C. (2015). Pedagogy: the unsaid of sociocultural theory. In Watkins, M., Noble, G., and Driscoll, C. (eds). *Cultural pedagogies and human conduct* (pp. 1–16). London, Routledge.

Williams, R. (1967). Preface to the Second Edition. *Communications*. New York, Barnes and Noble.

Williams, R. (1977). *Marxism and literature*. Oxford, Oxford University Press.

2 Cultural Studies and the Pedagogy of Community-Engaged Research

Rob Garbutt

Introduction

Of all that community groups do, the Annual General Meeting (AGM), with its election of office bearers and reports from the president and treasurer, can be one of the least inspiring. It is a largely administrative affair that punctuates the passion that brings people together. The December 2011 AGM of the *Aquarian Archive* had some of that, apart from an ongoing tussle over the role of president. What piqued my interest, though, was a reminder about a looming celebration: the 40th anniversary of the *Nimbin Aquarius Softlick*. This was a 10-day counterculture festival in May 1973 organized by the Australian Union of Students in the village of Nimbin on the far-north coast of New South Wales. Somewhat misleadingly badged as "Australia's Woodstock", the Aquarius Festival (as it is locally known) transformed this conservative rural region from sleepy Summerland into the fire-stick twirling Rainbow Region. Forty years on the Festival still resonates.

With a pronounced nod to Lawrence Grossberg's (1994) formulation of pedagogy and cultural studies, this chapter sits in the midst of the 'pedagogy of culture' and the 'culture of pedagogy', by way of research and teaching, community and university. It assays these constitutive elements and their interactions through the author's involvement in *Aquarius and Beyond*, as both an ongoing research project into the Aquarius Festival and its ripples through the Rainbow Region, and through the author's involvement in the 2-day community conference in 2013 that marked the 40th anniversary. The community conference provides the specific focus of this chapter.

The conference, one participant announced to me the night before the gathering, was an "eminently respectable cover for a group of ageing hippies to have a reunion". Before starting, the outcomes had already exceeded the intentions. As relative outsiders, the conference organizers created a space of hospitality in the Nimbin Town Hall where the village heard stories of itself told by locals and others, and where Nimbin in the present tense told its stories to many who were returning, some after a 40-year absence. As the conference unfolded, so too did reunions and reconciliations.

And just as *Aquarius and Beyond* yielded its joyous and awkward moments of reflection for many of the participants, so too did it provide the organizers with moments of intensity that stimulated ideas and reflections on the relationships between university, community, research, and pedagogy. Furthermore, because of the community-engaged nature of the conference, historical events and specific locations folded themselves into these thoughts and reflections. The result, in this chapter, is a *geophilosophical* investigation in miniature of what, how, and who cultural studies teaches when it is brought to bear on a community-engaged research project.

To begin, then, some scene setting is called for.

Cultural Studies in Particular

One of the distinguishing features of cultural studies is its close attention to *contexts* (Grossberg 1994: 5). The context for this chapter is a particular cultural studies formation within the cultural studies project (Rodman 2015); this locally influenced inflection of the global project intersects with more recent enthusiasm for community-engaged modes of research within the academy. This is the pedagogy of culture in which I became immersed when, midway along the course of my life, I stumbled into cultural studies at Southern Cross University.

The cultural studies formation at Southern Cross University (SCU) was strongly influenced through the scholarship of Baden Offord who from the late 1990s to 2014 played the lead role in the fostering cultural studies practice at the university. The cultural studies undergraduate major in the Bachelor of Arts degree was largely shaped by Baden's insights regarding how to connect the promises of cultural studies to local students' interests. This had direct connections to the theoretical interests of scholars at the Birmingham Centre such as Stuart Hall and Raymond Williams. However, and crucially, this scholarship was also strongly influenced by the critical pedagogy of Paulo Freire and Henry Giroux, and imbued with the ethos of the public intellectual as espoused, for example, by Edward Said (1994). Cultural studies at SCU is, therefore, an intellectual and political intervention with activist leanings.

This cultural studies practice has, of course, a particular institutional context. Southern Cross University is a small, rural-regional, multicampus university that is just over 20 years old. Its size and its geographic location enable personal engagement between faculty and students. The student population is composed of many mature-aged students as well as those straight from school. Most are the first in their family to enter university (Garbutt and Kayess 2014). Thus, the pedagogy of cultural studies has been a key concern at SCU, with the situation demanding a pedagogical approach that engages with everyday life experiences that are locally meaningful. Teaching deracinated theory—the sort that Graeme Turner critiques as "Cultural Studies 101" (Turner 2009)—would hold little relevance or interest for most of the university's cultural studies students. The units in the undergraduate major incorporate such activities as field trips to connect theory with the everyday world (Garbutt, Biermann and Offord 2012), with the term *engagement* integral to SCU cultural studies as a "way of being in the academy" in the sense that personal-political agendas are positioned as up for negotiation (Ang 2006: 186–7; Johnson et al. 2004: 25). Beyond the classroom, opportunities are sought to involve the wider university and the local community in less-formal educational experiences on areas of research interest such as critical race studies and critical disability studies (Biermann, Garbutt and Offord 2010). Thus, at SCU, cultural studies has a strong affinity with the discipline's pedagogical origins and political motivations (Rutten et al. 2013: 444).

Furthermore, the smaller-scale regional population in which the university is located affords a blurring of the lines between community and university. It is important not to overstate this: the academy is a foreign place for many people who find its practices, discourse, and spaces exclusionary. Nevertheless, research agendas are often founded in community concerns, and the region's history from the mid-1970s of environmental and community activism provides fertile ground for community-inspired research. The publication of *Belonging in the Rainbow Region* (Wilson 2003) and two international conferences organized around activating human rights that brought together activists *and* scholars are evidence of this simultaneously local and international research that engage beyond the academy (Goh, Offord and Garbutt 2012; Porter and Offord 2006).

So while community-engaged cultural studies research can be viewed as a pragmatic concession to neoliberal research agendas focused on *usefulness*, *relevance*, and the quest for new sources of funding (see Allon 2006: 36–37), I argue that at SCU engagement is a critical response and an organic aspect of being a cultural studies academic in a regional university: of strategically sharing the "wealth" of the university, in all its aspects, in response to community need. It combines a cultural studies "mode of interest in the world" with a "mode of involvement with others" (Allon and Morris 2006: 12).

It is within this context, disciplinary *and* institutional, that *Aquarius and Beyond*, the community conference and the longer-term research project, was and is still situated: within a university that is drawn into relevance with the community around and beyond it; where cultural studies research engages directly with people outside the academic realm as well as within it; and where the cultural studies pedagogy is decidedly democratic, has the potential to enable personal transformation, and is acknowledged as occurring within the academy's physical boundaries as well as without. This is a cultural studies that develops "by allowing the world outside the academy to ask questions of us as intellectuals" (Grossberg 1997: 264).

Community ⇔ University

The cultural studies story could be told another way.

Every day the numbers of tourists arriving in Nimbin dwarfs the population of around 500 people. Each shop in the village is occupied and during business hours street parking is not easily found. For tourists, the main street is a source of astonishment, mostly reactions to the village's reputation for a relatively visible drug market, particularly marijuana. But there is much more besides that which captivates: shops sell an array of hippy clothing, nostalgic and new in design; candles from the local Nimbin Candle Factory are favorite souvenirs; the bookshop swells with esoteric titles; the availability of alternative healing modalities dominates the single traditional pharmacy; cafes carry a vast array of organic, vegetarian, and vegan options; environmental concerns feature in the street posters; and life in all its richness seems to pour onto the footpaths and street.

The countercultural energy that gives life to this creative outpouring is not solely commercial: it is an ethos that pervades much village activity. Behind the scenes the Rainbow Power Company has been enabling people to decrease their dependence on the coal-fired power grid for 30 years and the Permaculture College spreads a similar message of sustainability and self-sufficiency. The Nimbin community has itself purchased the old high school site for its community center, as well as other buildings including the community art gallery and town hall. Most recently the community purchased a weatherboard cottage to demonstrate retrofitting a house for sustainable living. These communal buildings are also the focus of a solar grid for the village power supply.

And among and intermingled with this rainbow of activity are traditional organizations: the chamber of commerce, the lawn bowling club, the hospital, the agricultural show society, and much more. Countercultures and mainstream cultures flow into each other, as well as having their moments of partition. And beside the rainbow of color there are pockets of despair, mental illness, drug dependence, and exploitation. Nimbin is a complex and confusing site beyond first sight. So how is it that a declining dairy town became a thriving countercultural center?

The local confluence of global economic and technological changes on one hand, and cultural change on the other provide the most rehearsed answer. By the 1970s changes to the northern New South Wales dairy industry had brought a decrease in the working population to small village-based operations such as in Nimbin. Improvements to transport links and more affordable cars enabled travel to the larger shopping center, 30 kilometers away in Lismore. It is a disputed but often made claim that Nimbin in the 1970s was a dying village. Many shops had been shut for some time. It was unclear to the villagers where the future lay (Garbutt 2014).

Nearby, but in a parallel universe, a group of paid and volunteering workers with the Australian Union of Students were looking for a festival site for the biannual *Aquarius Festival of University Arts*. The 1971 Festival in Canberra had been criticized for having a planned program that was too "bourgeois", and an unofficial program that was too entrenched in oppositional protest. The pitch by the 1973 Festival Director, Graeme Dunstan, and Cultural Director, Johnny Allen, was for a 10-day countercultural festival with affirmative politics. The festival themes would be "survival on earth and a living affirmation that we do not need to be sold our culture" (May Manifesto, cited in Jiggens 1983). There would be no program, and it would take place on a greenfield site away from the mainstream where experiments toward a new social future could be carried out (Dunstan 1971).

Because of the declining agricultural economy during the 1970s, the NSW far-north coast with its abundant, cheap, subtropical, green fields was becoming known as a countercultural Shangri-la. Nevertheless, a suitable greenfield site for a festival was not easily found and by late 1972 the organizers were desperate. With too little time to turn farmland into a festival venue, a compromise was needed and Col James, an architecture lecturer from Sydney University, saw this situation as an opportunity to "recycle a town". When the idea was put to Fred Cullen, the president of the Nimbin Show Society, he knew that a festival for 5000 students needed the entire village to be involved in the decision making. A village meeting was called in January 1973 (Dunstan and Allen 2013).

Over 180 people came to the meeting. Graeme Dunstan had done a lot of storytelling in the preceding days and at the meeting did so again. Billy Garner (1973) wrote in the counterculture magazine *The Digger*, how:

> [Dunstan] gives a public recitation of The Dream. … He says that he wants the country culture and the city culture to meet. It's not to be a rock festival, not just a collection of performances, but 'an enlarging of the community for ten days', a sort of a bazaar of alternative lifestyles. Then he offers a simpler bait: a burst of spending; the beginning of craft industries; tourists; a bit of fame for everyone as Nimbin gets onto the map. Above all he claims it will bring young people back to the country.

Bob Marsh, the local police sergeant, was unable to attend the meeting but in a letter read out by the meeting chair implored the community to vote yes. The outcome was that all but four or five gave their assent to the Aquarius Festival coming to Nimbin later that year in May.

In the remaining months prior to the festival, a number of vacant buildings were bought by the Australian Union of Students and transformed into a festival headquarters, food cooperative, café, and meeting place. Students were given subsistence pay in the form of *Nimbuns*, exchangeable for food, while preparing festival infrastructure, taking on community liaison roles, and traveling the nation in performing troupes for publicity. The Sydney-based Bush Video installed Australia's first open-access cable television network across which each day's events would be streamed across wired-in monitors with footage shot by participants who took advantage of video "portapaks" (Allen 1973; Jones 2011: 248–9). A learning exchange was developed for the sharing of skills and knowledge, from natural therapies to weaving, but including such things as bridge lessons from the Lismore Bridge Club.

Throughout the lead-up, Dunstan and Allen put considerable energy into spreading the word "on the lips of the counterculture" (Dunstan and Allen 2013). The word-of-mouth invitation was important because of the festival's experimental form. As they wrote in the May Manifesto, "there will be no program; you are the program. But …", Johnny Allen emphasizes:

> [W]e spent a very active year […] going from campus to campus, community to community, inviting people to come and explaining to them how we wanted them to come. We wanted them to come in small self-sufficient tribal groups. We wanted them to find ways of manifesting their lifestyle and what they cared about. […] So it was really quite an effort to turn the conventional festival on its head.
> (in Dunstan and Allen 2013)

It is for this reason that the organizers and many Aquarians eschew the idea that the *Nimbin Aquarius Festival* was Australia's Woodstock, as its ethos was opposed to the idea of having celebrities on stage entertaining a crowd around the clock. Aquarius was a deliberative social experiment with the purpose of creating the society to come.

A concrete expression of this open and experimental social process at the *Aquarius Festival* was the establishment of one of the Rainbow Region's largest intentional communities at Tuntable Falls. While this community was not the first "alternative" community in the region, it presaged an influx of post-Aquarius lifestyle migrants, attracted by the "The Dream" that there is an alternative. As a result, the *Aquarius Festival* left indelible marks on the village. At its best, this has developed into a community that is collaborative, supportive of difference, and creatively sustainable; but conversely, it is also sometimes beset by issues arising from economic deprivation and the drug trade (McGee 2014).

Nimbin is the center of a countercultural change that has rippled through the wider region. The counterculture has nestled in beside a conservative rural community, both of which coexist and engage with each other, sometimes willingly, at other times "if we must", and that hybridize to produce a regional "vibe". For example, the community's history and skill in environmental protest and community organizing resulted in an unusually disparate coalition of interests coming together to successfully resist the coal seam gas industry on prime agricultural land (Hartman and Darab 2014). Or, to take another focus, the Rainbow Region, unlike many rural areas in Australia, has been able to embrace sexual diversity so that it has a significant and visible Gay, Lesbian, Bi-sexual, Trans-sexual and Inter-sex (GLBTI) community, with the *Tropical Fruits New Years Eve* party being one of the largest GLBTI events held outside the capital cities of Australia (Tropical Fruits Inc. 2013).

It is during this post-1970s period that Southern Cross University in Lismore grew from a Teachers College to a University (Bass 1992). The countercultural presence in the Rainbow Region and the subtropical setting often attract a somewhat "countercultural" group of academics and proto-academics (though none might use that specific term). And just as there are individuals such as Baden Offord who have infused cultural studies with a distinctive foci and ethos, so too has the local cultural formation and its landscape played a pedagogical role in this same disciplinary process.

University ⇔ Community

I have sketched this scene to explicitly situate the Aquarius Festival 40th anniversary event *Aquarius and Beyond* in terms of cultural studies at Southern Cross University, and in terms of the university within its region.

Aquarius and Beyond began as not much more than enthusiasm and interest. As a university-based member of the *Aquarian Archive*, a volunteer organization dedicated to archiving materials from the NSW far-north coast counterculture, I raised the opportunity for a 40th anniversary collaboration in late 2011: a forum at the university perhaps? The idea received positive nods. Such an event would be not only a way to expand the archive's collection but also an opportunity to develop a research project examining a significant cultural experiment on the university's doorstep.

A group of SCU staff and students began planning an event and by May 2012, at the first community-organized meeting at Nimbin Hall to plan the 2013 anniversary, we were ready with a proposal for *Aquarius and Beyond*. We framed it as a:

> market of ideas styled as a multiversity event [...] bringing together a range of expressions, reflections and projections into the future: from academic short-papers to performances, from pamphleteering to speaker's panels and soapboxes, and all points in-between.
> (Southern Cross University 2012)

The idea and the university were openly welcomed by the Nimbin community and we were given a prime spot in May after the *Nimbin MardiGrass* (the annual drug law reform rally) and directly preceding the Masked Ball.

Given this timing and our welcome, it was clear that an event held within the safe, convenient, and *cheap* confines of the university campus in Lismore would be an anathema to the Aquarian and community spirit. The university needed to go *to* Nimbin. From a critical pedagogical point of view this seems obvious—begin where the people are and make education accessible, in this case in geographical terms. It would, however, be one of many instances where convenience or cultural blindness—the enculturated, institutionalized blindness that comes from being in the academy—would be challenged. In this case the convenience of the university setting was because of the established and free facilities. To move to the Nimbin Town Hall, the site of that village meeting which voted "Yes" to the Australian Union of Students changed the financial and logistical equation. What was to be a simple and free day became a little more complex and a lot more wonderful.

Meanwhile, support for *Aquarius and Beyond* within the wider "Aquarian community" was growing. For many original participants, most now in their 60s and 70s, the desire and space to revisit as well as give due critical regard to a significant moment in their lives had come round. Importantly, too, Graeme Dunstan and Johnny Allen were actively supportive, and this gave our event an Aquarius stamp of approval. When, in 2012, Johnny began a "My Nimbin Aquarius Story" Facebook group that gathered over two hundred and fifty members, word spread about *Aquarius and Beyond*, this time on the new-media-lips of the counterculture. The "Call for Papers and Expressions of Interest" elicited so many responses that the planned 1-day event expanded to 2 days. Its timing on the Thursday and Friday before Saturday's 40th Anniversary Masked Ball, yielded a neat travel-friendly package of reflection, reunion, and revelry.

To quickly detour to one end of this tale, *Aquarius and Beyond* was a success. People came to what ended up becoming a "community conference"— something resembling an academic conference but substantially handed over to community speakers. Unlike most conferences, audiences grew throughout the 2 days with people coming in from the street to fill Nimbin Hall with up to one hundred and fifty people.

The first day became a critical reflection on the past, with an abundance of storytelling and song. The joy and the life-changing nature of the festival and times were on display. Mixed-in was the acknowledgement that the issues of the 1970s had remained live: the nature of social relationships and institutions and the connections between economy, ecology, and lifestyle were just two of these. And there were places for critical pause: the gendered and racialized assumptions of the times provided two points of focus and debate, as did the issue of new sexual freedoms and its limits in terms of power, exploitation, and abuse. The ability of participants to listen and speak, celebrate, and critically reflect was one sign of the hope and critical optimism that pervaded the event.

The second day considered post-Aquarius Nimbin, now and into the future. For example, on this day pre-Aquarius locals, some now into their 80s, reflected on life in Nimbin before Aquarius and now. Their focus on relationships between cultures rather than on a "straight/hippy" divide was revelatory. A panel of "children of Aquarius", many now with families of their own, spoke of what they had learned about child-rearing, freedom, and its limits, among other things. Natalie Myer, from the Nimbin Neighbourhood and Information Centre, gave a grounded account of maintaining and modifying the Aquarian countercultural ideal in more intensely economistic and regulated neoliberal times. Others reflected on the regional history of activism that has produced a community rich in practical knowledge of organizing for change, and which has resulted in such things as environmental victories and new communal property ownership laws. These technologies of care have been exported to others around the nation and beyond (Page 2014; Ricketts 2012).

Community members and academics spoke, together. Some sang. History was fashioned and sometimes spun. There was a storytelling dinner cum soiree. Archives of audio, video, and material objects were developed. And, *we broke-even*. After a final communal reflection, the closing session wrapped up with Aquarius minstrel Paul Joseph on ukulele leading a spiral dance to the Aquarius hymn, "May the Long Time Sun Shine Upon You (all love surround you, and the pure light within you guide your way home)" (New 2013: 4:14ff).

Aquarius and Beyond provided a community, for whom the place of Nimbin is significant, space to tell stories about itself *to itself*. It was an education for post-Aquarian arrivals in the region to hear about the festival and its build-up, but perhaps more significantly to experience "The Dream" through the spirit of the storytellers, and to consider how and in what form that dream is still active and viable. And it was an education for all to share in Nimbin in the present day and the struggles and hopes that continue. Nimbin itself is a pedagogical site: beyond the headlines of drug busts and beyond the commercialized hippy-dom is a community that takes conscious living seriously: being there among a collection of its people is an "always already" emplaced and engaged education.

Research ⇔ Pedagogy: University ⇔ Community

Cultural studies scholarship has been framed as a political "intervention" into social and cultural practices in an attempt to advance social justice (Bowman 2007). A public intervention, such as *Aquarius and Beyond* generates and demands ethical and scholarly rigor by opening academic cultural practices to the glare of public scrutiny: this is revealing for self and institution. Via social media, critique ensuing from such scrutiny can be rapidly shared, generative in its effect, and demand responsiveness that is enervating and sometimes frightening. And with *Aquarius and Beyond* scrutiny was amplified because "the public" in question was participating in the intervention, with this "public" skilled in cultural critique and intervening on their own terms.

The 2-day community conference was explicitly pedagogical. But it soon became apparent that the larger research project within which the conference was embedded was similarly pedagogical. The research outputs derived from this conference are an obvious manifestation of this, but so too was the research process itself. The act of research engaged during this conference provided concrete expression of what universities do when they research, and how and why they do it. It is in this sense that research as intervention has ethical implications that can reverberate beyond a single project.

It is here too that cultural studies practice, a practice for which ethics "organizes [its] political horizon" (Zylinksa 2005: 3), is well suited to community-involved research. Initially this derives from valuing everyday life in its multiplicity: a refusal to essentialize any one aspect of culture. Moreover, the discipline's sensitivity to the power-relations that are integral to cultural practices and processes (including the power-relations that imbue a research project itself) inform a cultural studies researcher's sensibility: humility is key in publicly pedagogical engagements, whether in the form of a research interview, or an event-planning process. This self-reflexivity provides researcher/interventionists with real-time feedback and checking mechanisms that build relationships. These both benefit the project and, at times, surface boat-rocking revelations about one's own practice and those of the academy. These public encounters are deeply pedagogical for all involved, if we are open to that potential. The following examples are intended as illustrations of these general points.

The decision to take the university to Nimbin significantly contributed to the success of *Aquarius and Beyond*. It was a surprise to many Nimbinites that we were able to hold and grow a crowd throughout the 2 days at what was, to all appearances, a conference. As Michael Balderstone, Nimbin Hemp Embassy President, told me, "It's a tough crowd; they don't stay if they don't like it" (2013: pers. comm., 24 May). Written feedback showed that hearing one's own history being told was a rare joy; to have time to meet and talk about local hopes, dreams, and realities was a stimulating pleasure. The familiar location at the Town Hall in the center of the village allowed the audience to grow organically as word spread on the street. The adult educational principle, sequestered by cultural studies, of beginning with people's lived experience as a source of learning and social transformation was confirmed once again.

Moreover, being in Nimbin enabled community involvement to flourish. When we wanted a stage that could work for both formal presentations and more relaxed panel discussions, the Nimbin Hemp Embassy willingly decked out the stage with sofas and a coffee table for a lounge-room feel. The Aquarius Foundation regularly decorated the hall for cabarets and balls, and so for the conference it was festooned with Benny Zable's banners of peace and imagination. A local group who had a portable photographic exhibition on local countercultural history was able to set up at the rear of the hall. The overall event was in its place and it was this that grounded all that happened: discussion was opened to the rigor of the street, and to the multiplicity of the place. It felt real.

The move to Nimbin did, of course, challenge us. Community accessibility, for example, is more than physical; financial considerations accompanied wider participation infusing event management and the budget with ethical dimensions. Our initial budget based on the norm of utilizing professional conference management together with credit card prepayment yielded a $150 entry fee to break even. The $150 fee would also effectively fence off the event from many locals who are on subsistence incomes. After a visit to Nimbin Neighbourhood and Information Centre for advice, I was given the clear message about "the way we do things here": we don't use credit cards; we make sure people get well fed; and we keep it local—local caterer, local produce, vegan, and vegetarian. I drove the 30 kilometers back to Lismore feeling as if I had arrived in Nimbin unsuitably dressed in a suit and carrying a patent leather briefcase.

The sensible option was to reorganize Nimbin-style. There would be no outsourced conference management and we would take cash only at the door. We organized a local caterer. Southern Cross University supplied, as an "in-kind" contribution, a technician and van packed with sound, lighting, and recording equipment for the conference; a video setup for one-on-one cultural history interviews; scanning equipment for document archiving; and a photographic studio setup for a "photobooth". After the initial setup all students ran all the technical services. With a budget recalculation and some wishful thinking we set the price at $30 for the 2 days.

And still there were issues. When I publicized *Aquarius and Beyond* with a $30 entry fee on the popular local Facebook grapevine "Nimbin Hookups", the second theme of the 1973 *Aquarius Festival*, "we do not need to be sold our culture" (May Manifesto in Jiggens 1983), was quoted in protest. Comments about the cost of "hearing our own history" quickly appeared with growing numbers of "likes". A rapid response was needed to preserve the integrity of and goodwill toward the project. From our organizers' point of view the fee was justified because of the known expenses, and yet there is still the issue that despite the 'oily rag' on which the event was run, the university does have resources and perceived riches, as do staff members such as me. To us $30 might be a trifle but on a precarious income the price was significant. So along with an explanation of why there was a fee, I took a leap of faith into "karma pricing", a locally well-understood price mechanism: pay the suggested price, what you think it is worth, or what you can afford. After tallying the door takings that ranged from a freshly picked flower to $150, we broke even.

Another instance where university culture had an exclusionary impact was the "Call for Papers" and "Expressions of Interest". Our hope was for performances of all kinds and 'papers' of all kinds. Nevertheless in my correspondence I did ask for a title and an "abstract or outline" of the contribution. In an email exchange with an influential community member who was worried about coming up with a title and an outline, I wrote to say not to "make a big thing out of it but just write in your own words what you want to talk about". I also suggested a title. I didn't think more of this until a number of miscommunications created enough fuel for an outpouring of feedback, which in essence, suggested that on the one hand I would use words like "collaborative event" in event emails, but that in effect this collaboration was token. For example, enquirers asked, "what support was there for community members to work out their own title for a talk and put together words for a so-called abstract or outline?"

On reflection, but too late for *Aquarius and Beyond*, I perceived an academic-shaped cultural void in the organizing. This void could have been addressed with preliminary workshops for those wanting to be part of the event but for whom the academic cultural artifacts of "title and abstract" were foreign objects. Here was a chance to take the educational and collaborative potential of the project another step forward by learning together about each others' cultural practices and ways. This lack of critical cultural awareness was an embarrassing revelation. While *Aquarius and Beyond* was successful, the opportunities for improvement of process are many.

These instances demonstrate how a community of onlookers provides a form of rigor that is not focused on robust methods and appropriately aligned theoretical frameworks, but on other aspects of process and ethics. The ethical implications of research-as-intervention become palpable as it manifests itself in relationships with people who are ready to call a process to account when it goes astray. The accounts here regarding the charges for attending *Aquarius and Beyond* and the process for developing the program are small instances where a light is shone onto oneself within university culture and the effect of that culture on the people who are being asked to interact with it.

Nevertheless, *Aquarius and Beyond* was a significant event for both the community and the larger research project. For the community it highlighted the village's key cultural role within the Rainbow Region, and provided a multivoiced and reflexive event, in place and with a concern for the present and future. For the ongoing research project that grew from the festival, we had in one location access to many of the key actors within that history, and most importantly, we developed relationships that would provide us with a group of peers that complements those of the academy. Then there are relationships with the community that are forged by together doing the things that constitute such education and research. Importantly, from a cultural studies perspective, what this affords is "theorizing [that can] happen 'in place' and not in isolation from the lived contexts of the everyday" (Tomaselli and Mboti 2013: 533).

Conclusion

In this chapter I have focused on the *Aquarius and Beyond* community conference, an event situated within a larger ongoing community-engaged research project. The event itself may be considered in a number of ways. In the context of the contemporary higher education sector within Australia it can be seen as a response to community-engagement agendas that focus research on utility and relevance to the wider community and society. Alternatively, within cultural studies, this project and the event might also be seen in terms of a turn away from textual analysis and toward ethnography: a methodological accompaniment to the utilitarian repurposing of university research. I argue that this is a limited analysis.

My argument for engaged cultural studies research is not an exclusive one. Engaged cultural studies research is one expression of an ecology of disciplinary modes of developing a research agenda. In a small regional university setting where community and university are intimately interwoven, combined with increasing demands upon the teaching-research cultural studies scholar, community-engaged research and teaching is not only a pragmatic possibility, but an ethical response. Given that many students at new generation universities are the first-in-family to attend university, community-engagement situates theory in relation to everyday experience. Techniques of critical analysis can be combined with an ethnographic approach to that which is accessible both beyond the classroom and within it. Research agendas readily emerge in this milieu. As a privileged institution amidst a plethora of local interests and needs, the academy should be at the service of the community. Not exclusively, of course, but as part of the reciprocity that constitutes everyday life and relationships.

These factors, combined with a critically aware countercultural current in the region, have nurtured a specific configuration of cultural studies at Southern Cross University—one that is overtly (self-)reflexive whether in terms of local and global concerns, self and others, everyday life and theory, or university and community. There has been a *geophilosophical* (and perhaps what might be called a minor *geopedagogical*) dynamic at work producing this cultural studies configuration.

Aquarius and Beyond is located within this milieu. The event functions as a research and pedagogical site; it is situated between university and community, and so is an intervention that has the potential to create effects in each domain. Indeed if all research is an intervention, then this aspect of cultural studies work is amplified when that research engages directly with communities. The research becomes pedagogical for all involved: it teaches communities about universities and vice versa, and the outcomes are neither predictable nor always complimentary. The risk that the research process itself might go horribly wrong, thereby decreasing the fund of community goodwill between the academy and the community, intensifies the research experience. From processes of collaboration, to the ethics of ownership of cultural knowledge, to the politics of representation while living as a researcher amidst the community of research participants, engaged research generates a critically reflexive research environment. Research outcomes are both substantive with regard to explicit research aims, and emerge from reflexively occupying the roles into which academic research interpellates all involved. And each role—researcher, researched, onlooker, expert—is variously occupied by the same individual at different times.

Thus, as an example of a research event, the *Aquarius and Beyond* community conference carries within it a countercultural impetus. It stimulates a critical reflection on recent regional history and on academic research and pedagogical processes. Community, place, and academy are put into relationship with each other and for the academy and cultural studies this opens our practices and processes to the outside. Opening any system to a wider environment involves risks, but it also multiplies the possibilities for enriching life. This is just one sense in which community-engaged research resonates with the very purpose of cultural studies as a critical pedagogical project. And just as it opens possibilities for that project, so too does it potentially enliven the communities in which it is actively situated.

References

Allen, J. (1973). After Nimbin—What? *Nimbin Good Times, Mushroom Man Edition*, 2.
Allon, F. (2006). Between Sydney and Hong Kong. *Cultural Studies Review*, 12 (2): 33–49.
Allon, F., and Morris, M. (2006). Introduction. *Cultural Studies Review*, 12 (2): 1–16.
Ang, I. (2006). From cultural studies to cultural research. *Cultural Studies Review*, 12 (2): 183–97.
Bass, R. (1992). *Teachers college to university*. Lismore, University of New England-Northern Rivers.
Biermann, S., Garbutt, R., and Offord, B. (2010). Cultural studies in action. In Riseman, N., Rechter, S., and Warne, E. (eds). *Learning, teaching and social justice in higher education* (pp. 85–99), Melbourne, University of Melbourne e-Scholarship Research Centre.
Bowman, P. (2007). *Post-Marxism versus cultural studies*. Edinburgh, Edinburgh University Press.
Dunstan, G. (1971). Which way Aquarius. *National U*, June 28: 5.
Dunstan, G., and Allen, J. (2013). Kaptain Kulture and Superfest present. Paper presented to *Aquarius and Beyond*, Nimbin Town Hall, May 11.
Garbutt, R. (2014). Aquarius and Beyond. *M/C Journal*, 17 (6).
Garbutt, R., Biermann, S., and Offord, B. (2012). Into the borderlands. *Critical Arts*, 26 (1): 62–81.
Garbutt, R., and Kayess, M. (2014). Fleshy academic literacy. *Fusion*, 5.
Garner, B. (1973). Nimbin lends itself to the counter-culture. *The Digger*, January 27–February 13: 3.
Goh, B.C., Offord, B., and Garbutt, R. (eds). (2012). *Activating human rights and peace*. Farnham, Ashgate.
Grossberg, L. (1994). Introduction. In Giroux, H.A., and McLaren, P. (eds). *Between borders*. New York, Routledge.
Grossberg, L. (1997). *Bringing it all back home*. Durham, Duke University Press.
Hartman, Y., and Darab, S. (2014). The power of the wave: activism Rainbow Region-style. *M/C Journal*, 17 (6).
Johnson, R., Chambers, D., Raghuram, P., and Tincknell, E. (2004). *The practice of cultural studies*. London, Sage.
Jones, S. (2011). *Synthetics*. Cambridge, MIT Press.
The May Manifesto. (1983/1972). In Jiggens, J. *Rehearsals for the Apocalypse* (p. 20). Brisbane, John Jiggens.
McGee, T. (2014). Reconsidering Nimbin 40 years after the Aquarius Festival. Accessed February 27, 2015, http://www.abc.net.au/radionational/programs/ockhamsrazor/5431260.

New, M. (2013). *An Aquarius legacy*. Accessed May 19, 2015, https://vimeo.com/66868356.
Page, J. (2014). Counterculture, property, place, and time. *M/C Journal*, 17 (6).
Porter, E., & Offord, B. (eds). (2006). *Activating human rights*. Bern, Peter Lang.
Ricketts, A. (2012). *The activists' handbook*. London, Zed Books.
Rodman, G.B. (2015). *Why cultural studies?* Chichester, Wiley Blackwell.
Rutten, K., Rodman, G.B., Wright, H.K., and Soetaert, R. (2013). Cultural studies and critical literacies. *International Journal of Cultural Studies*, 16 (5): 443–56.
Said, E.W. (1994). *Representations of the intellectual*. London, Vintage.
Southern Cross University. (2012). *Initial call for papers and expressions of interest*. Lismore, Southern Cross University. Accessed May 1, 2015, http://sassevents.scu.edu.au/aquarius/paperscall.html.
Tomaselli, K.G., and Mboti, N. (2013). Doing cultural studies. *International Journal of Cultural Studies*, 16 (5): 521–37.
Tropical Fruits Inc. (2013). Our story. Accessed April 14, 2015, http://www.tropical-fruits.org.au/about-us/our-story.
Turner, G. (2009). Cultural Studies 101. *Cultural Studies Review*, 15 (1): 175–87.
Wilson, H. (ed.) (2003). *Belonging in the rainbow region*. Lismore, Southern Cross University Press.
Zylinksa, J. (2005). *The ethics of cultural studies*. London, Continuum.

3 Learning to be Men
Masculinities, Pedagogy, and Science Fiction

Linda Wight

Like many cultural studies practitioners, my research, learning, and teaching are concerned with critiquing and contesting taken-for-granted assumptions that posit that human identities and social structures are fixed, natural, and inevitable. These are assumptions that can contribute to social disadvantage, oppression, and inequity. My research has focused in particular on problematizing hegemonic ideals of masculinity and in exploring the potential for science fiction to critique and offer alternatives to these dominant models. This chapter reflects on the embodied experience of doing this form of cultural studies in the classroom, of exploring these ideas in the context of a pedagogical exchange with undergraduate university students enrolled in a fantasy and science fiction course. Both the experience of masculinity—for men and women—and the activities of learning and teaching are deeply embodied. The purposes of this chapter are therefore twofold. First, I argue that science fiction is a useful tool for encouraging students to develop their awareness of how popular culture functions as a form of public pedagogy that frames how each of us experience masculinity. While some science fiction takes hegemonic ideals of gender for granted and encourages us to do the same, other texts problematize these assumptions by showing us the potential for bodies to be lived and experienced differently. Second, by reflecting on my own embodied experience of teaching science fiction in a university classroom, this chapter aims to encourage teachers to think about how we actually do cultural studies with our students and to move beyond conceiving of the classroom as a purely intellectual space to also embrace the bodily dimension of our practice.

Learning Masculinity: Popular Culture, Public Pedagogy, and the University Classroom

Cultural studies theorists have long identified popular culture as a form of public pedagogy, both as a crucial site for the production of hegemonic identities and as a potential site for critique and imagination of counter-hegemonic possibilities (Sandlin, Schultz and Burdick 2010: 3; Wright 2010: 141). Public pedagogies include those "spaces, sites, and languages of education and learning that exist outside of the walls of the institution of schools" (Sandlin, Schultz and Burdick 2010: 1), and it is largely from and in these spaces that boys and men learn how to perform hegemonic masculinity. Hegemonic masculinity stands as the form of masculinity that is positioned as ideal in a particular culture at a particular time (Connell 2005: 77). Violence, physical strength, rationality, sexual virility, and the suppression of emotions have been—and to various extents continue to be—some of the common markers of this idealized construction in Western societies. Each of these traits is closely connected to a particular conception of the male body, either emphasizing what male bodies should do, or placing limitations on how male bodies should be displayed and experienced. Lynne Segal (1990) notes that hegemonic masculinity is also commonly "defined through a series of hierarchical relations: rejection and suppression of femininity and homosexual desire, command and control over (often seen as 'protection of') the 'weak' and 'inferior'" (205). This hierarchy rests on the assumption that men's bodies are essentially different from and superior to women's, and therefore demands that men repress any experience of their body that might undermine this dichotomy, such as the experience of physical vulnerability. Raewyn Connell (2005: 79) points out that the number of men conforming to the hegemonic blueprint in its entirety might be quite small; however, she argues that the majority of men perform complicit masculinities that support the hegemonic ideal because of the perceived benefits it offers, not the least of which is social approbation.

Since the experience of masculinity is so deeply embodied, it is therefore crucial to attend to the way popular culture frames, directs, and limits this experience. Thomas J. Gerschick and Adam S. Miller (1995) observe that the body is often the "central foundation of how men define themselves and how they are defined by others" (183). As a result, men who aspire to the hegemonic ideal experience great pressure to ensure that their bodies look and behave in ways that are sanctioned by the dominant culture. Each day we are bombarded with idealized images of male bodies in the public realm. Henry Giroux (2006) argues, for example, that movies use "images, sounds, gestures, talk, and spectacles in order to create the possibilities for people to be educated about how to act, speak, think, feel, desire, and behave" (118). Antonio Gramsci (1971) points out, however, that hegemony is never absolute, and popular culture can also encourage contestation of and resistance to dominant modes (in this case, dominant modes of masculinity). Thus men who experience a disconnection between their own bodily experiences and the masculine ideal to which they are encouraged to aspire—a disconnection that may stem from their experience of race, class, sexuality, age, disability, or myriad other factors—may turn to popular culture as "a site of contestation and a site of utopian possibility, a space in which emancipating politics can be fashioned that 'consists in making seem possible precisely that which, from within the situation, is declared to be impossible'" (Giroux 2004: 60, citing Badiou 2001).

The university classroom is not the only space in which students may engage critically with the images of hegemonic and contestatory masculinities with which they are confronted in popular culture. Indeed, advocates of public pedagogy have argued strongly and legitimately "that schools are not the sole sites of teaching, learning, or curricula, and that perhaps they are not even the most influential" (Sandlin, Schultz and Burdick 2010: 2). Nevertheless, the university classroom may offer teachers and students alike a crucial space and time in which to focus on interrogating the way popular culture contributes to our embodied experience of masculinities. For some who have never thought about, let alone questioned, their investment in particular masculine ideals or popular culture texts, this can be a confronting experience. Some of my students, for instance, expressed concern that they had never consciously attended to the way *Terminator 2: Judgment Day* (James Cameron 1991) can be read as idealizing a particular image of a paternal and caring but still violent and dominant masculinity until they had viewed and discussed the film in class and through this particular theoretical lens. Giroux (2004) notes the importance of promoting this kind of critical dialogue and a culture of questioning and insists that "educators, cultural studies theorists, students, and activists face the task of providing a language of resistance and possibility" (76). Once again, such a task need not be undertaken in the university classroom, however for those students who have largely taken gender for granted, the study of masculinities as they are represented in science fiction may provide them with a critical tool—"a language of resistance and possibility"—with which to interrogate the popular constructions of masculinity that they encounter in their lives on a daily basis.

Interrogating Masculinity in and Through Science Fiction

Science fiction—often referred to as the literature of ideas—is an ideal tool by which to develop students' "language of resistance and possibility" because it takes itself seriously as a genre that is concerned with intellectual speculation. Joanna Russ (1972) labels science fiction the genre of "what if?" (79), recognizing the potential of the genre to imagine worlds, societies, and identities different to those we currently take for granted. In a similar vein, Ursula Le Guin (1979) calls science fiction the genre of "thought-experiment[s]" (156), the purpose of which is not to predict the future, but rather to describe and defamiliarize the present world. Of particular interest to me is the potential of science fiction to defamiliarize hegemonic masculinity, to reveal how gender is culturally constructed, and to open up the possibility of experiencing and embodying gender differently by allowing readers and viewers "to experience and recreate a new or transformed world based on a set of assumptions different from those we usually accept" (Annas 1978: 145).

Since the 1970s a number of science fiction writers—particularly those working within the burgeoning field of feminist science fiction—have employed a wide range of tropes to draw attention to the damage that contemporary ideals of masculinity pose to both women and men; to emphasize that such ideals are culturally constructed and therefore changeable; and to imagine alternative ways of embodying masculinity, or indeed of rejecting altogether the gender binary which currently frames how bodies can be experienced and lived. For example, a number of science fiction writers have imagined either all-female societies, or societies in which men and women are kept strictly segregated, in order to draw attention to the way women living in real-world patriarchal cultures are constrained from behaving in ways that are deemed masculine, and to imagine how both men and women might perceive and interact with their world and other individuals differently if allowed access to the full range of human behaviors and activities, rather than being constrained to enact only one side of the masculine-feminine binary. Other science fiction writers and filmmakers imagine societies in which familiar masculine and feminine social roles are reversed. By positioning men in an inferior social role—defined, for instance, as lacking intelligence, foresight, and self-control; barred from education and certain professions; and valued only for their sexual and reproductive capacities—these writers and filmmakers draw attention to the meaning that is invested in the sexed body and the ramifications this has for individuals' performance of, or exclusion from, particular social roles. Furthermore, these thought experiments in role reversal defamiliarize the culturally constructed gender hierarchy operating in the real world which we are encouraged to accept as natural, universal, and inevitable. Yet other science fiction texts emphasize the contingency of dominant gender ideals by imagining alien cultures which demonstrate the possibility of alternative social structures and definitions of gender, or indeed cultures from which gender as a framework for embodied existence is absent altogether.

While my pedagogic approach to teaching masculinity and science fiction embraces and emphasizes the genre's transformative and critical possibilities, it is important to acknowledge that much science fiction has taken, and continues to take, dominant gender ideals for granted. Veronica Hollinger (2003) observes that, "although s[cience] f[iction] has often been called 'the literature of change', for the most part it has been slow to recognize the historical contingency and cultural conventionality of many of our ideas about sexual identity and desire, about gendered behavior and about the 'natural' roles of women and men" (126). Science fiction has long been considered a genre written by men for men and boys, and although this perception is changing, many of the most well-known texts uncritically promote particular heroic models of masculinity, often in the form of the 'male warrior'. The warrior narrative invests masculinity firmly in the capacity of the male body to enact violence and teaches that "violence is legitimate and justified when it occurs within a struggle between good and evil" (Jordan and Cowan 2007: 82). Furthermore, the reward for successful performance of this role is also experienced through the body via sexual access to women; another opportunity for the warrior to prove his masculinity through the demonstration of sexual prowess.

Nevertheless, these more conventional texts may still form the basis for fruitful classroom discussion of the way hegemonic masculine ideals are framed and celebrated in popular culture texts. In addition, those texts that do question the assumption that contemporary gender roles are inevitable and universal may be used to encourage students to reflect on the ways they themselves think about, experience, and embody gender. As noted above, science fiction of this type alerts us to the potential for bodies to be lived and experienced differently, "expand[ing] and enhanc[ing] a field of possibilities for bodily life" (Judith Butler cited in Meijer and Prins 1998: 277). By studying science fiction texts that imagine separatist societies, role reversal societies, or societies in which men and women are undifferentiated by gender regardless of their biological sex, students may begin to consider the possibility of resistance to gender norms in their own social context. As David Couzens Hoy (1999) points out, "critical resistance ... flows from the realisation that the present's self-interpretation is only one among several others that have been viable, and that it should keep itself open to alternative interpretations" (11).

The possibility of critical resistance is further enhanced by those science fiction texts that draw attention to the contingency and mutability of the sexed body itself. Hegemonic masculinity is heavily invested in the idea of the stable male body which is clearly differentiated from the female body, so science fiction which emphasizes how easily the body may be transformed undermines the very foundations of the sexed binary on which this ideal depends. For example, some science fiction writers imagine male or female bodies developing the sexual characteristics of the other sex, either transforming completely or coming to rest in an indeterminate middle ground, challenging the assumption that all human bodies are either strictly male or female. Some writers imagine such changes to be the result of natural evolution, while others explore the possibility of technological manipulation. The latter allows for classroom discussion of technological advances in our own world that similarly reveal the contingency of the sexed body; for example, hormonal and surgical technologies that allow transsexuals to transform their bodies to better align with self-perception. These stories may also be used in the classroom as a springboard for discussion of the existence of intersexuality in our own world; the challenge that such nonbinary bodies pose to gender ideals and social structures that are heavily invested in the gender binary; and the efforts of various social institutions to erase such threatening bodies from the public consciousness, whether through surgical alteration of newborn babies, legal requirements to choose and adhere to one gender and comport one's body appropriately, or the almost complete omission of intersexual characters from popular culture texts.

Such discussions form a crucial component of my undergraduate course on fantasy and science fiction. In this course the interrogation of masculinities is framed as an important consideration within the broader question of what it means to be human, recognizing that conceptions of human identity are deeply influenced by cultural constructions of gender. One of the first questions asked when a child is born is *"is it a boy or girl?"*, the answer shaping both how that child is taught to embody a particular gendered identity, and others' embodied interactions with him or her.

In my fantasy and science fiction course, students engage with these ideas by reading and discussing a wide range of science fiction short stories, novels, and films organized around some of the dominant subgenres and tropes of science fiction: time travel, alien encounters, artificial intelligence and posthuman life, computers and virtual reality, utopia and dystopia, and gender and sexuality. Presenting gender and sexuality as a separate theme risks some students assuming that it is a concern relevant to only a small group of texts, such as those identified by critics, writers, or readers as "feminist" science fiction. Nevertheless, dedicating a week to the topic does allow for close study and discussion of the kinds of gender-bending science fiction outlined above. Furthermore, I attempt to discourage the impression that gender and sexuality are peripheral to the majority of popular culture texts by integrating a focus on gender into each week's discussion. For example, in the week on alien encounters, one of the topics that students discuss is how alien masculinity is presented in the science fiction film, *District 9* (Blomkamp, 2009). Noting the physical similarities of the aliens to the humans (both are bipedal, have two arms that extend from the shoulders, and two eyes positioned at the front of the head), students discuss how imagining aliens with bodies that approximate the human can result in writers and filmmakers also imposing human sex and gender norms on alien beings. In *District 9* the alien protagonist, Christopher, is identified as male both by his name and by his positioning as the protector of his people who have been stranded on Earth and condemned to a life in slums. Christopher fulfils the familiar role of masculine warrior when he breaks into a heavily defended human military facility to steal the fuel for the escape shuttle he intends to fly back to his home planet to seek aid for his oppressed people. Christopher also adheres closely to another dominant model of human masculinity that is idealized in many science fiction texts—the scientist. Much science fiction celebrates the male inventor who triumphs over obstacles and adversaries to save the world due to his superior intellect and scientific knowledge. This description can easily be applied in *District 9*; Christopher is portrayed as intellectually superior to the rest of his species who, for the most part, are depicted as mindless scavengers. Only Christopher has the technological knowledge and skill required to repair and pilot the space shuttle. Students discuss in class the advantages and problems of depicting aliens who so closely approximate human hegemonic norms. On the one hand, many note that this allows them to sympathize with Christopher and comprehend his motivations and actions. Many feel this is important, given that *District 9* has often been read as an allegory that draws attention to the processes, social structures, and belief systems that underlie apartheid and the problematic treatment of human refugees. Others recognize, however, what is taken for granted—perhaps unintentionally—in science fiction films that feature anthropocentric aliens. In this case, *District 9* implies that a particular embodied experience and performance of masculinity is universal, regardless of whether the man has human skin and hands, or a grey-green armored hide and claws. As this example shows, using as a pedagogical tool a popular cultural text with which many students are already familiar may help them to develop a "language of possibility and resistance" with which they can interrogate dominant constructions of masculinity in their everyday world.

Doing Science Fiction and Masculinities in the Classroom

Recognizing the potential of science fiction as a pedagogical tool, however, does not necessarily address how this potential is actually realized, and the pedagogical exchange experienced, in the physical classroom. As noted at the start of this chapter, the classroom is more than a site of intellectual exchange. My intimate awareness, experience, and use of my body, for instance, shapes how I perceive my role in the classroom, how I teach, how I communicate with my students, and how I listen, respond to, and interact with them (Bresler 2004: 9). Similarly, my students' interactions with me and the materials and activities with which they engage in the classroom are informed by their own embodied experiences and perceptions. Thus it is important to reflect upon how my pedagogy is embodied in the classroom when I teach science fiction, and how an awareness of this can contribute to a more meaningful and deeply grounded pedagogical exchange.

As a cultural studies scholar I tend to be critical of attempts by social structures and authority figures to impose a particular belief system or viewpoint on others whose own opinions and experiences are thereby devalued. In the university classroom, however, it is easy to fall into the trap of positioning myself—physically and intellectually—as the expert who imparts "the truth" about the science fiction texts under consideration to my students. One strategy I employ in an attempt to counter this tendency is to physically reconfigure the classroom, thereby altering the way the students and I interact. Ignoring the signs plastered on the walls that instruct teachers *not* to move the furniture, I have the students shift the desks and chairs so that instead of them being seated in a series of rows facing me—"the seer on the stage"—we are seated in a circle. Furthermore, rather than seating myself at the front of the room, I take a different place in the circle each time in an effort to foster an atmosphere of open exchange and dialogue.

Nevertheless, my role as teacher inevitably establishes me as an authority in the classroom. As the teacher I identify the key concepts that I believe it is important for the students to understand; choose the science fiction texts they will study; plan the learning activities and assessment; guide the discussion by asking particular questions and making certain responses; and pass judgment on students' learning by marking their assignments. To some extent, it is important for me to acknowledge and accept this authority. Lawrence Grossberg (1994: 17) raises the possibility of an "earned elitism" which acknowledges that we as teachers bring important experience, knowledge and skills to the classroom. My teaching draws on almost 10 years of research in science fiction and masculinities; therefore, it would be naïve and indeed poor practice to relinquish my responsibility for drawing on my expertise to construct meaningful learning experiences in the classroom. To do so would also deny my deep and genuine passion for this particular field of cultural studies.

bell hooks (1994) insists on the importance of embracing passion in our classrooms. Observing that often "individuals enter the classroom to teach as though only the mind is present and not the body" (1994: 113), she argues that an empowering pedagogy involves teaching from the body with passion, energy, and even love: "to restore passion to the classroom or to excite it in classrooms where it has never been, we must find again the place of eros within ourselves and together allow the mind and body to feel and know and desire" (1994: 118). My pedagogical approach accepts that one of the most important responsibilities I have in the classroom is to feel and express excitement and passion for the texts and ideas my students and I are exploring. Allowing my own passion to be expressed through my body—the energy with which I move about the room; the attention and interest on my face when I listen to my students' ideas; and the excitement in my voice as I explain a concept, talk about one of my favorite science fiction texts, or respond to a student's unique interpretation of a text—allows this to happen.

My passion for particular texts and ideas, however, carries the risk of me adopting a hierarchical pedagogy whereby I am positioned as the ultimate arbiter of what counts as "good" and "bad" science fiction. As Henry Giroux (1992) warns, this can have the effect of silencing and disempowering students:

> [R]ather than providing a place for young people to speak, the study of popular culture becomes a form of border crossing in which the Other becomes a resource for academic appropriation and valorisation. What begins as a critical project is often reduced to an intellectual practice that merely privileges the authoritative persona of the 'seer'. (243)

I encourage students to introduce their own textual examples to the discussion in an effort to provoke the expression of their own passions and to influence the direction and focus of the learning experience. This is one of the benefits of approaching the study of science fiction through the framework of key subgenres and tropes. The students draw on examples of relevant popular cultural texts with which they already feel a passionate connection—some of which I may not be familiar with or have not considered in this light—making these discussions a valuable learning experience for all of us, myself included.

Furthermore, I seek to follow Giroux (2006) in keeping my own pedagogic assumptions at the forefront of my mind by inviting critique of the same in the classroom. Giroux (2006) outlines his pedagogical approach to teaching cultural studies as follows:

> [A]s part of an attempt to read films politically, I make it clear that I bring a certain set of assumptions, experiences, and ideas to my engagement with films ... Not only do I encourage a critique of my own interpretations and analyses of film, but I also urge students to develop their own positions as part of a critique and engagement with varied positions, including my own, that develop amid class dialogue and in conjunction with outside readings and critical reviews. (125)

Similarly, when I first introduce the topic of masculinities in the classroom I am explicit about my theoretical and political perspective. I openly acknowledge that as a feminist scholar I approach the study of masculinities in science fiction from the assumption that hegemonic ideals of masculinity can be damaging, not only to the women who are positioned as inferior, but also to men who either cannot or have no desire to approximate the hegemonic ideal. I also explain my belief that hegemonic masculinity can come at a cost for those men who seem to benefit from it the most. For instance, difficulties forming close emotional relationships through feelings of immense pressure to live up to the roles of protector and breadwinner and struggles with the demand to not disclose any weakness or fear and to endure physical harm as a result of the need to demonstrate the ability to withstand pain and illness without complaint, actually make men vulnerable.

I encourage students to question and critique my assumptions and to raise the possibility of alternative perspectives. As a female scholar I am never as acutely aware of my sexed body as when I am discussing masculinities with my students. In particular, as I interact with my male students I acknowledge that their embodied experiences are invariably different to mine. As Brian Attebery (2002: 153) observes, the universe we perceive depends on who we are and what shapes our bodies take. Thus I acknowledge that my own perceptions about the damaging potential of hegemonic masculinity are shaped largely by my research and by my own embodied engagement with masculinity and the men in my life, rather than by first-hand experience of the pressure to conform to particular models of masculinity that are valorized in popular culture.

Rather than viewing these differences, however, as a barrier to learning and teaching, I encourage students to reflect upon and share their unique embodied perceptions of masculinity in order to engage them in a more meaningful learning experience. As Kenneth Mostern (1994) notes,

> the critical pedagogue is always someone who teaches from where the student is at, rather than from where the teacher is at. This does not mean that the teacher denies his or her pedagogical intentions or specific expertise, but merely that s/he respects the myriad expertise of the students that s/he does not share. (256)

Encouraging each student—male and female—to reflect on and express what it feels like, physically and emotionally, for him or her to engage with masculinity, establishes a personal ground from which the student can critically reflect on the way masculinity is constructed in the science fiction texts under discussion. In any case, my role is not to convince my students to agree to one particular conception of masculinity, but to prompt their thinking with questions that allow them to "gain some understanding of their own involvement in the world, and in the making of their own future" (Grossberg 1994: 18). Such questions may include: *are you aware of particular models of masculinity that are celebrated in popular culture? Do you feel pressure to live up to these ideals? Do you think hegemonic ideals of gender impact upon how you behave, how you use your body, how you dress and think about your appearance? Are you aware of popular culture texts that critique dominant models of masculinity and present alternatives? Do you sometimes feel a gap between your experience of your own body and the images that dominate popular culture? How has your experience and perception of your body changed over time and in different contexts?*

These last two questions, in particular, encourage students to recognize that just as some science fiction texts may offer resistance to monolithic conceptions of a fixed and stable masculine ideal, so too can their own bodies be understood as sites of potential resistance. The unruly body is not simply a passive surface upon which culture imposes its gendered meaning; rather, it is an active agent; one that may refuse to behave in the ways that are mandated as desirable by the dominant culture (Connell 2005). Elizabeth Grosz (1990) points out that,

> the body is the strategic target of systems of codification, supervision and constraint, [but] ... the body and its energies and capacities [also] exert an uncontrollable, unpredictable threat to a regular, systematic mode of social organisation. (64)

For men, this resistance is often most obvious during periods of illness or physical breakdown when the body forces men to acknowledge the physical vulnerability and weakness they have been taught to deny. Resistance may also stem from the experience of physical desire for someone or something that dominant culture deems inappropriate, or simply from an awareness that the real physical body—a body that tires, sickens, and ages—can never live up to the unrealistic ideal that is promoted in some popular culture texts. For female students, resistance may stem from an awareness that their bodies sometimes behave in ways that society has deemed to be masculine. These kinds of classroom activities that encourage students to reflect on their own embodiment of gender morphs science fiction from something that performs tricks of intellectual speculation into something that students can engage with deeply and meaningfully as a pedagogical tool that helps them to develop an awareness of their own experience of masculinity and the possibilities for resistance that this provokes.

Conclusion

Learning and teaching are deeply embodied activities. It is important that teachers of cultural studies reflect critically on how our pedagogy is embodied in the classroom and how this impacts upon both our own and our students' experiences of the pedagogical exchange. This experience will be most rewarding and productive when teachers embrace the bodily dimension of our practice, bringing passion and energy into the classroom and interacting with students in ways that foster an atmosphere of excitement, acceptance, and open dialogue. Acknowledging that our own perceptions and pedagogies are informed by our embodied experiences, we may also encourage our students to recognize themselves as embodied subjects who bring unique insights to the learning exchange. This recognition may be particularly crucial in courses—such as my fantasy and science fiction course—which ask students to critically interrogate cultural constructions of gender. Hegemonic gender ideals seek to authorize how male and female bodies may be lived and experienced, but university courses such as the one discussed in this chapter can encourage students to recognize that these ideals are neither natural nor inevitable and that bodies may be perceived and lived differently. Cultural studies teachers may draw on any number of pedagogical tools to draw students' attention to the way gender ideals are constructed and contested in popular culture. Science fiction, however, is uniquely placed to engage students with thought-experiments that imagine how gender might be experienced differently, or indeed erased altogether, in other cultural or social contexts. While students may engage critically with these texts outside the university institution, teachers can still play an important role in helping students to develop the "language of resistance and possibility" (Giroux 2004: 76) needed to interrogate the popular constructions of gender they encounter in their lives. This responsibility further feeds my passion for teaching, a passion that will always be central to my pedagogical approach.

References

Annas, P.J. (1978). New worlds, new words: androgyny in feminist science fiction. *Science-Fiction Studies*, 5 (20): 143–56.
Attebery, B. (2002). *Decoding gender in science fiction*. New York, Routledge.
Blomkamp, N. (dir.). (2009). *District 9* [film]. TriStar.
Bresler, L. (2004). *Knowing bodies, moving minds: towards embodied teaching and learning*. Dordrecht, Kluwer.
Cameron, J. (dir). (1991). *Terminator 2: Judgment Day* [film]. TriStar.
Connell, R.W. (2005). *Masculinities*, 2nd ed. Berkeley, University of California Press.

Gerschick, T.J., and Miller, A.S. (1995). Coming to terms: masculinity and physical disability. In Sabo, D., and Gordon, D.F. (eds). *Men's health and illness: gender, power, and the body* (pp. 183–204). Thousand Oaks, Sage.

Giroux, H.A. (1992). *Border crossings: cultural workers and the politics of education.* New York, Routledge.

Giroux, H.A. (2004). Cultural studies, public pedagogy, and the responsibility of intellectuals. *Communication and Critical/Cultural Studies.* 1 (1): 59–79.

Giroux, H.A. (2006). *America on the edge: Henry Giroux on politics, culture, and education.* New York, Palgrave Macmillan.

Gramsci, A. (1971). *Selections from the prison notebooks.* Hoare, Q., and Nowell, G. (eds and trans). London, Lawrence and Wishart.

Grossberg, L. (1994). Introduction: bringin' it all back home—pedagogy and cultural studies. In Giroux, H.A., and McLaren, P. (eds). *Between borders: pedagogy and the politics of cultural studies* (pp. 1–25). New York, Routledge.

Grosz, E. (1990). Inscriptions and body-maps: representations and the corporeal. In Threadgold, T., and Cranny-Francis, A. (eds). *Feminine, masculine and representation* (pp. 62–74). Sydney, Allen and Unwin.

Hollinger, V. (2003). Feminist theory and science fiction. In James, E., and Mendlesohn, F. (eds). *The Cambridge companion to science fiction* (pp. 125–36). Cambridge, Cambridge University Press.

Hooks, b. (1994). Eros, eroticism, and the pedagogical process. In Giroux, H.A., and McLaren, P. (eds). *Between borders: pedagogy and the politics of cultural studies* (pp. 113–16). New York, Routledge.

Hoy, D.C. (1999). Critical resistance: Foucault and Bourdieu. In Weiss, G., and Haber, H.F. (eds). *Perspectives on embodiment: the intersections of nature and culture* (pp. 3–22). New York, Routledge.

Jordan, E., and Cowan, A. (2007). Warrior narratives in the kindergarten classroom: renegotiating the social contract? In Kimmel, M.S., and Messner, M.A. (eds). *Men's lives*, (7th edn., pp. 272–83). Boston, Pearson, Allyn and Bacon.

Le Guin, U.K. (1979). *The language of the night: essays on fantasy and science fiction.* New York, G.P. Putnams' Sons.

Meijer, I.C., and Prins, B. (1998). How bodies come to matter: an interview with Judith Butler. *Signs: Journal of Women in Culture and Society*, 23 (2): 275–86.

Mostern, K. (1994). Decolonisation as learning: practice and pedagogy in Frantz Fanon's revolutionary narrative. In Giroux, H.A., and McLaren, P. (eds). *Between borders: pedagogy and the politics of cultural studies* (pp. 253–71). New York, Routledge.

Russ, J. (1972). The image of women in science fiction. In Cornillon, S.K. (ed). *Images of women in fiction: feminist perspectives* (pp. 79–94). Bowling Green, Bowling Green University Popular Press.

Sandlin, J.A., Schultz, B.D., and Burdick, J. (2010). *Handbook of public pedagogy: education and learning beyond schooling.* New York, Routledge.

Segal, L. (1990). *Slow motion: changing masculinities, changing men.* London, Virago.

Wright, R.R. (2010). Unmasking hegemony with *The Avengers*: television entertainment as public pedagogy. In Sandlin, J.A., Schultz, B.D., and Burdick, J. (eds). *Handbook of public pedagogy: education and learning beyond schooling* (pp. 139–50). New York, Routledge.

4 Ramping Up Cultural Studies
Pedagogy and the Activation of Knowledge

Baden Offord

> As a queer person with cerebral palsy (CP), Jacki Brown grew up very aware she was in the minority and this sparked a passion for social justice issues which she was able to explore when studying cultural studies as part of SCU's Bachelor of Arts ... "I don't feel like I'm isolated anymore, even with the big challenges in my life. For me, undertaking this degree really has been transformative. I devoted most of my cultural studies experience to exploring disability and queer sexuality. It really worked for me and gave me agency in the world".
>
> (Jax Brown, Undergraduate Brochure, Southern Cross University, 2015)

> Jax was named one of the top 25 LGBT people to watch in 2015, she is a disability and queer rights activist, writer, spoken-word performer. She co-produces Quippings: Disability Unleashed, a disability performance troupe in Melbourne. Jax has been published on Daily Life, The Feminist Observer, Archer Magazine: The Australian Journal for Sexual Diversity, formally for ABC's Ramp Up. Jax is a graduate of Southern Cross University with a BA in Cultural Studies, which examined the intersections between disability and queer identities. She presents workshops on disability and sexuality for university departments, disability organisations and women's health organisations. Disability rights continue to be a driving force in Jax's life as does a commitment to raising awareness of the issues effecting people with disability and how we can create change.
>
> (ABC Open, 2015)

A Bespoke Cultural Studies Pedagogy

In his recent book, *What's Become of Cultural Studies*, Graeme Turner (2012) makes the argument that cultural studies teaching has rendered "it vulnerable to the accusation that it has become elitist, as canonical, and as mystificatory as those disciplines it was set up to displace" (8). He makes the case that "we need to remind ourselves of the original attributes of cultural studies teaching—such as respect for an interest in the cultural knowledges and experiences of its students" (2012: 8). This chapter responds to these concerns through a reflective account of the pedagogic experiences I have had in teaching cultural studies between 1999 and 2014 at Southern Cross

University (SCU), which is a rural and regional public university located in far northern New South Wales, Australia.

I want to respond to Turner's salient comments by providing an account about a kind of bespoke cultural studies teaching that developed and continues at this university where I worked, which I believe shows that cultural studies teaching does have alternative renderings to those he has mainly observed—that is, where there has been and is a fundamental respect for "the cultural knowledges and experience of its students". In the following I want to discuss the cultural studies teaching I am familiar with through a focus on the central concerns that informed and helped to create a pedagogical environment that activated knowledge as encounter, exchange, and responsibility, and where the meaningful inclusion of students' lived experience became germane to its pedagogy.

I say this program was bespoke because the pedagogy of cultural studies that emerged was very much due to its context, as the university's students primarily came from low socioeconomic backgrounds, and the location of the main campus at Lismore placed it squarely in a rural and regional area, nestled in what is known as the "rainbow region",[1] a region diverse in demographics with a rural industrial base mixed with creative industries, organic farmers, sea-changers, herbalists, hippies, ferals, intellectuals, and hipsters. A curious mix of the rural and con-urban. What is also important about this context is that cultural studies came to be established in a university that was very young, having been established in 1994, when SCU morphed from a College of Advanced Education. As cultural studies was instituted across the Australian academic landscape in the 1990s, often through what was called 'the new humanities', it found a home at SCU quite readily as an open, nontraditional and experimental space. So the cultural studies pedagogy that has become the signature of SCU was in this sense tailor made to its cultural, political, social, and demographic context.

In many ways the advent of cultural studies was a part of a key moment in the sweeping changes that were affecting the humanities quite profoundly across Australia and the Anglophone world at the end of the 20th century and beginning of the 21st century. But as discrete cultural studies programs have come and gone across the university sector as Turner (2012) points out, SCU's has, remarkably, continued to maintain a space at the university and even flourish for 17 years.

Over the length of its existence, the program has become a multi–award winning teaching program with several national individual and team teaching citations. As a result of strong links that were developed, often organically, with the community, the teaching methodology became intertwined and integrated with activities within and outside the university. Field trips into the community became a key aspect of doing cultural studies, where students engaged with local Aboriginal rangers and custodians on country, witnessed court cases at the local courthouse, walked into local rain forest remnants with eco philosophers, and learned about the significance of beach culture at the Byron Bay Surf Life Savers Club. One particular subject (unit) in the cultural studies program, *Borderlands*, provided a powerful postcolonial engagement with a local town called Casino, students walking its multiple war memorial roundabouts, entering into the 'white' historicized space of the local folklore museum, visiting a now often forgotten Aboriginal reserve, and having a coffee at the local Italian café (for a theoretical discussion of this field trip, see Garbutt, Biermann and Offord 2012).

The integration of cultural studies scholarship with community-engaged learning became a key way of contextualizing theory and practice. Undergraduate and postgraduate cultural studies students became actively involved as participants, collaborators in a range of regional, national, and international conferences, including *Activating Human Rights and Diversity* in 2003 and *Activating Human Rights and Peace* in 2008. In 2006 cultural studies students helped to lead and participate in the first regional, student-focused university conference held in New South Wales on disability, *Out of the Spotlight: Disability in the Regions Conference.* In 2010, SCU hosted the Cultural Studies Association of Australasia's annual conference at Byron Bay, which addressed the theme of 'A Scholarly Affair,' a notion of some pedagogic importance to the cultural studies program at SCU where students were encouraged to see themselves as knowledge producers and scholars. Understanding that a purpose of cultural studies was to consider positionality, representation, and power relations and to communicate their implications and dynamics, underscored the students' role as intellectuals and ethical interventionists.

Another noteworthy facet is that as a specific pedagogical approach at SCU, cultural studies was embedded into its Bachelor of Arts degree from 1999 as a core critical approach to education. In the heady days of the establishment of a School of Humanities, Media, and Cultural Studies (which is now known as the School of Arts and Social Sciences after several other name changes), cultural studies was viewed as a crucial approach to knowledge production and an essential pedagogy for a critical and socially inclusive education. All this occurred despite an often hostile and precarious environment characterized by ongoing university restructures and uncertainty, rationalization of programs and degrees, disruptive technologies, corporatization, managerialism, standardization, emphasis on 'work ready' graduates, vocational degrees and outcomes, and *anti*–cultural studies Ministers of Education. As Henry Giroux, John Erni, Stephen Ching-Kiu Chan, Meaghan Morris, and others have noted vociferously, over the last few decades there has been an ongoing desiccation of the humanities generally and a significant challenge to its relevance within what is referred to as the 'knowledge economy'.

My view is that the cultural studies program at SCU has survived, I think, mainly due to its pedagogical self-conception and attention to its context, framed through an ethics of location. As explained above, having an open academic space available for cultural studies to thrive and to be sustainable has been essential. I'm not sure that this would have occurred at an older or established university in the same way, which is also to suggest that cultural studies at SCU echoes, in a very modest way, the original Birmingham motivation. Core ethical concerns with identity, place, and belonging, and of understanding the importance of full participation in society by all people, underpinned the curriculum design, development, and teaching practice. Theory was made to be tactile and therefore to engender a living social praxis in relation to the discipline of cultural studies. Following Stuart Hall's (1991) insight that "theory is only a detour on the way to something more important" (42), we saw cultural studies pedagogy as vital to that possibility of contributing to "something more important". The cultural studies that came about at SCU actively intervened into the pedagogical and scholarly space that was available by "providing the possibility and hope of a counter-hegemonic education that is valuable beyond measurement and that is life-changing" (Garbutt and Offord 2012: 4).

The cultural studies I refer to in this account, then, is characterized by a critical and ethical approach to knowledge. It coheres around how the pedagogic comes to be *activated* through the self and hinges on the capacity to understand the connection between subjectivity and the world, which always has a simultaneous political implication. Cultural studies was instituted at the university as a discrete discipline for the purpose of explicit and identifiable curriculum inclusion and recognition. The concern was to ensure that there was the space to enable a critical pedagogy of cultural studies. Following Nick Couldry (2001), the approach to cultural studies was based on his definition that it was, as a discrete discipline, "an expanding space for sustained, rigorous and self-reflexive empirical research into the massive, power-laden complexity of contemporary culture" (1).

In conjuring the idea of 'activation', which brings to mind the point of the pedagogical exchange—the activation of new understandings, encounters and relationships—we regarded the pedagogical encounter as a highly generative one that activates the relationship *between* the self and other. The term 'activating' as a consequence was a foundational pedagogical concept of this program, linked to both the operations found in the dialectical encounter between self and other (which we acknowledged was also the gist of human rights education), and that motivation to as a consequence make a "principled exposure" to use Paul Gilroy's (2000) terminology, of that encounter. As Susan Giroux (2010) puts it, "the pedagogical encounter has a crucially philosophic, existentially unsettling, and semiotic nature" (49). This was at the heart of our conception of the teaching of cultural studies.

The way the pedagogy of cultural studies developed at SCU, therefore, was not merely about preparing students to be 'work ready' or 'vocationally savvy' but it was a pedagogy concerned with what Raymond Williams (1967) once argued was about "the whole environment, its institutions and relationships ... the field in which our ideas of the world, of ourselves and of our possibilities, are most widely and often most powerfully formed and disseminated" (15–16). In other words, our approach to cultural studies was to institute an educational practice that would extend to the life world of students, preparing students to understand themselves in relation to, and as participants with, the community and the world around them. The hope was that this would enable their potentialities for both engaging with labor, but importantly, in the meaningful everyday experience of life.

This is how I would characterize the purpose of cultural studies pedagogy—to activate knowledge as Stuart Hall conceived it, to bring it to life, make knowledge coherent, relevant, and connected, always contextualized and based on self-reflexive, social praxis. The cultural studies program that was established at this university was inherently driven therefore by a commitment toward social justice, challenging the status quo, moving the center to the margins, and imagining intellectual practice as transformative and generative of these things. For those of us involved in this development, we knew that cultural studies as a disciplinary as well as anti-disciplinary field was crucial to the ways in which students understood notions of the self, identity, place, community, and belonging, through an engaged contextual and critical understanding.

In the remaining account, my aim is to consider some of the salient features of the cultural studies pedagogy that we practiced, which I believe has contributed to making it bespoke in the way I have described above. In the next section, I set the context a little more in terms of teaching cultural studies and its ongoing challenges. The resilience of cultural studies at SCU is not a story of triumph, but one of successfully negotiating the instrumentalist demands of a modern tertiary environment in which the core relationship that exists between student and teacher is increasingly mediated, marginalized, and fragmented. I then go on to discuss a specific feature that has informed and directed the mobilization of the cultural studies pedagogy at SCU. This is the conception of cultural studies pedagogy as a form of human rights education, one that is in a sense, activist and self-reflexively oriented. The argument will be made that cultural studies pedagogy lends itself to the most effective, rigorous, and appropriate way in which human rights education can be enacted, one that is characterized by principled exposure and ethical intervention into knowledge production. In the penultimate part of the chapter, I turn to a brief case study of one of the subjects taught in the cultural studies program, *Unruly Subjects: Citizenship*, to illustrate the features just described. I conclude with a personal reflection.

Beyond the Impossibility of Teaching

It needs to be emphasized, as Graeme Turner (2012) does, that cultural studies pedagogy sits within a precarious and volatile educational and political environment. It finds itself increasingly dependent on finding available spaces in which to be present. Caught in a widespread instrumentalist approach to pedagogy, which is now entrenched through metrics and regulations, teaching itself has become what Edward Said (2005) presciently noted some years ago, something that is "really impossible" to do (90). I think he was expressing his frustration about the inherent paradox and contradictions of modern tertiary education. He made this observation as a response to the instrumental and corporate university requirements of producing students who were able to negotiate the expectations of a standardized and accredited vocational future, while at the same time promulgating, instituting, and scaffolding a rhetoric where students should be enabled to be innovative and analytical knowledge producers informed by their ability to be critical thinkers. This conundrum of higher learning—producing 'work ready' vocationally equipped and specialized students who are also imbued with a critical acuity toward knowledge—has become a key feature in the politics of education and its contemporary struggles. What I think Said lamented was the inherent flaw of a tertiary education, where knowledge production is based on an educational project that is outcomes based, where pedagogy has been reduced to singular performance, not as it ought to be as Henry Giroux (2004) states, "embodied in the lived interactions among educators, audiences, texts and institutional formations" (61). How do we teach, and therefore, how do we learn, in a way that is fundamentally transformative and critically attentive to the limits and possibilities of knowledge, if the project of higher learning is merely to produce students (those who are now frequently referred to as clients and consumers) who are 'work ready' and vocationally prepared?

The struggle over modern education, whether it is in the primary, secondary, or tertiary contexts, has all but been lost to the corporate, scientized, and hyper-technologized approach to teaching and learning. This ascent of technology-driven education, which has been rationalized through managers and the language of the neoliberal marketplace, has entrenched attitudes, beliefs, and dispositions toward knowledge that has made teaching and learning a rehearsal of reductive thinking and standardized practice. This perfect storm, I suspect, is behind Said's lament of the impossibility of teaching.

The implications for the humanities and social sciences are especially profound. We are witnessing a time where education, in its most important sense of empowerment, innovation, and transformation (which lie in the understanding of what being human might mean), is lost to the corporate machine of progress, where what is valued and supported, is not the capacity to be self-reflective and to understand and transcend the limitations of knowledge, but where knowledge is reduced to de-contextualized and de-humanized valences of performance and achievement. The proliferation of 'one size fits all' standardized education has reified the most difficult of challenges in contemporary Western societies, where political strategies of living with difference have become assimilated into redundant, zombie-like habits of management, now frequently substantiated through the language of traditional values, border security, free trade, terrorism, and risk.

In all this, what is the promise of cultural studies pedagogy? How does it make a difference to the world and what does it contribute to the purpose of education? In what ways does it help to transform society and to equip students and individuals with the necessary tools to understand themselves and the society that they are in? What does cultural studies as a pedagogic activity provide as a means of encountering everyday life and complexity, recognizing epistemic valence and difference, discovering knowledge and its relationship to power? Given cultural studies and its concerns for the marginal, minor, excluded, forgotten, and subjected citizen, how does its pedagogy critically enable and produce generative, sincere, and genuine democratic practice?

Together with my cultural studies colleagues we considered these questions deeply. We have written elsewhere on the anomalous and frequently challenging predicament of cultural studies as a noninstrumentalist pedagogy within an audit-based and instrumentalized education. We have argued that the "imperatives of cultural studies are germane to any principled socially inclusive pedagogy" (Biermann, Garbutt and Offord 2010: 98), and these go well beyond the constrictions of a tertiary environment. Indeed, our argument would be that cultural studies pedagogy is precisely the kind of critical educational and humane approach that we need to sustain a democratic society that is culturally and socially diverse. As Stuart Hall (1992) has noted:

> [T]he work that cultural studies has to do is mobilize everything it can find in terms of intellectual resources in order to understand what keeps making the lives we live, and the societies we live in, profoundly and deeply anti-humane in their capacity to live with difference. (17–18)

We are well aware of the challenges that occur in our teaching practice, but our experience has shown us that we are able to find critical pedagogic spaces, often strategically and creatively working with aspects of that instrumental environment within the institution that allow and even sometimes actively support the cultural studies project. For example, through gaining national teaching awards, showcasing interdisciplinary best practice, helping the institution fulfill key performance indicators in relation to social justice, student equity, human rights, and so on, the project receives support. The cultural studies program at SCU has been able to be at the vanguard of the university's quest for interpreting and understanding socially inclusive pedagogy, something that it considers important. Through a series of Higher Education Equity Projects funded by the Commonwealth, the cultural studies program for over a decade was able to produce creative spaces for student engagement and learning. This included 'Inter-activate' in 2002, which educated students from specific disadvantaged groups about empowerment through Internet-activated citizenship; 'Student Talk 2004', involving student reflection on cultural diversity and social inclusion; 'Interrogating

Whiteness 2006', a year-long series of roundtables and exhibitions on race and inclusive citizenship; a 2007 symposium 'Diversity in Education: Beyond Tolerance'; 'Enhancing a Culture of Equity: Understanding the Student Experience,' a symposium in 2008; 'Everybody's Business: Human Rights and Social Justice in the 21st Century', a SCU/Richmond River High School collaboration in 2010. All these activities derived from the cultural studies teaching program and involved ways of integrating cultural studies scholarship and social justice with community-engaged learning practices. These were creative, community spaces for cultural studies pedagogy supported by the institution, activities that made it possible to activate knowledge, to bring theory and practice together, and to ensure that in the university cultural studies was perceived as a valuable demonstration of assisting it in its contribution to the public good.

Cultural Studies as a Form of Critical Human Rights Education

As mentioned, the cultural studies pedagogy that developed at SCU has been in an environment influenced strongly by concerns for social justice. This concern has translated into the cultural studies program conceiving itself as a form of critical human rights education. I don't think the conjunction made between cultural studies and human rights is really that exceptional, but it has not always, to my knowledge, been so explicitly situated within a tertiary undergraduate program of teaching. When Lawrence Grossberg suggests, "cultural studies takes its shape in response to its context" (cited in Turner 2012: 161), I would argue that this is precisely what happened at SCU.

There are many aspects of *doing* human rights and social justice that are not just resonant with *doing* cultural studies. In applying this to a form of critical human rights education, cultural studies is appropriately positioned as a critical activist scholarship. Glenn Mitoma (2008) has argued for the centrality of cultural studies in human rights research: "Cultural studies" he says, "can provide some of the most compelling readings of [the] ... post-colonial encounter, pushing beyond the sterile dualism of 'cultural relativism vs. universalism' toward a critical engagement with the processes of both culture and the universal" (2008: 8). For John Erni (2010), "[c]ultural studies has long been attentive to the complex interpenetrations of power, agency, and the social imaginary" (227). And, as R. J. Coombe (2010) argues, "[t]o the extent that issues of social exclusion, inequality, identity, power, and representation engage us, cultural studies are practically invested in human rights discourse and praxis" (233).

Cultural studies as an approach to human rights and social justice is also highly attuned to the complexity of analysis that is required if the value of the concept is to be understood as profoundly contextual. In this sense, cultural studies as a scholarly discipline has an important role in ethically (actively) intervening while also being attentive to the dangers of producing or sustaining neocolonizing knowledge(s). The best type of cultural studies educational scholarship, therefore, is aware of the hegemonic nature of dominant knowledge(s) and methodologies offered across the arts, humanities, and sciences.

In the formulation of the cultural studies program as a critical human rights education, we drew on the mutual benefits of incorporating human rights thinking and social justice practices that had been recognized in critical and transformative pedagogy. As I have noted with my colleague John Ryan,

> These two interweaving fields—human rights and social justice—have a long history in pedagogical praxis (Choules 2007; Freire 1972). When social justice issues occur, such as exclusion of people on the basis on race, sexual orientation, disability, class, religion or age, they have immediate value and relevance to a student's experience. Social justice as a framework invokes, for example, questions of privilege, power, social recognition or discrimination, thus bearing witness to the language of human rights.
>
> (Offord and Ryan 2012: 31)

From my point of view, cultural studies teaching, therefore, has an implicit interest and relevance in relation to human rights education as it underscores the symbiotic but also tension-filled connections between academic and activist, between theory and practice, between the declarationist and the critical. One of the roles of cultural studies in fostering human rights thinking is found through its signature study of culture and everyday life, describing and analyzing how human rights problems, values, and issues are negotiated on the street, by, in, and through the media, in performances, practices, sites, texts, and so on, wherever meaning is being produced, regulated, consumed, represented, resisted, and contested.

Cultural studies pedagogy has the potential, I believe, to enact and fulfill UNESCO's (2007) statement on what human rights education requires:

> Human rights education implies the learning and practice of human rights. A holistic approach to human rights education means that human rights are implemented at all levels of the education system, and that they are taught through both content transmission and experiences. Therefore, human rights education should not only be theoretical but should also provide opportunities for young people to develop and practice the skills to respect human rights and citizenship through "school life", i.e. all aspects of school as a living, social environment with its collective rules, interpersonal conflicts, time and opportunities for co-operation, and through opportunities for spontaneous initiatives by the pupils outside the actual teaching activities.

60 Baden Offord

Empowering marginalized students to have a critical voice and an active presence in learning, creating pedagogical spaces for all students to listen openly and then establish dialogue and analysis of what causes social exclusion, is a key element of the practice that emerged at SCU. This approach has fostered collaborative, peer-supported student learning, the implementation of networks between students, staff, and the wider community, and an increased awareness and appreciation of diversity and difference within the university.

Unruly Subjects: A Case Study of Cultural Studies as Pedagogical Intervention

> *Walking the Lismore CBD has brought my own privilege in society to my awareness. I discovered how deeply discourses of social, cultural, religious, political, and economic discourses are entrenched in the way that I view myself and construe my sense of individuality and freedom.*
> —Student Reflection

> *When you are on a cultural studies field trip you're no longer seeing the world on automatic pilot, so to speak, but you are really looking at the world through a different kind of lens. Suddenly, things that seem very ordinary to you and that you wouldn't pay attention to suddenly seem very extraordinary.*
> —Student Reflection

As I have noted above, a key feature of the cultural studies pedagogy at SCU has been its focus on the student's agency and how it is activated through specific learning spaces that are fundamentally about turning the world upside down, where the so-called normal, taken for granted arrangements in society, which are evident both subjectively and objectively, are seen as strange and odd. This shaking of the tree, so to speak, a radical and critical enquiry into how things are, is seen as crucial to the purpose of cultural studies. Denzin (2009: 381) has commented that "critical pedagogy subjects structures of power, knowledge, and practice to critical scrutiny, demanding that they be evaluated 'in terms of how they might open up or close down democratic experiences' (Giroux and Giroux 2005: 1)".

At SCU, the possibilities of an 'opening up' or 'closing down' of democratic experience has been pivotal to the cultural studies approach to curriculum. Consequently, one of the subjects that students undertake in the cultural studies program is explicitly geared toward notions of participation and active citizenship. This unit (subject)—*Unruly Subjects: Citizenship*—was developed for students to examine how power, identity, and belonging are situated in relation to sites, practices, texts, and representations. Juxtaposing the unruly subject with the various political and cultural formations of citizenship was used as a catalyst of learning about the inherent complexities of belonging and participation in a democratic society. Attempting to understand how Nelson Mandela as terrorist became the epitome of the global citizen, or how the Australian musician Peter Garrett moved from unruly politics and activism to being a Government Minister illustrates this conundrum well. The unit explores power relations found in several core institutions such as education, religion, media, the family, law, and the market. It does this through a combination of cultural theory, cultural pedagogy, and lived experience. The unit, like all the subjects in the cultural studies program at SCU, constructed a learning environment that wove the theoretical into the tactility, or experience of everyday relationships. Students gain insight into the possibilities of agency as well as understanding the limitations and challenges that also exist.

Unruly Subjects: Citizenship has had an interesting history. Initially conceived in 1999 and taught as a unit within the Cultural Studies major since that time, in 2008 in the wake of a review of the Bachelor of Arts, the unit was made into a core (mandatory) subject for all students to undertake even if they were not taking the Cultural Studies major. As a cultural studies teacher I thought this was of course a valuable thing and would ensure that the Bachelor of Arts curriculum was informed by cultural studies theories, methods, and practices. The unit had been identified as a very effective demonstration of socially inclusive pedagogy, one that was clearly doing human rights education as well as valuing interepistemic dialogue, critical self-reflexivity, and the importance of lived experience. Yet, a request was made by the university to change the name of the unit to *Subjects and Citizens*. The term 'unruly' was regarded as too unsettling for a mandatory unit of study. After some negotiation and realizing that this was decisively not a 'hill to die on' moment, we agreed to the change. At the time we realized that the only change that was required was the name, so throughout the unit, unruly remained a key concept. Ironically, in 2012, following another review of the Bachelor of Arts, we suggested that the unit be renamed *Unruly Subjects: Citizenship*, and it was reinstituted without any comment.

One of the hallmarks of this unit is the meaningful inclusion of lived experience of the students and their engagement with difference. Building upon the important contribution that cultural studies has made to the humanities, which is how it brought the culture of the everyday into critical legitimacy, this unit demonstrates the centrality of the meaningful inclusion of lived experience as a key feature of the teaching of cultural studies. This has been a particular strength of the program. Students learn that citizenship is a highly contested concept that is influenced by economic, political, social, cultural, and religious discourses. Citizen-students find that they are at the intersection of all these discourses, created through relations of power and knowledge. There are several ways that the lived experience of students is meaningfully included in the teaching. One way is that students are invited to give lectures where they have both the experience and a developing scholarship. In 2013, for example, in the week of the topic on 'Disability and Citizenship', two cultural studies students who identified with disability activism, Shari Robinson and Jacki Brown, gave a lecture, discussing accessibility, equity, and opportunities for disabled people as well as disability rights, politics, and activism, and examining the intersections between disability and queer identities (see the YouTube video of this lecture at: https://www.youtube.com/watch?v=BEOjbmSeNNY). Students found this intervention by one of their peers to be incredibly powerful. The conjuncture of student lived experience, student voice, critical theory, and disruptive hierarchy (where the student becomes the teacher) activates both individual and collective knowledge and agency.

Students also engage with an 'on the street assessment', where they learn to be reflexive and develop meta-cognitive skills in and about themselves as well as their fellow citizens and communities. For example, in the 'Central Business District (CBD) Walk', a key assessment in *Unruly Subjects*, which takes place halfway through the unit, students are required to visit a CBD (at Lismore we would go together) to critically examine the hegemonic institutions in society firsthand—law courts, church, council chambers, shopping malls, police station, and the street. Walking down a street in a CBD brings home the immediacy of power relations. Do we feel comfortable, secure, or safe when we walk in public spaces and arenas? Are we represented in the shops we go? Are there people staring at us because we are different in some way? Does the performance of gender implicate the way we are addressed and perceived? And so on. The unit's objective is to bring not just empathy for others, but a critical, principled exposure of what is considered normal and everyday life. As Douglas Kellner (n.d.) puts it,

> Hence, a critical cultural studies must make visible how representations construct a culture's normative views of such things as class, race, ethnicity, gender, sexuality, place, occupation, and the like, and how these representations are appropriated to produce subjectivities, identities, and practices.

Students then write a paper reflecting on the power relations—a unit objective—surveillance and other regulatory mechanisms that demonstrate forms of social and cultural formations of citizenship. This assignment is frequently an 'aha!' moment for students. They see the 'opening up' or 'closing down' of democratic practices firsthand. They connect theory to context.

Speaking Personally

> *Studying is above all thinking about experience, and thinking about experience is the best way to think accurately.*
> —Paulo Freire (1985: 3)

I write this chapter 1 year after leaving SCU. And as I look back on the 17 years I taught cultural studies to many wonderful cohorts of students, I've come to view the experience of being a part of a localized form of cultural studies pedagogy as transformative, indeed life changing. In this last section I want to reflect on my ongoing commitment to cultural studies as a discrete discipline, a project and a valuable form of critical human rights education. But in making my comments, I wish to re-emphasize the importance of 'the pedagogical encounter' as principled exposure and how it is 'crucially philosophic and existentially unsettling,' to invoke Susan Giroux's words once again.

My commitment to cultural studies does have a personal story attached to it. I came to the discipline circuitously after a traditional humanities education in history, Indian studies, and Southeast Asian studies. But I also came from the margins of society, of mixed Maori and Pakeha heritage, from a family that suffered, like others, intergenerational trauma caused through the ongoing effects of colonialism. My immediate family came to Australia from Aotearoa/New Zealand as migrants in the early 1960s, and the story that dominated our narrative was marked by sexual abuse, alcoholism, financial hardship, and a culture of suicide. I was 18 when my father took his life and 49 when my brother ended his. My mother, sister, and myself all attempted to do the same at one time or another. In the mix of it all was the fact that I was queer. And yet, death became my greatest friend. Through the lived experience of suicide I actually came to see life as the most precious and fragile thing. After a stint of living in India for several years, and influenced by my friendship with one of Mahatma Gandhi's colleagues, Achyut Patwardhan (who founded the Socialist Party of India early in the 20th century), I returned to Australia to enter into the world of academia on his advice. It took almost a decade in the traditional humanities to discover cultural studies and when I did I was already saturated by anarchist, Buddhist, Hindu, and Taoist philosophies. I was pleased to find in cultural studies a discipline that was profoundly questioning of authority and how knowledge was produced.

This personal story has contributed to how I have approached cultural studies. Although I became aware of the canon and the who's who of the contemporary global cultural studies pantheon, it seemed to me that there had already been cultural studies thinkers in other times and places with the same concerns and interests. I see Rabindranath Tagore, for example, as relevant as Michael Leunig when it comes to examples of critically reflexive analyzers of knowledge and culture. There is no lock on what cultural studies might be.

Another important touchstone that has influenced the way I have approached cultural studies is something that Toni Morrison has articulated so accurately, that "racism is a scholarly affair" (1998). This insight completely embodies for me the potential of the academic project to be enabling, transformative, expansive, and liberating but also profoundly dangerous, threatening, reductive, and myopic. What was startling about this insight was that reason, logic, and rationality were the basis of the academic project itself and could be used to support any position. I found in cultural studies, however, in its overarching critique of disciplinarity, a space from which to look at Morrison's thesis with coherence. And although I believe the contemporary field of cultural studies has its share of dead-ends and cul de sacs, cultural studies' critique is what distinguishes it as an interdisciplinary project within and outside the academic world.

There is of course no certainty that the cultural studies program at SCU will continue, particularly given the exigencies facing universities in a neoliberal climate. I do know that the teachers who now teach the program are also committed to socially inclusive pedagogy and issues of social justice. They are also invested in critical pedagogy, which is heartening. But I also know these teachers are vulnerable as some of them are on sessional contracts and exposed directly to the vicissitudes of vocationally oriented outcomes. And it's not easy to explain to management that cultural studies is potentially *the discipline* of our times—interdisciplinary, agile, self-reflexive, and contextual—most suited to the complexity of a modern, technology-oriented knowledge economy that values democracy, human rights, and social justice. And, as such, it may well be the kind of pedagogy that could contribute to bringing substantive, meaningful social change.

But, I do think it is possible to create space for cultural studies teaching and to teach cultural studies, as I have discussed in this chapter. The most critical space in a university is in fact the space that is created between the teacher and the student. This is where the most potential for *activating* knowledge—that is, the activation of new understandings, encounters, and relationships—can take place. This is where teaching cultural studies introduces students to how their experience is the "stuff of culture, agency and self-production" (Giroux 1997: 110). I think this is one of the most valuable aspects of doing cultural studies. It aspires for "something more important" than theory, as Stuart Hall puts it.

That 'something more important' is what I believe is the true potential of cultural studies teaching, and it happens in the space found in the pedagogical exchange between student and teacher. This exchange, moreover, is collaborative, and there are no guarantees about what questions, answers, and directions might emerge.

To return to Graeme Turner's (2012) book, *What's Become of Cultural Studies*, he argues that in the future,

> cultural studies teaching needs to do more to draw upon its students' own capacities, while demonstrating cultural studies' potential to create new understandings of aspects of experience our students may well have taken for granted. This is going to take a much more serious commitment to an engaged, lively, student centred pedagogy than we now commonly encounter. (175)

In reviewing my experience at SCU, I think this kind of teaching was happening, and it was based on a serious commitment to creating and sustaining meaningful spaces for cultural studies teaching to work. Having said that, Turner's instruction is entirely relevant as it goes to the very heart of how cultural studies teaching ought to be done. My commitment to cultural studies as a framework of doing critical pedagogy has come about precisely because of the way that it activates agency, for both the student and the teacher. As I explained above, the impact of cultural studies on my own life has been profound, and affected the way, for example, that I now understand and see things like suicide, a key narrative that has defined my life. I would have never thought 17 years ago that in 2015 I would be a keynote plenary speaker as a cultural studies/human rights scholar at the Suicide Prevention Australia National Conference, speaking on the topic of 'The Meaningful Inclusion of the Lived Experience of Suicide'. This, for me, was an 'a-ha!' moment. The speech I gave was, to my knowledge, the first time a cultural studies scholar had presented a plenary at this conference. My view is that suicide is something that can be understood and prevented through understanding the cultural, political, economic, and social context(s) of the everyday. This experience of speaking at what is normally a biomedical- and psychology-oriented convocation was for me an example of how cultural studies as a project can contribute to social change in many, surprising ways.

This brings me to how I opened this chapter, with reference to Jackie (Jax) Brown, one of my former cultural studies students. Jax's story is instructive of what I have been attempting to say about cultural studies as a critical and creative, socially inclusive pedagogy, one that is motivated by human rights and social justice concerns that are enunciated and practiced through the meaningful inclusion of lived experience and activating knowledge. The way(s) that cultural studies pedagogy worked to provide Jax with the intellectual space to explore her place in the world is compelling. Her activation of knowledge, power, and identity through her engagement with cultural studies provided her with a language together with the intellectual resources, creative agility, and critical perspectives, to ethically intervene into the discourses of 'normal-land' around questions of disability and queerness.

I've attempted in this chapter to respond in some measure to the concerns raised in Turner's (2012) book, specifically his observations on teaching cultural studies. From my point of view, it's time to ramp up cultural studies, to stake a claim for its relevance in the 21st century university and beyond, to enable and activate the pedagogic space, and to realize that it does need to respond to what I have termed its ethics of location. In this chapter I have reviewed, for instance, the bespoke cultural studies pedagogy that emerged at a rural and regional university. As Lawrence Grossberg has noted about Stuart Hall's conception of cultural studies, "it is not definable as any thing in advance, other than a project, premise and practice" (2015: 9). How cultural studies teaching might look in other locales and contexts is up for grabs.

Note

1. For a range of perspectives about the cultural politics of this region that emerged from a collective of cultural and media studies scholars and historians, see Wilson, *Belonging in the Rainbow Region*.

References

ABC Open. (2015). *Jackie (Jax) Brown*. Accessed September 1, 2015, https://open.abc.net.au/people/19463.

Biermann, S., Garbutt, R., and Offord, B. (2010). Cultural studies in action: principled socially inclusive pedagogy and higher education equity projects. In Riseman, N., Rechter, S., and Warne, E. (eds). *Learning, teaching and social justice in higher education* (pp. 85–99) Melbourne, Melbourne Electronic Scholarly Publishing.

Brown, Jackie. (2015). *Undergraduate guide: humanities and social sciences*. Lismore, Southern Cross University.

Chan, S.C-K. (2012). Doing cultural studies: critique, pedagogy, and the pragmatics of cultural education in Hong Kong. In Morris, M., and Hjort, M. (eds). *Creativity and academic activism: instituting cultural studies* (pp. 105–24). Durham, Duke University Press.

Coombe, R.J. (2010). Honing a critical cultural study of human rights. *Communication and Critical/Cultural Studies*, 7 (3): 230–46.

Couldry, N. (2000). *Inside culture: re-imagining the method in cultural studies*. London, Sage.

Denzin, N.K. (2009). Critical pedagogy and democratic life or a radical democratic pedagogy. *Cultural Studies <=> Critical Methodologies*, 9 (3): 379–97.

Erni, J.N. (2010). Reframing cultural studies: human rights as a site of legal-cultural struggles. *Communication and Critical/Cultural Studies*, 7 (3): 221–29.

Freire, P. (1985). *The politics of education: culture, power and liberation*. New York, Bergin and Garvey.

Garbutt, R., Biermann, S., and Offord, B. (2012). Into the borderlands: unruly pedagogy, tactile theory and the decolonising nation. *Critical Arts: South-North Cultural and Media Studies*, 26 (1): 62–81.

Garbutt, R., and Offord, B. (2012). A scholarly affair: activating cultural studies. *The Review of Education, Pedagogy and Cultural Studies: Special Double Issue*, 'A Scholarly Affair: Activating Cultural Studies,' Garbutt, R., and Offord, B. (eds), 34 (1–2): 3–7.

Gilroy, P. (2000). *Between camps: race, identity and nationalism at the end of the colour line*. London, Allen and Lane.

Giroux, H.A. (1997). *Pedagogy and the politics of hope*. Boulder, Westview Press.

Giroux, H.A. (2004). Cultural studies, public pedagogy, and the responsibility of intellectuals. *Communication and Critical/Cultural Studies,* 1 (1): 59–79.

Giroux, S.S. (2010). *Between race and reason: violence, intellectual responsibility, and the university to come*. Redwood City, Stanford University Press.

Grossberg, L. (2015). Learning from Stuart Hall, following the path with heart. *Cultural Studies* 29 (1): 3–11.

Hall, S. (1991). Old and new identities, old and new ethnicities. In King, A.D. (ed). *Culture, globalization and the world system* (pp. 41–68). London, Macmillan.

Hall, S. (1992). New ethnicities. In Donald, J., and Rattansi, A. (eds). *Culture and difference* (pp. 223–27). Sage, London.

Kellner, D. (no date). *Critical pedagogy, cultural studies, and radical democracy at the turn of the millennium: reflections on the work of Henry Giroux*. Accessed April 1, 2015, http://users.monash.edu.au/~dzyngier/critical_pedagogy_Kellener.htm.

Mitoma, G. (2008). *Human rights and cultural studies: a case for centrality*. Cultural Critique. Accessed March 2011, http://ccjournal.cgu.edu/past_issues/glenn_mitoma.html.

Morris, M., and Hjort, M. (eds). (2012). *Creativity and academic activism: instituting cultural studies*. Hong Kong, Hong Kong University Press.

Morrison, T. (1998). *Uncensored*. ABC Television.

Offord, B., and Ryan, J. (2012). Peace building education: enabling human rights and social justice through cultural studies pedagogy. In Goh, B.C., Offord, B., and Garbutt, R. (eds). *Activating human rights and peace: theories, practices, contexts* (pp. 27–44). London, Ashgate.

Said, E. (2005). *Power, politics, and culture: interviews with Edward W. Said*. London, Bloomsbury Publishing.

Turner, G. (2012). *What's become of cultural studies?* London, Sage.

UNESCO. (2008). *Human rights education statement*. Bangkok: UNESCO.

Williams, R. (1967). Preface to second edition. In Williams, R. (ed). *Communications*. New York, Barnes and Noble.

Wilson, H. (ed). (2003). *Belonging in the rainbow region*. Lismore, Southern Cross University Press.

Section II
Alterity, the Other, and the Pedagogical Exchange

5 Creative Practice as Pedagogy
An Ecology of Experimentation

Kim Satchell

Wednesday (11 February) Field Notes
Auto-choreography—a pedagogy of place

Gun metal grey with sunny
    breaks moody ocean
emitting a pungent after-thought
people opt for the shade
little tern ply waves hover an'
the sun appears polished
the focal point folds the void—
    blue inky black
nights a whirling dervish of light
inhabiting a smile beneath the
    colours of an
a cosmos that functions
perhaps there is a discrepancy
the suffering engineered
arousing unspeakable giants
not as if death does not stare me back
remembering the after-birth
shimmering momentarily
    awaken to love
rises on the waves
beachcombing shape-shifting
appearing as something else then joy
leave-taking

crumbles all over the shore
petrol or is it birth
birds bait fish
fall as angels
formidable in the sky

grey go the days
and dark

ornamental parasol
nonetheless for being pretty
at work
by a human carousel
in the daydream of life
in the face
of a tenuous body

surfs coasts
disappears in the folds of existence
soul of them clouds
vanishing
with all the remains of peace

Excerpt from: Seven Walks toward a Coastal Philosophy: The Field Guide for the Transformation of Everyday Life (unpublished manuscript).

We-things build a road to us others, we-animals blaze the trail toward the soon-to-be intelligent us [....] I love you sometimes, the way a dog does his bitch, by pure sense of smell, the way an octopus undulates its eight arms, the way a tree entwines its branches in the wind.
(Serres 2011a: 57)

The post-Kantians concentrate on a universal encyclopaedia of the concept that attributed concept creation to a pure subjectivity rather than taking on the more modest task of a pedagogy of the concept, which would have to analyze the conditions of creation as factors of always singular moments. If the three stages of the concept are the encyclopaedia, pedagogy, and commercial professional training, only the second can safeguard us from the heights of the first into the disaster of the third—an absolute disaster for thought whatever its benefits might be, of course, from the viewpoint of universal capitalism.

(Deleuze and Guattari 1994: 12)

What, then, of Frederic Jameson's notion that it is easier to imagine the end of the planet than the end of capitalism?

(Taussig 2004: 312)

If I had invented writing, I would have done so as a perpetual revolution [...] for example these grafts of poetry onto philosophy, which are anything but confused, or certain ways of using homonyms, the undecidable, or the ruses of language, which many read in confusion because they fail to recognise the logical necessity. Each book is a pedagogy aimed at forming its reader.

(Derrida 2007: 31)

After all, what would be the value of the passion for knowledge if it resulted only in a certain amount of knowledgeableness and not, in one way or another and to the extent possible, in the knower's straying afield of himself.

(Foucault 1990: 8)

The beginning of the 21st century is an unfolding enigma of contradictory impulses and puzzling dilemmas. A coming of age of the ages, if the first two decades provide any evidence to go by, people, technology and the environment are becoming enmeshed in conditions of unprecedented consequence. There is a tension between organizing human life and understanding more-than human life as a self-organizing complex, engaging people in an implicit and explicit reliance (and responsibility), a pedagogy fraught with a willingness to learn, willful ignorance, and loathsome denial. Consider the inextricable relationality of bodies and the environment, including all living organisms and forms, life in the Anthropocene (the effect of human activity on a geological scale). Why not then paradoxical notions of pedagogy in relation to cultural studies? In order to invigorate generative responses—predicated upon seeking emerging and efficacious approaches to the current milieu, characterized by dramatic change, upheaval, and crisis. In the age of the network the micro-political is no personal matter and so it appears everything is everyone's business.

Pedagogy continues to hold significance for cultural studies, as a formation and diverse project seeking to respond to important concerns without perpetuating existing problems (Grossberg 2010; Turner 2012). The conjunction of rapid population expansion, the proliferation of technology in every sphere, and the strain of resource exploitation upon biological diversity, call not only for critical analysis but also for creative practice (Serres 2014, 2015). In the context of the unprecedented challenges these determinants are posing to reproduce, the same orthodoxy is ludicrous. The futility of opposing change or harking back to some previous arrangement is also evident (Massey 2006). Nonetheless, the stakes of making change operative and ameliorative could not be higher. Riding the wave of change in any kind of weather, one day difficult, then impossible, but what next (Deleuze 1997)? The following proposition is a double articulation of pedagogy and cultural studies cognizant of these circumstances but nonetheless advancing modes of existence and micro-politics, as a collectivist morphology of orientations and practices (Connolly 2002; Grossberg 1992).

Figure 5.1 Look at me now: Headland and South Solitary Island. Photograph Kim Satchell.

This chapter takes pedagogy as a protean term imbued with significance as a site of contestation and conflict. Pedagogy is the central thematic of a discussion that turns a double key (reversible after the pattern of a key for an antique French clock—one end for winding, the other for adjusting the time) of an argument for the quality of pedagogy constitutive of creative practice, the substance of an ecology of experimentation, of creative practice constitutive of pedagogy. The argument unfolds and folds with reference to philosophy as pedagogical exercises (*études*), drawing on two preeminent continental philosophers and post-structuralist thinkers, Gilles Deleuze and Michel Serres. The projects of each converse productively, constructing a fluid conceptual framework, employed here to support an alacrity of thought and action. This is a move bringing them into useful proximity with cultural studies and pedagogy, continuing the engagement with Deleuze already evident in the field (Gregg and Seigworth 2010; Grossberg 2010; Hickey-Moody 2013).

This chapter also seeks to promote the current modest reception of Serres within cultural studies, in a more robust manner, coupled with the burgeoning availability of Serres' corpus in English translation (Yates 2005). The account presented within this chapter will thematically weave together the currents of Serres' thought on pedagogy, but also upon ecology and movements in cultural studies toward the environmental humanities, specifically in the current work of Stephen Muecke (2014, 2105). The final aspect of the discussion fleshes out these ideas in the context of a mode of coastal philosophy and fieldwork, at the confluence of space, place, and ecology (Satchell 2007, 2008a, 2008b, 2010a, 2010b, 2012, 2013). The sum of these pedagogical exercises amounts to a *minor* pedagogy, in a Deleuzean-Guattarean manner, recognizing and employing creativity in the flux of the everyday and inexorable change.

The idea is to employ pedagogy as the focal point to assemble a range of terms and their inversions, beginning with "the pedagogy of the concept" to both set the scene and put things in motion (Deleuze and Guattari 1994: 12). Deleuze and Guattari (1994) afford pedagogy significance in regard to the creation of concepts, seen as principally the work of philosophy (along with laying out a plane, plan, or diagram). This is notable and prescient in regard to the ongoing economic rationalization exacted on higher learning by the uncertainties of the global market, perpetually in or on the verge of crisis (Serres 2014). The dramatic changes to the world of work through information technology require a logic entailing people's participation in an economy dominated by the technological advance of the global market and the World Wide Web. Deleuze (1995: 136) contests the words 'concept' and 'creative' as the province of philosophy, rather than information technology, communications, and advertising whose primary aim is to sell market capitalism as both means and end. Alternately Deleuzean-Guattarean philosophy experiments with modes of existence and possible worlds, to elude the assumptions of the dominant economic logic and call forth "the people to come" (Deleuze and Guattari 1994: 218). The appeal of such an inventive philosophy is that it works by connection and encounter, the 'double-becoming' of geo-philosophy (new earth and new people) immanent to existence and the workings of the material world riven with interpotentiation, from the virtual to the actual (Deleuze and Guattari 1994). At face value a touch anthropocentric, however the type of people called for are those aware of themselves as co-mingled bodies, in new modes of existence and relationship with the earth (Bogue 2009; Serres 2008, 2012, 2014).

Creative Practice as Pedagogy 75

The value of positing the pedagogy of the concept is arguably strategic, tasking philosophy with the responsibility to find new modes of existence through the creative practice of becoming immanent with the unfolding earth and cosmos—in short a practical philosophy for a new ecology. The emphasis shifts from the pedagogue to the quality of ideas as creativity, to the quality of relationships as symbiosis (what the body can do in terms of affect and being affected considerate of a relationality to other living organisms and to the world), learning to live otherwise (Deleuze 1988a, 1988b). Deleuze's whole project in philosophy can be viewed as pedagogical exercises (Stivale 2008). The pedagogy of Deleuze's (1995) conceptual arsenal goes back to his own self-confessed apprenticeship in philosophy and is borne out in a smoldering involution through a practice of style that involves, starting in the middle of things, looping around and arcing forward characterized by his now famous seminars at Vincennes, but no less in the curvilinear and 'multilinear complex' of his thought and multifarious writings (Bogue 2004; Deleuze 1993, 1995: 161; Stivale 2008). The pedagogy of the concept is a hard-won reality including the risk and misinterpretation of creative thought, madness, and suicide—dice throws, or in surfing parlance, 'critical take-offs' on waves of consequence (Deleuze 1983).

Figure 5.2 Eagle ancestor totem. Artwork Kim Satchell. Photograph Shekinah Satchell.

The signature creativity of Deleuze prompts a speculative turnabout from the term 'pedagogy of the concept' to *the concept of pedagogy*. This logic opens the terms into productive association and multiplicity within a burgeoning ecology of experimentation (Hayden 1997). As a conceptual practice Deleuze's (Deleuze and Guattari 1994) philosophy takes up the pedagogy of ancient philosophy, he discusses with Guattari in terms of association, friendship and rivalry, while also invigorating pedagogy through practice, with extensive preparation for conducting courses, enthusiasm and verve (in his thought and style) with the quintessential requirement of creation (Bogue 2004; Deleuze 1995, 1983; Stivale 2008). Following this line of thought Deleuze's (1992) expression of philosophy and pedagogic practice is evident in his encounters drawn from wide-ranging fields and thinkers (Deleuze 2007). The inversion of the terms concerns the laying out and folding of a plane, the second activity in the practice of philosophy they discuss in terms complimentary to their definition of a map "that must be produced, constructed" (Deleuze and Guattari 1987: 22, 1994). Consider the term *Le pli*, the French for fold, Deleuze (1988a, 1988b, 1993) explores in regard to Leibniz, Foucault and the associated *pli* words in his work on Spinoza, that are evident in his teaching, interviews, dialogues, conversations and writing (Deleuze 2007). Reading Spinoza he says is having "a feeling of a gust of air behind you", there are also the Leibniz turnabouts, coming into port only to be tossed back into the open sea and the fold in relation to Delueze's reading of Proust, Foucault, Leibniz and the Baroque, or even his work on Lewis Carroll and Francis Bacon, and so on (Deleuze 1988a, 1988b, 1990, 1993, 1994, 2000, 2003, 2007; Deleuze and Parnet 2007: 15). Characterized is the expression and outline of Deleuze's looping and enveloping thought, practices, teaching, reading, and writing, that constitute a broader project and labyrinthine body of work (Stivale 2008). Deleuze's (1995, 1997) ideas produce a concept of pedagogy that forms a fecund assemblage, shot through with life, vitality, and encounter.

Deleuze's (1988a) practical philosophy affects the concept of pedagogy and in turn pedagogy for cultural studies in regard to three overlapping concerns with mutual significance. My contention is that cultural studies pedagogy practices (at best) a reading, writing, and toolbox (toolbook) approach to pedagogy (learning dialogue) as an assemblage, which responds to a contemporary milieu (both varied and differentiated by a range of epistemic and ontological locations—to negotiate) (Morris 2005). In the same way Deleuze's thought relates to the immanence of the earth and cosmos, a variable opening whole, as a process of differentiation as a "logic of multiplicities" that must be made and is always in the making (Deleuze 1995: 147; Deleuze and Guattari 1988, 1994; Hayden 1997). Conley (in Deleuze 1993) asserts the concept of the fold in Deleuze's work is a culmination of ostensibly his philosophical poetics. For example Deleuze (1993) says of the 'cryptographer' one "who peers into the crannies of matter and reads into the folds of the soul" (3). "This art of inventing the key to the enveloped thing" (Leibniz cited in Deleuze 1993: 143) is what Deleuze does with the concept of the fold, he reads and writes a vitalist pedagogy; ideas enumerated, folded and unfolding across a range of works as tools of thought, weapons, and pedagogical practices.

The concept of the fold in Deleuze (1988b, 1993) is manifold both as a toolbox and a complex. There are two aspects that bear here upon his pedagogy and on the consilience of a range of concepts that constitute his broader project. Namely the complex of terms associated with 'perplication' the use of the fold outlined in several places and the fold in relation to thinking inside/outside, thinking with Foucault that Deleuze (1988b) does in the context of radically theorizing processes of self-formation and transformation through subjectification (Deleuze 1994: 187). The fold in motion as expression involves a double movement, folding, unfolding, and refolding that also embodies notions of thought and envelopment (as in a network of energetics), allowing for a dynamic process considering anything, and what it can do. Deleuze reiterates in many instances, beginning in the middle and working out both contrapuntal with the fold, the rhizome-producing assemblage, a minor literature as a collective enunciation and a refrain (*ritornello*) as place-making. The fold as thought for example begins in the midst of perplexity and unfolds through explication, thinking, "the thing *explains itself*" (Deleuze 1990: 68, his emphasis) unfolding as explication, thus folding through implication that involves and involutes to evolve through further explication, complexity, and multiplicity (Deleuze 1993). The fold associated deftly with experimentation and thinking is always coming about, zigzagging as in tacking in sailing with inverted loops to catch the wind, following a line of flight, auto-choreographed in concert with various elements ("like a taxi, queue [*lingne d'attente*], line of flight, traffic jam, bottleneck, brushes with the police. To be an abstract broken line, a zigzag which glides between") (Deleuze and Parnet 2007: 32). The fold as toolbox and complex is about learning to live in the world negotiating a state of envelopment and a series of envelopments in variations of motion of habitation and inhabitation.

On the edge of these folds the thinker surfs, sails, and flies as in Deleuze's (Deleuze and Parnet 2007: 15) invocation of a "witches broom", on a line of flight riding the line between life and death "life-experimentation" (Conley in Deleuze 1993; Deleuze 1988b; Deleuze and Guattari 1994; Deleuze and Parnet 2007: 47). In this respect the world is dynamic and labyrinthine, as is the soul and thought on the outside, developed in regard to Foucault and the fold of thought getting on the outside through the subjectification of a series of initiations, crises, exercises, 'askesis', and becomings aimed at complex self-formation—life as a work of art(fulness) (Deleuze 1983, 1988b, 1995; Foucault 2005). The fold is adequated as a moving fold between two-folds, conceptually as an idea to turn inside out and become attendant to the work of self upon the self, while turning outside in as a co-mingling of a panoply of entities on the site formerly known as I, but now another through

78 Kim Satchell

Figure 5.3 Kim Satchell on a finless surfboard design, gliding in the barrel.
Photograph Nicky Schmidenberg.

becoming-other (Deleuze and Guattari 1988). On the outside of thought affords the perspective or point of view of what was formerly the subject, to approach the unthought of thinking as a thinking otherwise, following Proust for a foreignness in one's own language and to act on the difference to a former habituation (Deleuze 1988, 1997, 2000). Deleuze (Deleuze 1993; Deleuze and Guattari 1988) explicates through Leibniz and with Guattari such a process as going from monadology to nomadology, a work on the self beyond oneself as subject, akin to populating a desert that becomes inhabited. In the foreword to *Negotiations* he states "philosophy throws us all into constant negotiation with, and a guerrilla campaign against ourselves" (Deleuze 1995: np). The ecology of experimentation this suggests becomes the laboratory of life, modes of existence, and creative practice that conspire for inventive responses to existential circumstances.

The pedagogy of such an ecology of experimentation exemplifies Deleuze as a voracious and seasoned reader, consummate in his reading of others' work in philosophy, literature, art, and science. No ordinary reading though, rather plugging in to a socket, intensive and affective, a flow directly in contact with the Outside (Deleuze 1988b, 1995). Such reading following his thoughts on Spinoza is an "affective capacity" involving "maximum and minimum thresholds" intensities, on the edge of the fold and "is reading with love" (Deleuze 1988b: 124, 1995: 9). The "pick-me up or pick-up" approach, encountering ideas when reading that pass through one another producing becoming, getting on the same frequency, a liaison, an exchange of fluids, jump-starts, hotwires, setting in motion (Deleuze and Parnet 2007: 10). In the book with Parnet they suggest reading the longer paragraphs faster and the shorter ones slower (Deleuze and Parnet 2007). These experiments are inventive, teasing out possibilities for new modes of existence within the complexity of impossible situations as weapons against, for, and within oneself. Deleuze (1995: 7) calls for new ways of reading and writing, and refers to his writing as "a flow and not a code", there is a vitality and encounter that taps into the flux as flow that sets off chain reactions of becoming (Deleuze 1983, 1997). Discussing Cixous' inventive work, Deleuze (2004) coins as "writing in strobe" (231) proposing a particular point of view and velocity of reading that brings disjunctive elements into coherence as a "book-as-drug" sensation. There is an unmistakable, affective "pick-me-up" in his writing that one gets or does not (Deleuze and Parnet 2007: 51; Stewart 2007). The notion of writing with (people, the world) equates with pedagogy providing an appropriate turning point to continue the discussion of pedagogy considering Michel Serres and his work.

There are instances where both Deleuze and Serres use the example of learning to swim to distinguish particular approaches to pedagogy. Deleuze draws the distinction between the ineffectual 'do as I say' and the 'do with me' teacher whose approach is "sensory-motivity" bringing the sign and heterogeneity into encounter with bodily movement, the water, waves, and learning (Deleuze 1994: 23). In a number of places Deleuze extols surfing as an activity embodying the immersive "getting into something" in motion; as Conley (in Deleuze 1993) points out, Deleuze is a "geo-philosopher" who surfs and coasts (Deleuze 1995: 121). Serres for his part too is maritime in philosophy traversing pedagogic impulses, across the biological and life sciences, across a post-humanities/sciences divide (North-west passage) (Serres 2012). Serres (1997) equates learning with swimming and education, as pertaining to the locus of the body and its engagement with the environment (Serres 2011b). There are some touching connections between Deleuze and Serres as philosophers and friends (Conley 1997; Deluze 1995). Each acknowledges the other on various occasions. There are numerous elements of their work that resonate one with the other, here also with my concerns around notions of the body (multiplicitous and co-mingled), the fold (fluidity, inside, outside, and between), writing particularly pedagogy and finally ecology, in relation to place-making. The motifs Serres (2012) weaves into his work have a vibrancy derived from writing in an ecological mode that draws directly on the dynamism and operation of life, biology, geology, within and beyond (Harrison 2013).

The interest Serres (2014, 2015) holds for pedagogy and cultural studies currently is the way he is attuned to contemporary dilemmas and the implicative role of human development from antiquity. As a thinker he purposefully weaves a language of materiality with the materiality of language—writing as an ecology of experimentation seeking the emergent and generative. Doubling back to the example of swimming, he turns upon on the idea of crossing-over a body of water, as an orientation to the outside achieved from the middle and in-between, to attain an altered state and reorientation (Serres 1997). He profoundly locates in the inverted (sides of the) body (including the brain) as both sensory-motive and neuro-muscularly facilitated, a reorientation to pedagogy for advanced learning (Serres 1997, 2008, 2011a). The example builds upon the sense of incompleteness in favoring only one side of the body, discovered in the consequent development of his own experience of left-handedness, and the crossing over of developing the right hand but losing none of the prowess of the left, indeed coming to be that of the "third-instructed", that opens "the infinite possibility of learning" (Serres 1997: 34). In work specifically related to themes on the body Serres (2011) states, "[f]reedom is defined by the body and the body by potential" and goes on to posit the "pedagogy of the possible" casting the discussion back in the open sea of "the possible of pedagogy" (52–53). How impoverished is the general consensus of accepted methods and constraints harbored in the institutions of the modern academy (Serres 2015)—methods oblivious to the form of a pedagogy unfolding from the body and in the curricula of living organisms and the earth.

Serres (2008, 2012) outlines these ideas (as recurring themes) with fractal intricacy and precision that develop and proliferate. Consider the example posited in the term 'Bio-Gea', life and earth building upon a rapprochement outlined in the *The Natural Contract*, calling for "mastery of the mastery", restraint in the human assault on life and the earth—a new becoming (Serres 1995: 38, 2012). Serres' (2008) attention to pedagogy and to place is beautifully illustrated in the notion "[a]ll pedagogy consists in making the little human who starts out as a parasite into a symbiotic partner of a fair exchange" (Serres 2006: 9). Another example he refers to when writing his pages, is the etymology of *pagus*—a peasant plot cultivated in the furrows and patchwork of a quilted earth (Serres 2008, 2011). The weaving of reading, writing, place, and ecology is the sort of pedagogy in which cultural studies has a future direction.

To what end and by what means are the pedagogic concerns of geophilosophy intended? If not geared toward living, elaborated as this might be in the midst of the contradiction and conceit of unenlightened human self-interest—the war and the peace—then to what? To think the finite world has infinite possibilities within it but not absolute certainty over the outcomes is a sobering but inspiring thought, in need of concepts such as

Creative Practice as Pedagogy 81

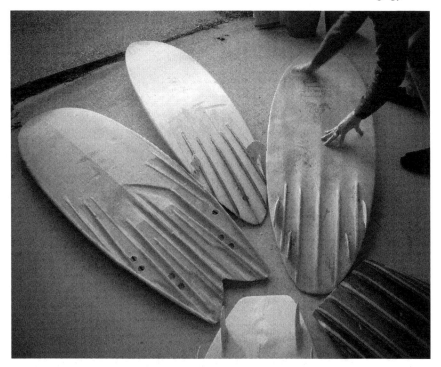

Figure 5.4 Strange handmade surfboard designs for auto-choreography and body English. Photograph Shekinah Satchell.

the threefold of borders (Satchell 2013). For Serres (2011) borders operate as inside, outside, and between; they are mediated in a range of ways; and they come in a range of mediums that enfold and envelop—soft, hard, and porous. Some are given, some are made, still others are realized and appropriated in constructs, ensembles, and assemblages. The body, clothes, transport, housing, a garden, roads, a quiet secluded place, a polluted river, towns, cities, countries, topographies, geographies, and ecologies all operate in the threefold; *inside, outside,* and *between.* In Casey's (2011a, 2011b) schema these are more boundaries than borders, whereas Serres (2011b) conflates and complicates them even further using the example of appropriations through pollution to make his case for a new contract with the earth. The way these borders or edges, fold, unfold, and enfold in regard to a fractalization or multiplicity of possibility, means possibilities for enriching dimensions of encounter and "polyvalent unity of conflictual programs and contractual proximity"—and of course, conversely the closing of possibility of the brute pedagogy of discipline and control, the earlier work of Foucault illuminated (Certeau 1984: 117; Deleuze 2007). For example the fractalization of surfers inhabiting a coastline or of learning in a classroom over a course of study where ideas proliferate, influence, and take hold in the practice of everyday life (differentiation), as Mandelbrot affirms things open up extraordinarily dependent on the type of instrument of measure, and the geometry of nature is riven with scale that can be woven (Deleuze and Guattari 1994; Mandelbrot 1967, 1982; Satchell 2013). This may seem poetic or quixotic considering the barriers, the obstacles, the negotiations, the mishaps, the problems, the breakdowns, the failure, sacrifice, and the cost—quality of life or impoverishment. These are evident in the pedagogy of culture and culture of pedagogy with the stakes of conflicting programs, different agendas, conflicts of interest, exploitation, manipulation, and recalcitrance, as much as good fortune, boons, productive associations, stature, autonomy, success, and privacy (Baldwin 1995; Certeau 1984).

The paradoxical relation of the pedagogy of culture and culture of pedagogy is an overlapping arena educators and cultural studies practitioners do well to heed, considering the way they are embedded in one another. This has become startlingly apparent, in three distinct ways: the proliferation of global culture through the Internet; the take-up of mobile technology including smartphones; and social media sites and the rationalization of education and training through online delivery. Willis (cited in Grossberg 1997: 381–2) foreshadowed these signs for education/training becoming "subordinated to technical instrumentalism and to the 'needs' of industry" stating "[w]e need an altogether new approach to education" (381–2). The pedagogy of culture has become a contested arena of hegemonic mediatization, networked possibilities, and cyber-world dangers. The convergence of metadata and supercomputing casts a darkening shadow on the overreliance on technology. There also seems to be an odd correlation between human world 'connectedness' facilitated by technology and the 'disconnectedness' with the more-than human world technology exacts upon its hosts. Equally distressing is the demoralization of the culture of pedagogy through rationalization and standardization (St. Pierre 2004). I think this is what makes creativity central to pedagogy, because plainly creation and invention are distinctive and necessary in worlds crushed by such oppressive forces and calamitous sequences of events, evident in local, regional, and global news streams daily (Deleuze 2007; Deleuze and Guatarri 1994; Serres 2008, 2015).

There are several specific and interrelated streams of creativity emergent in the conjunction of these 21st century dilemmas, as a pedagogy of culture and culture of pedagogy germane to the micro-political. Emergent forms of creative practices for living, enacted as a culture of pedagogy, are precipitated by survival and ethical responses to disaffectedness with anachronistic forms of politics and greed—a "grassroots action" (Hawken 2007). Another form of creative practice that may emerge would be the use of standard and alternative technologies in ameliorative ways to synchronize and synergize—a hi/low tech hybridity synergized with savvy consumers (bio-regionalism) (Braungaut and McDonough 2002; Lynch, Glotfelty and Armbruster 2012).

Figure 5.5 Fish ancestor totem. Artwork Kim Satchell. Photograph Shekinah Satchell.

What then of the culture of pedagogy, a question that I sense will be played out at human and more-than human level, built in the ruins of former institutions and new forms of organization (Serres 2015). So while this may read for some as speculative fiction or for others fabulist extrapolation, I want to turn to a specific example that makes the passage between the pedagogy of culture and the culture of pedagogy plausible through interesting applications. Stephen Muecke, a cultural studies scholar, writer, and translator, currently teaching in an environmental humanities program provides some possible directions to consider.

Stephen Muecke's work offers a case in point for experimental work in pedagogy in the context of cultural studies and the environmental humanities. The focus here though is on the experimental character and the impetus of ideas as pedagogical exercises, in thought and learning contexts. Such experimentations as Muecke's (2015: 1) "Ecologising Modern Institutions: A Speculative Fiction" are based on the premise that while he is abroad "something wonderful has happened", the Abbott Government (at the time of writing the current, conservative government in Australia) has been ousted and the Greens (an Australian national political party) swept to power in a double-dissolution. The upshot is a newly elected government with a mandate to 'ecologise' the existing institutions (he discusses in three examples); science, law, and the humanities. While these thought experiments are brief they open interesting lines of inquiry about some practical forms of subjectification that open onto different futures. Muecke's (2014) teaching practice in the Environmental Humanities Program at UNSW, in the unit ARTS2247 "Indigenous People and the Environment", outlined in

"'Rebooting': An Eco-Pedagogy" offers further evidence. Drawing students from a range of disciplines (economics, law, developmental studies, social sciences, biological sciences), the course uses "post-critical pedagogy" based on group-project work in three distinct parts: first, they examine their field of study considering what to retain; second, do research specific to an environmental issue; and third, analyze their field in the context of the research to consider possible adjustments to maintain relevance for the future. Toward the end of the semester "diplomats from the future" arrive as experts from 2035 (played by scholars from two other universities in Sydney, Australia) to assess each group's "diplomatic brief" (a 7500 word document) where they are assessed on a range of skills and their approach, response to the specific issue, and the needs of the future. This experimental sort of approach to learning is creative and generative of the exchange between the pedagogy of culture and the culture of pedagogy, adaptive to relevant contexts of learning and everyday life issues that matter, an exemplary instance of putting the environmental humanities in action (Rose and Robin 2004).

The last aspect of this chapter concerns my own work, drawing on studies in creativity and writing in an ecological mode, to provide place-based accounts of a multispecies sense of place (Satchell 2013; van Dooren and Rose 2012). These ideas have been developed as creative research (practice-led research and research-led practice), providing textual evidence to supplement a conceptual framework supported by immersive fieldwork (Smith and Dean 2009). The pedagogy of place and the place of pedagogy bring these concerns full circle, intent on learning from place and the place of encounter with the more-than human. In the ambit of this chapter a return to the theme of geo-philosophy, of earth and territory pivotally revolving around a place to live and work—recursive, accumulative, and life-affirming (Deleuze and Guattari 1994; Serres 2008). A number of creative practices, as pedagogical exercises and everyday practices, figure co-extensively with a body of work and life as a work of art (Deleuze 1995). The studies turn in shorthand, upon beachcombing and 'shacking-up', as modes of existence and "technologies of self" (Foucault 1997, 2005). These are fundamental as an embodiment of a coastal philosophy and consequent pedagogy, engaging in modes of existence with creative practice as an ecology of experimentation, otherwise quite ordinary pursuits thoughtfully rendered into complex relations with the confluence of space, place, and ecology (Certeau 1984; Hillier 2012). Beachcombing and shacking-up are complimentary aspects of a vernacular culture I refer to as *coasting*, associated with the coast, to states of flow and 'temporary autonomous zones' TAZ, as well with outsiders, runaways, renegades, castaways, and surfers of a certain ilk (Bey 1991; Evers 2004; Isham 2004; Maréchaux 2009; Satchell 2006).

Beachcombing is an activity people often attend to inadvertently, on holidays or a picnic, as a pursuit though beachcomber's lives revolve around the site of the beach and the coast in a more thoroughly idiosyncratic way. The beachcomber attends to all manner of things from the weather, birds,

Creative Practice as Pedagogy 85

Figure 5.6 Catch of the day. Artwork Kim Satchell. Photograph Shekinah Satchell.

fish, plants, and animals, to the ebb and flow of the tide, the state of the foreshore erosion or rehabilitation, the flotsam and jetsam of marine debris including the remains of material flushed from the watershed and borne seaward and back to shore (Brewster 2009). A ragpicker of the sea, collecting the remains of materials to be repurposed, upcycled, and recrafted into use, anything from adornment to furniture and even architecture (the 'shack') lies within the purview of the beachcomber (Benjamin 1997; Braungaut and McDonough 2013; Nin 1970). The patina of these items often gives them an alluring quality, a certain weathered look and at times the happenstance of extraordinary design. But these are as much objects to think with as with to work. The material comes without cost, the reward of ferreting objects out of obscure places or swift responses to weather events. Rosalie Gascoine (cited in Bottrell 1977: 39) discusses her own assemblages as "forces in equilibrium", developing the Japanese aesthetic *Ikebana* (closeness to nature) by rambling in the woods and storing her found objects in the yard from which to create, confirming an affinity already seasoned in my daily practice at the beach. The beachcomber and collector have some common traits akin to the hoarder but are far more canny and inventive (Bennett 2010, Hamilton 1974). This is a practice that is consonant with Michel Serres' (2008) call for inquiry to "make use of what is cast aside" (287). As a conceptual persona for philosophy, the beachcomber's unassuming activities are wonderfully suited and apposite (Deleuze and Guattari 1994). The conceptual framework adopted for this pedagogy of place is tentatively summarized in the form of seven walks formulating coastal philosophy, the underlying frame of a series of field notes and written texts (Satchell 2013).

The seven walks are a composite of '*randonnée*' (wandering and recursive walking), beachcombing engendering place-sensitive accounts of chance, encounter, and intimacy with the local foreshores and headlands (Ingold 2004; Muecke and Pam 2012; Serres 2008: 259). Walking provided a composite activity, as a creative practice, a contribution to a mode of inquiry, the articulation of a coastal philosophy. The underlying frame for these walks develops the themes of ethos, acumen, and genius—three themes embracing seven orientations. A framework for a pedagogy of place and the outline for a written text. The first theme concerns the Epicurean idea of *lathe bioasa* (the "hidden life") going unnoticed, leading a quiet unassuming existence, attendant to the surrounds in an unobtrusive manner, just going about your business learning to live (Arendt 1978). The second involves *far niene* (doing "sweet nothing") restive idleness, relaxed, open to contingency and the conditions that present themselves with their own dictates (Robertson 2004; Rousseau 1979; Saint-Amand 2011). The third is *reverie* (daydreaming), becoming lost in thought or otherwise led in a voluntary volition of the play of thought (Bachelard 1969a; hooks 1995; Rousseau 1979). The fourth relies upon *curiosity*—a piqued interest that does not tire of novelty and focused attention (Foucault 1997; Mathews 2005). The fifth is *perspicacity* honed on the attention to detail that gives way to insight, a further marker of the symptomologist and cryptographer (Benjamin 2006; Deleuze 1993, 1997). The sixth *pareidolia* (multiple readings) seeing alternate readings of random patterns of information or stimulus, a face in the wood or a horse in the clouds, land-forms can take on alternate forms from different perspectives becoming mimetoliths (landforms resembling other forms) (Gelb 1999). The seventh walk consummates the previous walks as *heirophony* (making sacred) or consecrating the bond with a place and the inhabitants, not in terms of holy and profane as dichotomous, but the luster of the sacred in the ordinary (Eliade 1972). The pedagogy of place these orientations cohere in, and are predicated upon, is notion that there is more to learn from places, in terms of their value and the regard with which they should be held, than hitherto thought or otherwise has been lost by some cultures (Serres 2012; Shannon and Satchell 2013).

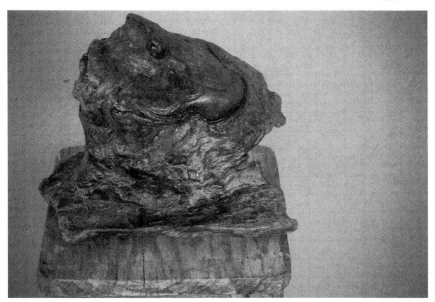

Figure 5.7 Self-formation: a practice of soul-making. Artwork Kim Satchell. Photograph Shekinah Satchell.

The appeal of the term *shacking-up* is the suggestiveness implied in a liaison and the playfulness of constructing a cubby-house in relation to place (Robertson 2003; Satchell 2008b, 2010b). The idea of shacking-up retains a modest and earthy connection with the pedagogy of place. The house in its locus is 'ambiguous' opening in and out to 'cosmic forces', within a territory that becomes the basis of a home-place for the arts, interlaced with 'inter-species junction points', a milieu for a multi-species sense of place (Deleuze and Guattari 1994: 185; Grosz 2008; hooks 1990). As Bachelard (1969b) so elegantly notes a house is somewhere to hold your dreams. While this may seem ethereal, on the contrary these dreams are substantiative, working with the language of materiality and the materiality of language, advocated throughout this chapter (Benjamin 2007; Deleuze and Guattarri 1994). The threefold of Serresean borders (in regard to the house and surrounds) in their dynamism and folds, play on the confluence of space, place, and ecology as co-habitation and inhabitation, where species meet, know, and become known (Harraway 2008). No greater luxury can be afforded but privacy and solitude to immerse one's own self in the care of his or her soul and the vocation of his or her work (Baldwin 1995). Just as Thoreau (1974) made an inventory of all the items he possessed at Walden to pursue simplicity and economy, a similar list provides evidence of diverse interests in the pursuit of creativity and pedagogy. Library, study, studio, workshop, shed, collections of books, records, tools, instruments and surfboards, along with materials such as canvases, paint, wood, stone, resin and foam, various projects at various stages, just as someone inhabits their house with its rooms and furnishing, they also inhabit and live with the assemblage of all these other objects, materials and the creative practices they entail sheltering and taking care of the soul (Benjamin 2007; Certeau 1984; Serres 2008). The ways these too become folded with cosmic forces "from House to universe ... from endosensation to exosensation ... that arise from within or come from outside and renders their effect on the inhabitant perceptible" making the ecology of experimentation palpable with a multispecies sense of place (Deleuze and Guattari 1994: 185–186). In the end shacking-up is (as is surfing and *just coasting*) a coastal philosophy—a joy, something that flows (Deleuze 1993, 1995; Satchell 2010b; Serres 1990).

In sum the place of pedagogy is apparent at every turn, at every stage of life, and with each endeavour: "the process is mutual so men learn while they teach" (Seneca cited in Foucault 1997: 215). The activity of learning is no better served than by someone striving for mastery over him- or herself and the development of his or her creative powers, succeeding to evoke compassion, care, and gentleness toward others, and developing humility that treads softly on the earth and ponders the welfare of other living things. The centrality of the place of pedagogy is borne out in the notion of guidance—each person is called upon to be both a guide for themselves and others toward making peace.

References

Arendt, H. (1978). *The life of the mind*. San Diego, Harvest.
Bachelard, G. (1969a). *The poetics of reverie: childhood, language and the cosmos*. Boston, Beacon Press.
Bachelard, G. (1969b). *The poetics of space*. Boston, Beacon Press.
Baldwin, B.J. (1995). *An autobiography in design*. New York, Norton.
Benjamin, W. (2006). *Berlin childhood around 1900*. Cambridge, Harvard University Press.
Benjamin, W. (2007). *Illuminations: reflections and essays*. New York, Shocken Books.
Bennett, J. (2010). *Vibrant matter: a political ecology of things*. Durham, Duke University Press.
Bey, H. (1991). *TAZ: The temporary autonomous zone, ontological anarchy, poetic terrorism*. New York, Autonomedia.
Bogue, R. (2009). A thousand ecologies. In Herzogenrath, B. (ed). *Deleuze, Guattari and ecology* (pp. 42–56). London, Palgrave Macmillan.
Bottrell, F. (1977). *The artist craftsman in Australia: a close look at the work of 40 top Australian craftsmen*. Ultimo, Murray.
Braungaut, M., and McDonough, W. (2002). *Cradle to cradle: remaking the way we make things*. New York, North Point Press.
Braungaut, M., and McDonough, W. (2013). *The upcycle: beyond sustainability—design for abundance*. New York, North Point Press.
Brewster, A. (2009). Beachcombing: a fossicker's guide to whiteness and Indigenous sovereignty. In Smith, H., and Dean, R.T. (eds). *Practice-led research and research-led practice in the creative arts* pp. 126–49). Edinburgh, Edinburgh University Press.

Casey, E.S. (2011a). Border versus boundary at La Frontera. *Environment and Planning D*, 29: 384–93.
Casey, E.S. (2011b). The edge(s) of landscapes: a study in limnology. In Malpas, J. (ed). *The place of landscapes: concepts, contexts, studies* (pp. 91–109). Massachusetts, MIT Press.
Certeau, M. de (1984). *The practice of everyday life*. Berkeley, University of California Press.
Conley, V.A. (1997). *Ecopolitics: the environment in poststructuralist thought*. London, Routledge.
Connolly, W.E. (2002). *Neuropolitics: thinking, culture, speed*. Minneapolis, University of Minnesota Press.
Deleuze, G. (1983). *Nietzsche and philosophy*. New York, Columbia University Press.
Deleuze, G. (1988a). *Spinoza practical philosophy*. San Francisco, City Light Books.
Deleuze, G. (1988b). *Foucault*. Minneapolis, University of Minnesota Press.
Deleuze, G. (1990). *The logic of sense*. New York, Columbia University Press.
Deleuze, G. (1992). *Expressionism in philosophy: Spinoza*. New York, Zone Books.
Deleuze, G. (1993). *The fold: Leibniz and the Baroque*. Minneapolis, University of Minnesota Press.
Deleuze, G. (1994). *Difference and repetition*. New York, Columbia University Press.
Deleuze, G. (1995). *Negotiations 1972–1990*. New York, Columbia University Press.
Deleuze, G. (1997). *Essays: critical and clinical*. Minneapolis, University of Minnesota Press.
Deleuze, G. (2000). *Proust and signs*. London, Athlone.
Deleuze, G. (2003). *Francis Bacon: The logic of sensation*. Minneapolis, University of Minnesota Press.
Deleuze, G. (2007). *Two regimes of madness: texts and interviews 1975–1995*. Los Angeles, Semiotext(e).
Deleuze, G., and Guattari, F. (1987). *A thousand plateaus: capitalism and schizophrenia*. Minneapolis, University of Minnesota Press.
Deleuze, G., and Guattari, F. (1994). *What is philosophy?* New York, Columbia University Press.
Deleuze, G., and Parnet, C. (2007). *Dialogues II*. New York, Columbia University Press.
Derrida, J. (2007). *Learning to live, finally: the last interview*. New York, Melville House.
Eliade, M. (1972). *Shamanism: archaic techniques of ecstasy*. Princeton, Princeton University Press.
Evers, C. (2004). Men who surf. *Cultural Studies Review*, 10 (1): 27–41.
Foucault, M. (1990). *The history of sexuality, Volume 2: the uses of pleasure*. New York, Vintage.
Foucault, M. (1997). *Ethics, subjectivity and truth: the essential works of Michel Foucault 1954–1984, volume 1*. New York, New Press.
Foucault, M. (2005). *The hermeneutics of the subject: lectures at the College de France 1981–1982*. New York, Palgrave Macmillan.
Gelb, M.J. (1999). *How to think like Leonardo da Vinci*. New York, Dell.
Gregg, M., and Seigworth, G.J. (eds). (2010). *The affect theory reader*. Durham, Duke University Press.
Grossberg, L. (1997). *Bringing it all back home: essays on cultural studies*. Durham, Duke University Press.

Grossberg, L. (2010). *Cultural studies in the future tense*. Durham, Duke University Press.
Grossberg, L. (2014). Theorising context. In Featherstone, D., and Painter, J. (eds). *Spatial politics: essays for Doreen Massey* (pp. 32–43). London, Wiley-Blackwell.
Grosz, E. (2008). *Chaos, territory, art: Deleuze and the framing of the earth*. New York, Columbia University Press.
Hamilton, L. (1974). *The pleasures of collecting*. London, The Claxton Publishing Company.
Harraway, D. (2008). *When species meet*. Minneapolis, University of Minnesota Press.
Harrison, M. (2013). The act of writing and the act of attention. In Harrison, M., Rose, D.B., Shannon, L., and Satchell, K. (eds). Writing creates ecology and ecology creates writing. *TEXT*, Special Issue 20: 1–11.
Hawken, P. (2007). *Blessed unrest: how the largest movement in the world came into being and why no one saw it coming*. New York: Viking Press.
Hayden, P. (1997). Gilles Deleuze and naturalism: a convergence with ecological theory and politics. *Environmental Ethics*, 19 (2): 185–204.
Hickey-Moody, A. (2013). *Youth, arts and education: reassembling subjectivity through affect*. London, Routledge.
Hillier, J. (2012). Liquid spaces of engagement: entering the waves with Anthony Gormley and Olafur Eliasson. *Deleuze Studies*, 6 (1): 132–48.
hooks, b. (1990). *Yearning: race, gender and cultural politics*. Boston, South End Press.
hooks, b. (1995). *Art on my mind: visual politics*. New York, New Press.
Ingold, T. (2004). Culture on the ground: The world perceived through feet. *Journal of Material Culture*, 9 (3): 315–40.
Isham, H. (2004). *Image of the sea: oceanic consciousness in the romantic century*. New York, Peter Lang.
Lynch, T., Glotfelty, C., and Armbruster, C. (eds). (2012). *The bioregional imagination: literature, ecology and place*. Athens, University of Georgia Press.
Mandelbrot, B. (1967). How long is the coast of Britain? Statistical self-similarity and fractional dimension. *Science*, 156 (3775): 636–38.
Mandelbrot, B. (1982). *The fractal geometry of nature*. New York, Henry Holt.
Maréchaux, L. (2009). *Outlaws: adventures of pirates, scoundrels and other rebels*. Paris, Flammarion.
Massey, D. (2006). Landscape as a provocation: reflections on moving mountains. *Journal of Material Culture*, 11: 33–48.
Mathews, F. (2005). *Reinhabiting reality: towards a recovery of culture*. Sydney, UNSW Press.
Morris, M. (2005). From criticism to research: the 'textual' in the academy. *Cultural Studies Review*, 11 (2): 17–32.
Muecke, S. (2014). 'Rebooting': an eco-pedagogy, ARTS 2247 *Indigenous people and the environment*. Environmental Humanities Program, UNSW.
Muecke, S. (2015). Ecologising modern institutions: a speculative fiction. Plenary given at *Fractious modernities: the (dis)contents of the now*, Centre for Advanced Study in English, Jadavpur University Calcutta, February 24–26.
Muecke, S., and Pam, M. (2012). *Contingency in Madagascar*. Bristol, Intellect Books.

Nin, A. (1970). *The diary of Anais Nin, volume 2, 1934–1939*. Boston, Houghton Mifflin Harcourt.
Robertson, L. (2003). *Occasional work and seven walks from the office for soft architecture*. Astoria, Clear Cut Press.
Robertson, L. (2004). *Rousseau's boat*. Vancouver, Nomados.
Rose, D.B., and Robin, L. (2004). The ecological humanities in action: an invitation. *Australian Humanities Review*: 31–32.
Rousseau, J-J. (1979). *Reveries of a solitary walker*. Hammondsworth, Penguin.
Saint-Amand, P. (2011). *The pursuit of laziness: an idle interpretation of the Enlightenment*. Princeton, Princeton University Press.
Satchell, K. (2007). Reveries of the solitary islands: from sensuous geography to ecological sensibility. In Haebich, A., and Offord, B. (eds). *Landscapes of exile: once perilous now safe* (pp. 97–114). London, Peter Lang Publishing.
Satchell, K. (2008a). In praise of surf spots. *Kurungabaa: Journal of Literature, History and Ideas for Surfers*, 1 (3): 10–13.
Satchell, K. (2008b). Shacked: the ecology of surfing and the surfing of ecology. In *Proceedings of Annual Conference of the Cultural Studies Association of Australia (CSAA)*, Adelaide, University of South Australia, December 6–8, 2007.
Satchell, K. (2010a). Auto-choreography: animating sentient archives. *Cultural Studies Review*, 16 (1): 104–18.
Satchell, K. (2010b). THIS: message in a bottle to Jimmie Durham. *Performance Paradigm*, 6: 53–65.
Satchell, K. (2012). Sing me Byron Bay. *Continuum: Journal of Media and Cultural Studies*, 6 (2): 249–61.
Satchell, K. (2013). Poetics of the weather: studies in creativity. In Harrison, M., Rose, D.B., Shannon, L., and Satchell, K. (eds). Writing creates ecology and ecology creates writing, *TEXT*, Special Issue 20: 61–68.
Serres, M. (1995a). *Angels: a modern myth*. Paris, Flammarion.
Serres, M. (1995b). *The natural contract*. Michigan, University of Michigan Press.
Serres, M. (1997). *The troubadour of knowledge*. Michigan, University of Michigan Press.
Serres, M. (2006). The natural contract revisited [transcript of lecture]. Institute for the Humanities at Simon Fraser University, May 6.
Serres, M. (2008). *The five senses: a philosophy of mingled bodies*. London, Continuum.
Serres, M. (2011a). *Variations on the body*. Minneapolis, Univocal.
Serres, M. (2011b). *Malfeasance: appropriation through pollution*. Stanford, Stanford University Press.
Serres, M. (2012). *Biogea*. Minneapolis, Univocal.
Serres, M. (2014). *Times of crisis: what the financial crisis revealed and how to reinvent our lives and futures*. New York, Bloomsbury.
Serres, M. (2015). *Thumbelina: the culture and technology of the millennials*. London, Rowman and Littlefield.
Smith, H., and Dean, R.T. (eds). (2009). *Practice-led research and research-led practice in the creative arts*. Edinburgh, Edinburgh University Press.
Stewart, K. (2007). *Ordinary affects*. Durham, Duke University Press.
Stivale, C.J. (2008). *Gilles Deleuuze's ABCs: the folds of friendship*. Baltimore, John Hopkins University Press.

St. Pierre, E.A. (2004). Deleuzian concepts for education: the subject undone. *Educational Philosophy and Theory*, 36 (3): 283–96.
Taussig, M. (2004). *My cocaine museum*. Chicago, University of Chicago Press.
Thoreau, H.D. (1974). *The portable Thoreau*. Bode, C. (ed). New York, Penguin.
Turner, G. (2012). *What's become of cultural studies?* London, Sage.
van Dooren, T., and Rose, D.B. (2012). Storied-places in a multispecies city. *Humanimalia*, 3 (2): 1–27.
Yates, J. (2005). "The gift is given": on the errant ethic of Michel Serres. In Abbas, N. (ed). *Mapping Michel Serres* (pp. 190–209). Ann Arbor, University of Michigan Press.

6 The Tactical Researcher
Cultural Studies Research as Pedagogy

Amanda Third

en·gaged
adj.
employed, occupied, or busy; committed, as to a cause; pledged to marry, betrothed; involved in conflict or battle; being in gear; meshed; partly embedded in, built into, or attached to another part, as columns on a wall.

As many commentators have noted, today's cultural milieu is characterized by complexity, as both a practical phenomenon and a pervasive "structure of feeling" (Ang 2011: 779). Under the reign of complexity, cultures globally are perceived to be facing large-scale, intractable challenges, such as climate change, global recession, youth unemployment, and elevated mental illness and suicide rates. These issues are characterized by "irreducible multiplicity, historical undecidability, and the simultaneous presence of contradictory elements, under the logic of both/and (rather than) either/or" (Ang 2011: 783–4). In this context, it is increasingly acknowledged that traditional, positivist ways of knowing are inadequate epistemological practices, and that large-scale, cross-sector, interdisciplinary collaborations are necessary if we are to make significant inroads into the matrix of complex issues shaping contemporary experience.

It is within the frame of complexity that cultural studies, alongside cognate cultural and social research disciplines, has begun to (re)assert its importance to the future globally[1]; an assertion that has not gone ignored, albeit some way from receiving widespread acceptance.[2] As Ien Ang (2011) has argued, to achieve broad-based and meaningful impact, cultural and social research must move beyond the critique of complexity to embrace 'cultural intelligence'. For Ang, cultural intelligence entails critically informed ways of navigating "complexity through appropriate modes of conceptual and discursive simplification ... by developing informed, empirically grounded accounts which substantiate the messy complexities in particular fields of practice; not for the purposes of critique ... but in order to open up new avenues for addressing the challenges involved" (2011: 788). Whereas Stuart Hall argues that cultural critique demands a 'detour through theory', Ang emphasizes that "cultural intelligence can only be gained through a *scrupulous detour through the empirical*, without which we cannot sufficiently appreciate and grasp the actual complexities at hand" (2011: 791, emphasis added).

One possible, though not exclusive, modality for impactful future social and cultural research lies in the 'engaged research' paradigm, which entails researchers, government, industry, not-for-profit organizations and user groups collaborating to define and set the research agenda, design and deliver the necessary studies, and implement the results. Working in the engaged research mode enables user-centered research to actively influence policy and practice agendas, not only—or even primarily—through the positioning of research outputs for ready uptake, but by fostering an active dialogue within a "community of practice" (Wenger 2000) that plays a powerful *pedagogic* role for research, policy, and practice alike.

Engaged research places new demands on the researcher; demands that often remain invisible amid (and sometimes ill-addressed by) universities' enthusiastic and growing interest in research that targets 'real world' impact. Drawing upon informal, semistructured interviews conducted between May and July 2015 with five Australian academics[3] who identify as 'engaged researchers' or researchers with a deep investment in 'community engagement' and "a disposition to qualitative and interpretive work" (A),[4] this chapter documents how such researchers are grappling with the shift to the engaged research paradigm in the context of a range of externally funded projects. In doing so, it thinks through the consequences for their sense of identity as researchers and for the status of humanistic and social scientific knowledge more broadly.

What Is 'Engaged' Research?

Superficially, engaged research can be read as a response to neoliberal research funding mechanisms and the corresponding demand that universities 'engage' beyond the domain of the academy and demonstrate their 'real world' relevance in an age wracked by "wicked problems" (Rittel and Webber 1973). However, we must be wary of easily dismissing engaged research on these grounds because, as I will demonstrate, it is also driven by a deep political and intellectual rationale, and its commitments to troubling knowledges can potentially lead to a revitalizing role for the humanistic and social scientific disciplines in public life. In its humanities, arts, and social sciences inflections, much engaged research derives its inspiration from the "critical mission ... [and] political and moral purpose" of the (non)discipline[5] of cultural studies, "which is about the public good before economic development, and which addresses the issues of the cultural distribution of power as a core concern" (Turner 2012: 12). Indeed, engaged research can be understood as one outcome of cultural studies' role as "a kind of academic *lingua franca* for the new humanities, a common theoretical and methodological language which may enable those disciplines engaged in cultural research to work with each other" (Turner 2012: 12).

Engaged research is conceived as a fundamentally collaborative enterprise in which researchers, government, industry, the not-for-profit sector, and user groups partner—over extended periods of time—to collectively identify the issues that require intervention; design research questions and methodologies; deliver a series of research project(s); and implement results in 'real world' settings. Engaged research is grounded in and reproduces a 'community of practice' (Wenger 2000) that centers on a dynamic process of knowledge production and exchange that calls the diverse expertise and experiences of collaborators into play. Engaged research places the dialogue between multiple stakeholders at the heart of the research model, as the site of productive engagement. In this context, the researcher becomes one of a number of specialized agents whose knowledge is activated—and potentially re-formed or reconstituted—in dialogue with others. While the engaged research process requires a certain degree of consensus among participants about the terrain of intervention, along with a commitment to broad-based change (what Wenger would call "joint enterprise" [2000: 229]), it is the careful management of differences—in experience, conceptual understandings, expertise, and approach—that drives the conversation forward.

Configured in this way, diversity is an engine of the potential success of an engaged research project.[6] Engaged research aims to channel conflict into the research process in ways that enable competing perspectives to bump up against one another, colliding and shaping one another in unexpected and fruitful ways. This demands "mutual engagement" (Wenger 2000: 229); deep levels of trust between participants, cultivated through respectful but robust exchanges, over long periods of time. While the engaged research mode is premised upon participants maintaining an openness to and engagement with alternative perspectives, sticking points and gridlocks inevitably arise. The point is not to resolve these differences (although this may be a positive by-product) but to hold them in tension and allow them to directly inform the research process in ways that resist the sedimentation of orthodoxies.[7] Rather than stumbling blocks, then, the engaged research mode embeds these agonistic moments as opportunities for mutual learning. Indeed, while the production of impactful outputs—in the form of reports, scholarly publications, best-practice models, resources and tools, and so on—are a crucial indicator of the success of an engaged research project, another important criterion of success is the mutual education of participants. At the end of a successful engaged research project, participants emerge with a "*shared repertoire* of communal resources—languages, routines, sensibilities, artifact, tools, stories, styles, etc" (Wenger 2000: 229, emphasis added). In the process of mutual education, research insights are not 'watered down' but activated in ways that demand high levels of rigour from the academic researcher. As Wenger (2000) notes—and I will return to this idea in a moment—"navigating the social landscape defined by communities [of practice] and their boundaries requires a strong identity" (239). Engaging in playful dialogue in the engaged research mode opens up the research process to interrogation and input from 'outside'. It simultaneously cultivates the possibility of a *sphere of influence* by which researchers are able to intervene in policy and practice debates in a direct manner that leads to enhanced uptake—a platform for research insights to mingle with and influence/be influenced by alternative perspectives. In other words, engaged research is a matter of pedagogy.

But how does the university-based researcher experience working in an engaged research setting? What kinds of adaptations, subversions, and contortions must the academic researcher perform to operate meaningfully in this setting? And how do such performances betray the limits of knowledge in contemporary society?

Engaged Orientations

The 'doer' is variably constructed in and through the deed.
(Butler 1990a: 181)

It is just before midnight. I am curled up on the couch under a blanket, my body folded awkwardly around my iPad. The screen emits a blue-ish glow in the semi-dark. My partner and son are asleep. Aside from the sounds of the house breathing, it is quiet. Sleep is tugging at my eyelids. I have eight hours of back-to-back meetings tomorrow, starting at 8.30 A.M. I have arranged it that way so I can take Friday 'off' to write. I would go to bed but this article about the discourse of the Ivory Tower is fascinating. And if I can seize this moment of quiet in which to digest it, it can be processed in the back room of my brain while I am in meetings tomorrow. ...

Called into being across spatial, temporal, disciplinary, and sectoral divides, the engaged researcher is acutely aware of the multifarious performances demanded by the diverse settings in which they must operate: "At a minimum, you are 'the expert', the negotiator, the translator, the devil's advocate, the diplomat, the mediator, the teacher, the student, and the radical who doesn't quite have their feet on the ground. Sometimes you are one of these things, and other times you are many of these things all in the same moment" (D). Or, as other participants expressed it, "there are multiple hats to be worn simultaneously" (B) and "you need to be many things to many people" (E). They noted that it had taken time, and a willingness to learn from mistakes, to develop the necessary research, management, and interpersonal skills to perform in their roles. As one participant stated, pointing to the need to develop a range of competencies that extend beyond the training that conventionally constitutes the academic's skill set: "As academics, we are not always well-trained or prepared for the demands of inhabiting these multiple personalities, whether it's sequentially or simultaneously" (D). This combination of factors sometimes resulted in an amplified sense for these researchers of, as Dana Pollock describes it, a "divided, even duplicitous, self" (2010: 465).

In pointing to the multiple performances required of them, the researchers I interviewed gestured toward the operations of *performativity* that shape engaged research and the identities it produces. Judith Butler defines performativity as the "reiterative power of discourse to produce the phenomena that it regulates and constrains" (1990b: 28). For Butler, performativity is iterative; it achieves its naturalized authority through "repetition and ... ritual" (1990b: xv). Importantly, though, in Butler's formulation, while the trajectory of performativity aspires to securing the subject's complicity with normative ideals, it nonetheless offers up the possibility of subversion. Subversive agency finds its locus in the possibility of disrupting the "practices of repetitive signifying" (Butler 1990a: 185) and asserting different ways of being, For Butler, then:

> The critical task is ... to affirm the local possibilities of intervention through *participating in precisely those practices of repetition* that constitute identity and, therefore, present the immanent possibility of contesting them ... *The task is not whether to repeat, but how to repeat* or, indeed, to displace the very norms that enable the repetition itself (1990a: 189, emphasis added).

The engaged researchers I spoke with viewed their 'engagement'—their willingness to *participate* in interdisciplinary and cross-sector dialogues—as the locus of their capacity to *activate* research and wield influence over ongoing debate, policy, and practice:

> You have to be part of the conversation if you want to see it change. You can't stand on the sideline and critique and expect to have an impact. But if you're going to be part of the conversation, you have to stay alert ... The trick is not to be co-opted by it. You have to keep making trouble, to keep gently disrupting the assumptions that underpin the conversation, to not let the dust settle (D).

We can understand this participant as being concerned with 'how to repeat', with troubling the "stylised repetition of acts" (Butler 1990a: 179) that constitute knowledge practices both within and without the university. The engaged researchers I interviewed all noted that a wide variety of research modalities—from desk-based philosophical theorizing to scientific laboratory research—were necessary for a rich and vibrant intellectual culture and the capacity for innovation. However, they felt drawn to engaged research as a mechanism for a form of repetitive 'troublemaking'[8] that can activate theory and empirical data and open up the possibilities for meaningful social change.

Among those interviewed, there was a perception that a certain 'orientation' to the world is necessary to carry out this kind of research: "You carry with you a certain way of seeing and orienting yourself to the world, a critical aesthetic, that predisposes you to this kind of research" (A). This idea of an 'orientation' was key to the ways these researchers conceived the *political* project of engaged research. As Sara Ahmed has explained, orientations "point us toward the future ... Orientations are effects of what we tend toward, where the 'toward' marks a space and time that is almost, but not quite, available in the present" (2006: 554). This 'tending towards'— this future-orientation—was palpable in engaged researchers' narration of their developing sense of the potential of 'new' epistemologies and practices for inspiring 'real world' change. Some explicitly cited social justice imperatives as the primary impetus for their work: "Social justice motivates me. My work is built around the cultural studies 'chestnuts' of power and representation" (A). Others described being motivated by more abstract ideas of "changing the world" (D) and "making a difference" (C). In this sense, all those I interviewed expressed a concern with undertaking research directed at producing 'cultural intelligence' (Ang 2011). As one participant expressed it, "it's about shifting thinking. It's not about recognizing gaps, which is a trait of academic work, but [about,] now that we have identified that gap, how can we move that forward and collectively reconstitute what we know?" (C). Another claimed that engaged research is most effective in achieving the kind of "slow change that is required in policy and practice settings" (B). Collectively, then, and intimating the performative dimensions of research, they framed engaged research in terms of *intervention*, calling to mind Mike Michael's (2012) observation that research does not simply reflect what is 'out there' but "is instrumental in, and a feature of, the 'making of out theres'" (26).

However, beyond the concern with mobilizing research and/or expertise to intervene in policy and practice-oriented dialogue, these researchers were also committed to the idea that engaged research delivers "fundamentally changed paradigms of knowing and knowledge production" (Pollock 2010: 465). The majority expressed dissatisfaction and/or frustration with the capacity of normative approaches to university-based knowledge production to impact a complex social world (B, C, D, E). This sentiment took shape in relation to a perception that entrenched knowledge practices were often inflexible and stifled creative approaches and outputs. In particular, disciplinary boundaries were subjected to critique: "I don't believe it is possible to work towards solutions to complex problems by working in disciplinary silos. The dominance of particular actors or regimes that reproduce inherited knowledge are part of the problems we are trying to tackle" (B). But so too, the idea of 'the academy' and 'the university' as bounded entities came under scrutiny. One interviewee suggested that researchers should be "encouraged to take more risks" (C) in conducting and promoting their work beyond the boundaries of the university, concluding that "researchers have to become more like activists" (C). In collectively highlighting the limitations of conventional knowledge systems, these engaged researchers expressed a desire to reconstitute the accepted conditions of legitimate knowledge production: "we need to transform the way we do things, the very way we think about and reproduce what constitutes valid knowledge" (D). Or, as another interviewee expressed it, "in this sense, there is a political orientation to my work. A commitment to contesting the terms of knowledge is important if we are to respond to complex problems" (B). From the interviewees' perspectives, then, it is this commitment to unsettling normative knowledge practices on an ongoing basis that gives the engaged researcher's (often phenomenologically fractured) identity coherence across time.

Ontologies of Discomfort

'I' am and am not a scholar, much less one who is genteelly 'engaged'.
(Pollock 2010: 464)

I am keenly anticipating the moment of sitting down to write. I have been thinking about these issues for years—not sporadically, but in an almost routinized manner, and out of necessity as much as, if not more than, an intellectual commitment to reflexivity. But the opportunity to commit these thoughts to paper has evaded me in amidst the multiple demands on my time. A sustained and rigorous scholarly analysis does not easily emerge from a crowded head space and the fragments of time snatched between meetings, data collection, the nurturing of partnerships, report writing, policy work, grant applications, and the #EndlessAdministration that accompanies the large-scale, interdisciplinary and cross-sector projects in which I am participating (and which—of course—is an increasingly prominent feature of any academic's everyday). It is not for want of trying, nor because of a predisposition to either perfectionism or procrastination (although, from an outsider's point of view it might seem legitimate to accuse me of both at times). I just haven't found the space, yet. ...

The engaged researchers I interviewed reported having a sense of 'not fitting anywhere' in particular. Although they often feel valued by their institutions and well respected by their colleagues in academic, government, corporate, and not-for-profit sectors, their dominant experience of themselves as researchers is structured by ontological discomfort:

Inside the university, I feel I'm regarded as a kind of irritant. I'm in a kind of conservative department and no one quite knows how to make sense of me. It feels often like my research is regarded with suspicion; like my research is not quite valid, that it must be corrupted by the funding or the relationships with 'the real world'. And then, when I sit in meetings with industry or government partners, I feel like a taxidermist's rare or extinct bird, a throwback from a bygone era who thinks on another plane, strangely removed from reality, but who occasionally throws a useful insight into discussion that makes them see things from the outside. But you could say that I don't ever feel quite at home either in the university or outside it. Perhaps this is why cultural studies appeals to me. It helps me make sense of this 'almost but not quite' sense of fitting in (E).

Importantly, for the engaged researcher, this sense of not-quite-at-homeness manifests less as an identity crisis than as the embodied experience of the broader conditions of contingency that shape knowledge production in a complex world:

> When you are dealing with complexity, you never really *know* anything. You have to be able to rely on the process and trust that your training and your capacities as a critical thinker will enable you to make the necessary intervention at the appropriate moment. 'Knowing' in a complex knowledge ecology is very ephemeral at best" (D).

Recalling Wenger's claim that one "requires a strong identity" (2000: 239), these engaged researchers expressed a willingness to sit with this uncertainty—and to allow themselves to be "vulnerable" and "exposed to the other" (D)—as a way of letting the research and the potential for new ways of thinking and doing things to unfold. Reflecting on the engaged research mode, Pollock has posited that this kind of uncertainty is generative of new knowledge possibilities in which "apparently fixed structures of relation swing open to surprise" (Pollock 2010: 465).

Echoing this idea, one interviewee claimed that, "if I start to feel comfortable, I start to get concerned. … Comfortable means you're not confronting the dilemmas head on; you've receded into complacency. Comfortable means the possibilities have closed down" (E). In these kinds of ways, the experience of discomfort had become, for some interviewees, a litmus test of their reflexivity, and a marker of their integrity and their capacity to contribute meaningfully to the engaged research process. The absence of discomfort, by contrast, pointed to a failure of process.

This experience of 'not feeling at home anywhere' is but one version of a variety of spatial metaphors (home as a place/not feeling at home *anywhere*) that were key to interviewees' ways of conceptualizing their engaged research practices.[9] For example, one interviewee noted that "the engaged researcher is *nomadic*" (D, my emphasis). Further, interviewees often distinguished between 'the university' or 'the academy' on the one hand, and "outside/beyond the university" (A, B, C, D, E) or "in the real world" (A, D, E) on the other. One talked about her "pathological *openness* to diverse ways of knowing" and the problems with knowledge practices that operate in "disciplinary *silos*" and "*close* down" opportunities for "*real world* transformation" (B, my emphasis). Others talked about "the boardroom" (D, E), "the meeting room" (C, D, E), "the partner organization's premises" (D), and "research participants' homes" (C). They collectively conceived of themselves as actors moving regularly across place-based boundaries, and this mobility was perceived not only as a key factor in the research and engagement practices they had developed (e.g., methods for "talking to people 'out there' in community" [A]) but also as foundational to their *political* project of contesting and shifting the boundaries of knowledge. Indeed, each couched their descriptions of their practices and experiences in ways that indicated that they perceive engaged research as fundamentally concerned with the *respatialization of knowledge.*

To articulate this project of respatializing knowledge, interviewees also frequently mobilized—albeit critically and/or tongue-in-cheek—another familiar euphemism for the university; namely, the Ivory Tower. Within mainstream discourse, the Ivory Tower has installed itself as the ultimate pejorative signifier of the university as a bounded and impermeable entity with limited relevance to public life and, for the apocalyptically inclined, a seriously limited shelf life (see Boker 2012). That is, the Ivory Tower is a figuration that orients understandings of the university and, by extension, knowledge. And, so too, it is a figuration that shaped—for some, none too subtly—the ways the engaged researchers I interviewed conceptualized their project of engagement. Given this, it is useful to make a brief detour to consider how and why the Ivory Tower operates within mainstream discourse, and what this can tell us about the ways that research, the university, and knowledge are being conceptualized, enacted, and valued in contemporary society.

On the Ivory Tower: A Parenthesis of Sorts

> *This is where I belong—one foot in and one foot out. Here and simultaneously at the university, when here raises the stakes of there, and there underscores the in-and-beyond-the-moment importance of what's happening here.*
>
> (Pollock 2010: 464)

> *I am yearning for a space, a room of one's own, a retreat from the ceaseless tide of tasks and the complex web of interactions (which at other times buoy and sustain both my work and my sense of self) in which to actively put the pieces of my thinking together and find the right words. So, here I am at a very noisy café close to home (the soundtrack is Robert Palmer doing a cover of Marvin Gaye) that does not have free WiFi (a very deliberate choice). My smartphone battery is running low, a timely technological subversion that mitigates my impulse to keep checking my e-mail. I am 'in the zone', alone in a bubble of calm but intense focus. I can feel my synapses firing in a deeply*

satisfying way; electrons rapidly discharging down unprecedented paths. I am differently alive. And I am simultaneously excited that this rare moment has arrived; triumphant that I have carved this space out; anxious that I will be disrupted; and just a little worried that I might have forgotten how to write 'academically'. After all, it has been several months since the last time I did this. ...

In 1949, in the context of heightened postwar tensions around the perceived threat of communism, the politically conservative medieval historian, Ernst Kantorowicz, wrote a statement refusing to comply with the University of California's Board of Regents' demand that all academics employed by the university sign an oath of loyalty to the United States or risk having their employment terminated. In the statement, he claimed that:

> There are three professions which are entitled to wear a gown: the judge, the priest, the scholar. This garment stands for its bearer's maturity of mind, his independence of judgment, and his direct responsibility to his conscience and his God. It signifies the inner sovereignty of those three interrelated professions: they should be the very last to allow themselves to act under duress and yield to pressure.
> (Kantorowicz 1949)

It is significant that Kantorowicz's bold statement in support of academic freedom constructs an image of the scholar as a cloistered figure: his statement coincides with the consolidation within Anglophone culture of the pejorative discourse around the university as an 'Ivory Tower', and the enduring efficacy of this discourse as a mechanism for both questioning and regulating the 'legitimacy' and (public) 'utility' of the university today turns, of course, upon a notion of the scholar as publicly funded but disengaged and 'out-of-touch' with the 'real world'.

As Steven Shapin (2012) documents, the modern discourse of the Ivory Tower is a reworking of the "ancient religious and secular debate over the active and the contemplative life—*negotium* and *otium*: is it better, more virtuous, more authentically human to be engaged with civic affairs or is it better—from time to time or always—intentionally to live apart from the polis?" (26). Originally connoting religious meanings (see Shapin 2012: 2–3), in the 19th century, the Ivory Tower began to be invoked in relation to aesthetics; in particular to argue for the value of artists' retreats as providing the necessary solitude for imaginative freedom and artistic creation. At this point in history, the Ivory Tower had both positive and negative connotations, depending on how one thought about artistic creation, the kinds of outputs it should produce, the conditions under which it should take place, and its responsibilities to 'society' (Shapin 2012: 5). However, beginning in the years leading up to the Second World War and consolidating in the early years of the Cold War, the Ivory Tower came to be reconfigured as a metaphor for the university as a cultural and "defective institution, needing correction and reform" (Shapin 2012: 14).

This was in large part the result of fierce contemporary debates about the role of the university and its knowledge products in national political life. The debates centered on the contributions of universities to the political and ideological struggle initially against fascism and Nazism and, increasingly, with the onset of the Cold War, also against communism. Notably, in the United States in particular, during the Second World War, universities were called upon to align themselves with national war efforts and demonstrate their ideological complicity with the aims of the state. Indeed, it was against this very idea of the university as an arsenal of ideological opposition to the perceived rising threat of communism that Kantorowicz mounted his impassioned defense of academic freedom. And he did so through recourse to an argument that reasserted the importance of the bounded and privileged space of the university for public life.

Simultaneously, contemporary debates asserted the necessity for *applied research* that would reach beyond the boundaries of the so-called Ivory Tower.[10] As Robert M. Hutchins, President of the University of Chicago, told staff and students in 1942, "when war has been declared, long run activities must be sacrificed to the short run activity of winning the war. We have stood for liberal education and pure research. What the country needs now is vocational training and applied research" (cited in Shapin 2012: 16). This trend toward the valorization of applied research consolidated further in the postwar period, and it marked a key moment in cordoning off the arts, humanities, and social sciences as the 'inevitable' residents of the Ivory Tower.

In this economy of peak political tensions, the arts, humanities, and social science disciplines were positioned very differently to those of the "natural sciences, engineering and professional schools" (Shapin 2012: 14). This was partly because of social scientific and humanistic academics' willingness to engage in critique of Western capitalist order and to entertain—albeit often highly critically—alternative worldviews. However, it was also because, in the context of the push toward applied research, the sciences found it much easier to migrate out of the Ivory Tower and be "kept ... on tap for military and commercial purposes" (Shapin 2012: 21), whereas the social scientific and humanistic disciplines, increasingly viewed as lacking relevance to the life of the nation, remained firmly within its crumbling walls. As Shapin notes, "the outcome, as the Cold War proceeded, was a fault line in the academy—between those whose inquiries had major constituencies outside the university and those whose inquiries did not" (2012: 22).

In this context, then, the Ivory Tower trope was mobilized to discipline the institution of the university in general, and to denigrate the arts, humanities, and social sciences in particular. Whereas, in the past, "practically everyone acknowledged that both engagement and disengagement were necessary moments in human life and in the making of knowledge", in the postwar Anglophone world, we have seen the consolidation of a "monologue [which] finds no worth in the Ivory Tower" (Shapin 2012: 26). Indeed, the discourse of the Ivory Tower as a fortress of decaying relevance today has become so totalizing that it is often difficult to remember that, as Simon Marginson (2011) reminds us, "universities have a notable capacity to hold in a bounded heterogeneity", and that the university often operates as "a semi-independent site for criticism and renewal of the state" (418).[11]

The Ivory Tower loomed large in the imaginations of the engaged researchers I interviewed—researchers who might present at first glance as the very antithesis of Kantorowicz's idealized figures of public office—and they saw themselves as actively engaged in and working across the knowledge boundaries and discursive containments this trope instantiates within the public domain. At the same time, however—and in a manner that harks back to the invocation of the Ivory Tower as a respite of creative disengagement in 19th century constructions—they also expressed a somewhat ambivalent desire, a nostalgia even, for the Ivory Tower as a locus of scholarly retreat and deep thought. The majority of interviewees regularly imagined an academic life in which a space of 'disengagement' featured more strongly. One said, "I have a yearning for a rather more autonomous approach that ... is easier to negotiate" (B), and another noted that, "I dream all the time about having a sabbatical where I can sit in a quiet office somewhere beyond the reach of my collaborators and the quotidian schedule of meetings and workshops and data collection and just bunker down and ... think and write about what it all means" (D). In particular, the Ivory Tower featured as a necessary space of peaceful reflection conducive to producing research outputs that line up with the university's preferred, and rewarded, modes of text-centric knowledge production. However, one participant in particular noted that the more solitary, scholarly life and research outputs afforded by the Ivory Tower also underpinned her reputation and efficacy in 'the outside world': "I need more time and space to do the deep thinking and writing and discussions to formulate what my unique contribution is and to translate that into academic outputs. It's important to have a reputation as an established scholar ... [so that industry partners] can assess and seek your unique contribution. It's part of your readability for those stakeholders" (B). Or, in other words, a positively inflected conception of the Ivory Tower was seen by interviewees as necessarily constitutive of both their personal scholarly identity, and their identity 'out there' in the research 'marketplace'.

However, notwithstanding these moments of appreciation of the benefits of the Ivory Tower, by and large, the researchers I interviewed rallied against the idea of the university as a cloistered entity with little public relevance. To make sense of the ways these researchers conceptualize the politics of their mobility across the discursive divide between the university and the rest of the world, I turn to Michel de Certeau's discussion of tactics and strategy.

Tactical Orientations

> *There is only the taking up of the tools where they lie, where the very 'taking up' is enabled by the tool lying there.*
>
> (Butler 1990a: 185)

> *I am deep in thought, fingers poised on the keyboard, when my phone dings. I jump. My four golden hours are up and I have 10 minutes to scurry home and get online to meet with a graduate student. And then there is a meeting with a research assistant, and a phone call to a partner organization who haven't paid their invoice. And then it will be time to pick up my son. Back to the 'real world'. ...*

How, then, does the engaged researcher trouble knowledge?

As I have already intimated, the engaged researcher's work is fundamentally preoccupied with a respatialization of knowledge that conceptualizes normative boundaries of knowledge as the terrain of action and change. Importantly, this process of respatialization does not aim at the colonization of new spaces. As one participant stated:

> We sometimes forget, in university life, that we are not the lone ethnographer, pith-helmet-equipped, heading off into the wild to partake in the extraction of data. I get tired of ... colleagues who talk about community engagement as a terrain to exploit. Have we not learned anything from ethnography over the last 100 years? (A).

Rather, resisting forms of knowledge that seek to dominate via staking spatial claims, engaged research promotes mobility and action across conventional knowledge boundaries (interpersonal, discursive, disciplinary, institutional, sectoral, professional, geographical, and so on). Engaged research is simultaneously unconcerned with boundaries (inasmuch as it seeks to elude containment within such borders) and intensely preoccupied with them (inasmuch as they are necessary to the conceptualization of the project of moving across, and of bringing into dialogue, discrete or bounded spaces). Envisaging knowledge as *mobile and mobilizing*, engaged research is primarily concerned to work *with* existing boundaries to generate new ways of knowing and of activating knowledge. As one participant noted:

> You have to work with the cognition that there are tensions that can't be dissolved ... There's a need to ... look at the research process to *work with those differences*. Engaged research doesn't try and dissolve all that messiness into a coherent project and to bring perspectives together. It aims to understand why some pieces remain separate but remain part of the whole, and to ask how the pieces can be explored differently (B).

Ideally, or perhaps inevitably, through the force of repetitious resistances, and usually over long periods of time, engaged research may gradually dissolve the boundaries across which it works, and be implicated in the instantiation of new ones. But by the time this happens, if it is successful, engaged research will already have identified the new boundaries, regrouped, and be mobilizing across them.

Configured as nomadic, not feeling at home anywhere, and unconvinced by the need to stake out a 'place', the boundary-crossing figure of the engaged researcher is constantly compelled to operate in ways that theorist of the everyday, Michel de Certeau, might define as 'tactical' (de Certeau 1988). In *The Practice of Everyday Life*, de Certeau, who is concerned with the politics and possibilities of opposition, contrasts 'tactics' with 'strategy'. He uses the term 'strategy' to refer to the organizational force of the everyday, which operates in alignment with the priorities of dominant order. Strategy occupies the terrain of the spatial: "It postulates a *place* that can be delimited as its *own* and serve as the base from which relations with an *exteriority* ... can be managed" (1988: 35–36).[12]

Against the totalizing organizational impulse of strategy, de Certeau argues, political opposition assumes the form of 'tactics'. Tactics are distinguished from strategy by their relationship to space and time. Unlike strategy, tactics have no enduring claim to the spatial realm of dominant order. Rather, tactics borrow the spaces of the other and use or, rather, reuse them to momentarily subvert that same order. As de Certeau suggests:

> A *tactic* operates in isolated actions, blow by blow. It takes advantage of 'opportunities' and depends on them, being without any base where it could stockpile its winnings, build up its own position, and plan raids. What it wins it cannot keep. This *nowhere* gives a tactic mobility, to be sure, but a mobility that must accept the chance offerings of the moment, and seize on the wing the possibilities that offer themselves at any given moment (1988: 36–37, my emphasis).

Although tactics operate on the principle of speed—across the plane of the temporal, seizing opportunities and 'surprising'—and while they cannot make a permanent claim to strategic space, they can nonetheless have permanent effects; the impact of tactical and troubling repetitions (and, here, I deliberately gesture toward Butler's argument about the subversive possibilities of performativity) is cumulative.

Reading them through de Certeau, it is significant, then, that engaged researchers report not 'feeling at home anywhere' and that they articulate the project of engaged research in terms of *mobility*. These qualities point to the tactical operations of the engaged researcher and were most explicit when they were describing their engagements in multistakeholder environments. The engaged research mode, as I have already indicated, centers dialogue: "it emphasizes the dialogues that are necessary between different kinds of knowledge and stakeholders, across different spaces and times, without trying to minimize what that means" (B). One interviewee, talking about her participation in an ongoing cross-sectoral project dialogue, talked about her approach in terms that explicitly referenced the temporality that characterizes de Certeau's conceptualization of the tactical:

> It's all in the *timing*. You have to be on guard, always ready to intervene, to push the boundaries, to throw out a challenge. It is this capacity to react—almost instinctually but with the full force of what you know activated in the moment—that is the mark of the engaged researcher (E).

In making such claims, the engaged researchers I interviewed expressed a strong degree of reflexivity about their role in shaping and managing dialogue between partners, and also signaled their 'troublemaking' ambitions.

In such settings, engaged researchers view themselves as intervening in dialogues with other 'expert citizens' (Bang 2010) to hold competing ideas, personalities, and epistemologies in productive tension in ways that potentially open up new perspectives. However, the engaged researchers I interviewed openly acknowledged that, in navigating dialogue with partners, the power relationships between the various agents are asymmetrical: "it's a very messy and uneven process" (E). They spoke about the ways they (alongside other actors in the dialogue) sometimes momentarily exercise authority within interdisciplinary and cross-sector dialogues, assuming an explicit agenda-setting role. To do so, they would wait for the right moment (the 'opportunity', in de Certeau's terms) and then, drawing on the 'weight' of their expertise, intervene (often this marked the moment of the 'surprise') to direct conversation. The researchers viewed their tactical interventions as targeted at surfacing assumptions and tensions between competing perspectives, with a view to working *with*—'on the terrain of the other'—these tensions to move conversations forward. The engaged researcher is never entirely sure what kinds of effects his or her tactical incursions will produce. This way of working inevitably produces moments of overt and covert conflict. However, conflict was seen, not as something to be avoided, but as a necessary part of the process. As an interviewee said, "you have to have a commitment to transparency, contestation and dialogue. Conflict can be more valuable than consensus or certainty" (B). Indeed, the power differentials at play render consensus impossible in all but momentary ways. As an interviewee suggested, "where these moments of agenda setting take place, they are not fixed or permanent but momentary and become open, again, to contestation ... So there are moments where alliances ... converge but then, just as quickly, fragment again or spin off in surprising directions" (B). Or to put it in de Certeau's terms, the engaged researcher does not 'keep what they win' but must surrender to the process and wait for the next 'opportunity'.

In the process of surfacing differences and mobilizing the generative potential of power differentials, then, engaged research operates as "an experimental system that is organized in a way such that the production of differences becomes the orienting principle of its own reproduction ... [creating] a kind of subversive movement" (Lury and Wakeford 2012: 6).

Interviewees pointed to the challenges of implementing this kind of research, highlighting that "engaged research is a much more fraught enterprise than is sometimes presented" (B). But they were also quick to acknowledge that "it can be a source of incredible creativity ... and new commitments" (B), and that working in this 'messy' way was preferable to research that "abides by institutional rules" and "can produce clean, timely and applicable research, but which often only addresses a fractional perspective, can become quite redundant very quickly, or which reasserts conventional ways of seeing and understanding that are part of the problem we are trying to resolve" (B). Engaged research does not unfold along a linear trajectory. Indeed, it operates to problematize forms of knowledge that assume linearity as a condition. Working *with* uncertainty and conflict, what is ultimately always already potentially at stake in the unpredictable and multidirectional vectors of engaged research is "the radical implosion of normative epistemologies" (Pollock 2010: 465).

Engaged Knowledges

> *Who devises the protocols of 'clarity' and whose interests do they serve? ... What does transparency keep obscure?*
>
> (Butler 1990a: xix)

> *Perhaps inevitably, I have to write to ask for an extension on the submission deadline. I have been careful to keep the editor informed about my progress, so he is gracious and forgiving when I request extra time. I cancel a range of nonurgent meetings for early next week. I start calculating the moments I might be able to use over the weekend to keep progressing the chapter: when my 3-year-old has his daytime sleep; when my partner takes our son to the supermarket to do the shopping; after dinner on Sunday night ...*

So, then, what kind of knowledge does engaged research produce?

In the first instance, engaged research produces large—even overwhelming or excessive—volumes of data, or, as one participant said: "occasionally the university asks how they can help with our big data sets and I just laugh" (C). The analysis of this data often focuses on short-term deliverables, such as a report, a journal article, or a set of policy recommendations or design specifications. Many of the engaged researchers I interviewed harbor intentions of returning to this data at a later date, but the pressures of funding and new projects often preclude this in practice: "There are mountains of qualitative and quantitative data that we never really address in full before we have to move onto the next project" (C).

All of the researchers I interviewed found the sheer quantity of data an ongoing challenge, not only in relation to the practicalities of managing large, rich, and multiplying data sets ("I am totally overwhelmed by little spaces in my office and in my computer where there are little bits of data ... I literally have hundreds of files" [C]), but also in relation to fulfilling their ethical obligations toward their research participants. The researchers' descriptions of their ethical responsibilities constellated in particular around a somewhat old-fashioned object of knowledge containment; namely, the filing cabinet, which was configured as a troubling—or more precisely, guilt-inducing—repository of an excess of 'voices': "When I think about what I should do with all this data, I just feel remorse. It's that feeling of 'I have spent all of this time with you, talking together and learning from you, and then I have put you in a filing cabinet'" (C). Or, as another participant expressed it: "I have a filing cabinet in my office where I keep all the transcripts and recordings from my qual[itative] work and it just carries on swelling with a proliferating cacophony of voices that call out to me, pleading with me to write them up further and *really* do them justice" (D). In this sense, as a form of research practice that is excessive to "linear and foreclosed modes of scholarly productivity" (Pollock 2010: 465), engaged research produces unwieldy and equally *excessive* amounts of data that problematize the idea of the neatly contained data set that can lead directly to 'clean' and decisive conclusions.

At the same time, such data sets were seen as the source of a summative wisdom, particularly when they were generated by a team of researchers who debated and discussed the accumulating data in an ongoing way:

> I am sitting on a mountain of data that I never can get to. But, actually, reporting on all of that data is no longer important ... It's about the ability to make sense of what the growing constellation of data is adding up to. I feel like, as a team ... we have come to this way of thinking about our subject and articulating it ... [that] can tell a coherent story about the whole (B).

Such claims surface the temporality of engaged knowledges. Engaged research produces *processual* knowledges—ways of knowing that defy finality, that resist the certainty of enduring conclusions. In a complex social world, the 'problem' is constantly transforming and, by extension, knowledge claims that respond to this complexity are always contingent, always mutating: "engaged research produces research methods, processes and findings that are always partial, fraught and sometimes contradictory" (B). Thus, while aspiring to 'solutions', engaged research operates with the knowledge that the moment of arrival will always be postponed. It posits that surrendering the idea of definitively knowing and thereby solving the problem, once and for all, produces the most workable interventions.

In this context, expertise—especially disciplinary expertise—takes on a specific utility; it is always up for grabs, its boundaries ripe for contestation. The engaged researcher must be prepared to surrender his or her expertise momentarily and allow it to be open to influence, while always holding it present. In an image that recalls Kantorowicz's robed scholar, one interviewee stated, "you have to wear your expertise like a garment. You can't wear it tightly, like a wetsuit that protects you from the outside conditions. You have to wear it more like a long, flowing robe that billows out towards, and touches, the other as you move alongside them but which is nonetheless fluidly bounded" (D). The aim, then, is not to reassert the boundaries of disciplinary knowledges but to activate them in dialogue. This requires paying attention to and playing with the tensions between certainty and uncertainty. This is crucial for it enables the knowledges generated by engaged research to have a future.

The settling of knowledges, the reproduction of certainty that is grounded in disciplinarity, is always to some degree retro-oriented, about proving what we already know. By contrast, the unsettling of knowledges orients us toward the future. This does not mean abandoning what we know. It means tactical moments of suspended belief, listening carefully, responding in good faith, all the while holding what we know close, but not too tightly. It entails strategic moments of commitment, the willingness to argue a point, to mount a rigorous defense. The engaged researcher 'knows' when he or she is unsettled, when the horizon of possibility stretches out in front of him or her, offering up solutions that have been hitherto unthinkable. "Knowing is a twitching of the senses, a sense of discomfort in our apprehensions of the future" (D).

The question that this mode of research constantly raises is that of the 'objectivity', 'rigour', and 'integrity' of the research. The engaged researcher is constantly called on to justify his or her modes of scholarship, exposed to radical questioning. Positivist frames would suggest that 'objectivity' is compromised in the engaged research mode; that our ways of knowing and articulating are always already 'infected' by our relationships with others. And, for certain, our relationships do impact the ways knowledge gets activated and interrogated. As one participant said, "neutrality is not possible" (C). Indeed, engaged research is explicitly invested in shaping the social world, with generating new epistemologies and social realities. But these aspirations, like those of the project of cultural studies from which it draws inspiration, are explicit. Engaged research seeks to:

> make transparent how the categories we mobilize also mediate the making of the social world and the 'ontological politics' of these practices. This is not only an invitation to be reflexive about how our interventions contribute to the making of some realities and not others. It is also a call to think about how we can interfere and creatively challenge accepted categories as well as illuminate the choices we make about the social worlds we help make happen.
>
> (Ruppert 2012: 45)

Far from abdicating the responsibilities of rigour, then, the engaged research mode compels it; it forces the researcher to know the edges of their knowledge inside out; to be prepared at any moment to articulate their ideas, or defend them. Distinct from the version of rigour that is grounded in notions of objectivity and the purity of scientific methods, the rigour of engaged research emerges from a process of being forced to confront the strengths and limitations of our thinking by engaging directly and dynamically with the other. Rigour is produced through multiple enunciations across time; it is the product of the ongoing project of grappling with the performative dimensions of research, of dealing with the consequences of a systematic campaign of 'troubling repetitions'. What emerges, then, is a rigour grounded in pedagogy and regulated by the *collective*; that is, "the creation of new, *partially shared* imaginaries without—and this is crucial—relying on one homogenizing translation into a dominant party's terms" (Lury and Wakeford 2013: 17).[13]

Returning to the Ivory Tower

> *The one who waits for the law, sits before the door of the law, attributes a certain force to the law for which one waits.*
> (Butler 1990a: xiv)

> *My phone rings and it is a representative from a youth-serving not-for-profit partner organization who are undertaking a planning process. "I can't wait to show you our new strategy document. I'm so excited", says the voice on the other end of the phone. "We've embedded that situationist theory stuff you were talking about in our new program to get young people politically engaged. I'll send you a draft. We'd love your feedback". I'm gratified that critical theory might have a practical application, but I do wonder if de Certeau would be pleased or whether he would roll in his grave, and the weight of responsibility kicks in. ...*

I have argued that working in the engaged research mode, with all of its attendant pleasures, pressures, and frustrations, offers cultural studies researchers—and those in social scientific and humanistic disciplines more broadly—the opportunity to intervene in policy and practice settings to great effect. The engaged research mode opens up a space for researchers to engage with complex social issues in their real world settings, to develop and experiment with novel methodologies in collaboration with partners, and in doing so, contribute groundbreaking insights to the public domain. However, beyond this, engaged research takes seriously the idea that research and teaching and learning are always intertwined. Engaged research is a multidirectional pedagogical practice (Pollock 2010: 465). It fosters robust dialogue and mutual learning among communities of practice, binding them together in the joint enterprise of interrogating the limits of existing knowledge, and forging new terrain for research, policy, and practice. The payback for the social scientific and humanistic researcher working in the engaged mode is the ability to move from cultural critique to cultural intelligence; to activate research in ways that directly contest and reframe scholarship, practice, and policy debates; to embed research insights into practice; and to learn from their collaborators.

As I have argued, engaged research entails the researcher operating tactically to enact troubling repetitions on the terrain of the other in order to expose the performativity of knowledge and open up the possibility of new epistemologies that can work with complexity to address 'wicked problems'.

However, the engaged researcher plays a risky—albeit perhaps necessary— game. Amid neoliberal funding imperatives and the consolidation of what George Marcus describes as the "hyper-desire to be relevant" (2003: 14),[14] the engaged researcher walks a tightrope between enacting troubling repetitions and playing into the forces at work in dominant culture that have contributed to the very problems engaged research critiques and intervenes in. Or, to put it differently, the question that constantly presents is precisely the question that Butler (1990a) poses in her analysis of performativity; namely, "what makes certain kinds of parodic representations effectively disruptive, truly troubling, and which repetitions become domesticated and recirculated as instruments of cultural hegemony?" (Butler 1990a: 177).

The engaged researchers I interviewed are acutely aware of the political push and pull associated with working at and with the intersections between diverse epistemologies and ideologies: "We don't want to become a service industry of applied research. We need to push back against the idea that research is used to meet the private agendas of corporations and increasingly the problematic agendas of governments that use [short-term research] contractors rather than public policy mechanisms" (B). But the line between troubling and hegemonic always threatens to dissolve (indeed, both impulses are always already at play). Sometimes the engaged researcher troubles on one front and then such troublemaking is appropriated by hegemonic interests on another. The engaged researcher must thus always have his or her wits about them and practice careful vigilance: "You can never be sure to what extent you are subverting the dominant and to what extent you are being co-opted. And, indeed, you can't control it. But you *can* remain vigilant about these things and take steps within the scope of your influence to counteract hostile appropriations. And that is the beauty of working in the engaged research mode. Because you're part of ongoing conversations, you don't only get 'one chance to blow', as Eminem might say. So you keep coming back, keep engaging, and keep on troublemaking at every opportunity" (E).

When the humanist Kantorowicz penned his letter to the University of California Board of Regents in 1949, the state of discourse around the university's 'relevance' in Anglophone cultures was such that it was still possible—and made sense—to reassert the bounded and privileged space of the university as a necessary locus of deep philosophical reflection and political and social conscience. However, at the same moment, amid the rising call for applied research and on the back of wartime 'discoveries' such as the atomic bomb and radar, the majority of Kantorowicz's scientific counterparts were entering into "a new, powerful, and durable compact with political power" (Shapin 2012: 18) and departing the Ivory Tower in droves. In this context, the scholarly conscience for which Kantorowicz was advocating—a conscience sharpened in and protected by the privileged space of the university—was in many quarters the ultimate casualty. As Shapin notes, while "you could do science with no clear links to power, profit or human welfare ... it was just this conception of science that was thought to be, and *was*, on its way out" (2012: 21, my emphasis). All researchers, including scientific researchers, must be vigilant about this possibility, and this vigilance might include, at times, calling for the necessity of the Ivory Tower.

Acknowledgments

I wish to thank the five researchers who participated in this project for their thoughtful reflections on what it means to be an engaged researcher. Thanks also to the range of partner organizations and young people I have worked with over the last 8 years in helping me formulate this take on the place of social and cultural research in addressing complex social issues, and to Andrew Hickey, Dimitris Vardoulakis, and Miguel Vatter for their invaluable input on the argument presented here.

Notes

1. For example, in the domain of youth media policy, commentators have argued that policy makers globally "need to listen to the findings of the best social scientists in our shared field in order to make better decisions. ... The relevant youth practices are shifting very quickly. Social norms in digitally mediated environments are extremely powerful. These norms ... pose special problems for those who seek to impose traditional methods of direct regulation. ... Social science research can help us to understand ... the substantial shifts in youth practice in order to be able to craft effective policy in this area" (Palfrey 2010: 6).
2. See, for example, the work of the Institute for Culture and Society at the University of Western Sydney, Australia (James 2015).
3. I bracket the 'non' here to gesture cultural studies' history of committed ambivalence toward disciplinarity, while acknowledging, as Graeme Turner does, that, as cultural studies has matured and taken on institutional status, it "does tend to behave very much like a discipline" (2012: 7).
4. The five interviewees are academics with a background in cultural studies, history, and/or sociology, and were employed in full-time and part-time capacities, in both ongoing and contract roles, at tertiary institutions located in urban and regional Australia at the time of interview. Four of them identify explicitly as cultural studies practitioners and the fifth identifies primarily as a sociologist but is employed in a cultural studies–dominated department.

5. Given that Australian academic circles are very small, to protect their privacy and ensure their willingness to speak frankly, care has been taken to ensure that none of the participants in this study can be identified using information provided here. However, all quotations are attributed to one of the five participants using A, B, C, D, or E.
6. It is for this reason that, while engaged research has much in common with 'participatory research', I prefer the term 'engaged' because it, in shifting the emphasis from 'participation' to 'engagement', acknowledges the conflicts and power relations that are central to the research process (see Arvanitakis and Hodge 2012).
7. In this way, the engaged research process takes seriously the challenge, which boyd and Crawford (2012) set out, of remaining vigilant about how emergent practices are shaping our ways of knowing and acting upon the world.
8. We should note here that, while it is yet to be argued systematically in the literature on the discipline of cultural studies, 'troublemaking' is by now commonly thought of as a key characteristic of the cultural studies project.
9. The experience of 'not feeling at home' is how the uncanny has often been described. See for example Freud (1973).
10. Although, we should note that this view was not without significant detractors (see Shapin 2012: 15–16). And, of course, the idea that the university is somehow disengaged from public life and disconnected from other institutions of power elides that universities have "always been sites of power and of service to Church or state" (Shapin 2012: 14).
11. Although he adds that, nonetheless, "the state is not always listening" (Marginson 2011: 418).
12. By establishing control of space, strategy simultaneously subordinates time to its agenda. De Certeau claims that strategy marks "a triumph of place over time … a mastery of time through the foundation of an autonomous place" (de Certeau 1988: 36).
13. We might, of course, also question the neutrality of positivist modes of knowledge. In the positivist mode, the interlocutors are different; they are structures, rules, instruments, modes of measurement, observational procedures. But they are arguably as equally invested as engaged research in shaping the social world; concerned with reproducing particular epistemologies.
14. And we should note here that Marcus attributes this 'hyper-desire for relevance' to cultural studies' advocation of the figure of the 'public intellectual' as a model for the 'new scholar' (2003: 14).

References

Ahmed, S. (2006). Orientations: toward a queer phenomenology. *GLQ: A Journal of Lesbian and Gay Studies*, 12 (4): 543–74.

Ang, I. (2011). Navigating complexity: from cultural critique to cultural intelligence. *Continuum: Journal of Media and Cultural Studies*, 25 (6): 779–84.

Arvanitakis, J., and Hodge, B. (2012). Forms of engagement and the heterogeneous citizen: towards a reflexive model for youth workshops. *Gateways: International Journal of Community Research and Engagement*, 5: 56–75.

Bang, H. (2010). Between everyday makers and expert citizens. In Fenwick, J., and McMillan, J. (eds). *Public management in the postmodern era: challenges and prospects* (pp. 163–91). Cheltenham: Edward Elgar.

Boker, J. (2012). *University of the future: a thousand year old industry on the cusp of profound change*. Sydney: Ernst and Young.

boyd, d., and Crawford, K. (2012). Critical questions for big data. *Information, Communication and Society*, 15 (50): 662–79.

Butler, J. (1990a). *Gender trouble: feminism and the subversion of identity*. New York: Routledge.

Butler, J. (1990b). *Bodies that matter: on the discursive limits of sex*. New York: Routledge.

de Certeau, M. (1988). *The practice of everyday life*. Berkeley: University of California Press.

Freud, S. (1973). The 'uncanny' [1919]. In *The Standard Edition of the Complete Psychoanalytical Works of Sigmund Freud*, trans. James Strachey, vol. 17. London: Hogarth.

James, P. (2015). Engaged research. In *Institute for Culture and Society: annual review*. Accessed August 15, 2015, http://www.uws.edu.au/__data/assets/pdf_file/0009/929898/2014_ICS_Annual_Review_Final.pdf.

Kantorowicz, E. (1949). The fundamental issue: documents and marginal notes on the University of California loyalty oath. Accessed July 19, 2015, http://www.lib.berkeley.edu/uchistory/archives_exhibits/loyaltyoath/symposium/kantorowicz.html.

Lury, C., and Wakeford, N. (2012). Introduction: a perpetual inventory. In Lury, C., and Wakeford, N. (eds). *Inventive methods: the happening of the social* (pp. 1–24). New York: Routledge.

Marcus, G.E. (2003). On the unbearable slowness of being an anthropologist now: notes on a contemporary anxiety in the making of ethnography. *Cross Cultural Poetics*, 12 (12): 7–20.

Marginson, S. (2011). Higher education and public good. *Higher Education Quarterly*, 65 (40): 411–33.

Michael, M. (2012). Anecdote. In Lury, C., and Wakeford, N. (eds). *Inventive methods: the happening of the social* (pp. 25–35). New York: Routledge.

Palfrey, J.G. (2010). The challenge of developing effective public policy on the use of social media by youth. *Federal Communications Law Journal*, 63 (1), Article 3.

Pollock, D. (2010). Doorjambs and the promise of engaged scholarship. *Quarterly Journal of Speech*, 96 (40): 462–68.

Rittel, H., and Webber, M. (1973). Dilemmas in a general theory of planning. *Policy Sciences*. 4: 155–69.

Ruppert, E.S. (2012). Category. In Lury, C., and Wakeford, N. (eds). *Inventive methods: the happening of the social* (pp. 36–47). London: Routledge.

Shapin, S. (2012). The Ivory Tower: the history of a figure of speech and its cultural uses. *British Journal of the History of Science*. 45 (1): 1–27.

Turner, G. (2012). *What's become of cultural studies*. London: Sage.

Wenger, E. (2000). Communities of practice and social learning systems. *Organisation Articles*, 7 (2): 225–46.

7 Questioning Care
Lisa Slater

Introduction

What worlds do you care for? Donna Haraway (2008) challenges her readers to become curious about the world-making effects of their caring practices. In this chapter I will examine the world-making effects of settler Australians' care for Indigenous peoples, and more broadly reflect upon pedagogies of care and the production of the contemporary caring subject. Haraway (1988) has long argued for situated knowledges. As much as we live in an interconnected, entangled world, peoples (or as Haraway might prefer, the more-than-human) also live different histories. To care is to make claims on life and the future (and in so doing draw upon particular pasts). In Australia, the art of caring for others or instituting good health and well-being continues to be modeled on settler liberal concepts of what *is* a good life and a healthy subject-citizen. In contrast, many Indigenous people have called upon settler Australia to recognize and take seriously alternative life worlds and thus to imagine different futures. To do so, we need to ask, what are the world-making effects of our caring stories? Cultural studies prides itself on a commitment to social justice, and I would argue that such an undertaking requires a radical innovation of how we understand and practice care. My intention is to not simply critique modes of caring for others but rather to run a bit of interference on care: to reflect upon what worlds are we caring for, so we might consider what worlds flourish and what worlds are diminished. To generate new political practices and anticolonial styles of care, we need to draw upon alternative genealogies of care.

As cultural studies academics, we care, and teach our students, about social justice. Lately, I've been speculating about what our students care for. Or perhaps more accurately, I am curious about knowledge politics, which is much more than revealing the politics or working to produce more accurate facts but rather understanding that the "[w]ays of studying and representing things have world-making effects" (Puig de la Bellacasa 2011: 86). The stories we tell about care—knowledge construction and circulation—have material consequences. When I say our students, I mean students of Australian universities, not just my students at the University of Wollongong. Where are we directing their affective force? Over the last few years when teaching undergraduate students, I have been surprised by their self-assured (if not even self-righteous) sense of what social issues are important and deserving of care. But more so, even if they are improvising as knowing, empathetic subjects, they are highly attuned to, and keen to learn, what issues should animate their sympathy and what is the correct response. They know that their care should be directed toward such issues as marriage equality, the environment, poverty, and homelessness, and if I tell them about sweatshops or the escalating imprisonment rates of Aboriginal people, they will care about that, too. They know not to care is to out oneself as ignorant, or worse a *brute* or *redneck*. To care about particular issues is the mark of the civil or the civilized.

We might ask, are we in an age of watered-down ethics (Puig de la Bellacasa 2010)? We cultivate awareness and we care about a long list of fashionable issues. Puig de la Bellacasa argues that concern for ethics has become a form of hegemonic thinking. She writes:

> That we live in the age of ethics is perceivable in an inflationist use of the word: from corporate ethics to everyday ethical living—garbage recycling, fair trade—from international relations to the life sciences, every human practice seems today to cultivate awareness of its ethical component. In most instances interest in the ethical translates in a local or global search for rules, recommendations or resolutions regarding a specific field or profession. (2010: 153)

She refers to this as biopolitical morality: forms of power aimed at controlling people's existence at every level of experience and subjectivity (2010: 155). In an era when the primary role of higher education is to produce workers for the knowledge economy, and to secure individual prosperity and social mobility, coupled with the frustration that many academics feel about the lack of student engagement in sociopolitical issues, demonstrations of some form of care and interest seem better than nothing. My concern is that despite our training and commitment to critique, as cultural studies scholars we might be, however inadvertently, conceding to biopolitical morality.

However, for many students, Indigenous issues can be some of the trickiest to negotiate. In general students are aware of the socioeconomic disparity between Indigenous and mainstream Australia, and left leaning politicized students are quick to blame past generations and the government. But most sense it's a minefield, and are wary. My colleagues who teach Indigenous studies (and from my own previous experience) tell me students largely want to learn about 'dot paintings' and an ancient culture but do not want to discuss contemporary issues, such as the ongoing impact of colonial and neocolonial practices, because they are considered *too political* and *confronting* (terms settler Australians readily apply). Over the years, I have noted the resistances of settler Australian students, which coexist with a particular enthusiasm for so-called 'traditional' Aboriginal culture. This cultural dynamic is found in broader Australia, and it is one for which I have developed an intellectual fascination. Of course, not everyone cares about Indigenous people. In Australia, this is only too clear. However, I would argue, concern for Indigenous well-being has become a moral barometer of our time. Thus, settler sensitivity, anxiety, around how to engage with Indigenous issues makes it a productive site for investigating the knowledge politics of care.

It would be fair to say, I've been doing a lot of thinking about care, worrying at care. In particular my interest is, what I am calling in a crude sociological category, "*good* white people": progressive settler Australians who want to engage with Indigenous peoples, cultures, and social issues. In short, care. They, or we, are deeply concerned about the so-called "Indigenous problem"; socioeconomic inequality, poor health, education, and housing, and racism, growing incarceration and suicide rates, the closing of remote communities, the 'loss' of culture, and the list could go on. There is a lot to worry about. Overwhelmed, the good white person asks, what can we do? Too often the effect is that 'we', settler Australians, imagine that we know what the problem is and, like the government, we must find the solutions (Cowlishaw 2013: 245). What is the cultural relationship? Tony Birch argues pity is the "emotion that drives the relationship between conservative and liberal-minded Australians alike in their dealings with Aboriginal people" (Birch 2014: 41). Largely, I agree. However, I think pity is an expression of good old-fashioned settler anxiety; variously understood as a sense of illegitimacy or guilt due to Australia's colonial past and ongoing white privilege (Gelder and Jacobs 1998). Nonetheless, Aboriginal people are objects for mainstream Australia to worry about but not to take seriously.

Good white people care about Indigenous people and culture. We are anxious to get 'it' right; our sense of self and belonging depends upon it. But more so, anxiety is an historical subjectivity—a social practice, an activity through which the subject is constituted. Foucault claimed that the study of the genealogy of the modern Western subject needed to be twofold. It is not enough to take into account technologies of domination,[1] we also need to consider the active practices of self-constitution, which Foucault calls technologies or *care* of the self:

> techniques which permit individuals to effect, by their own means, a certain number of operations on their own bodies, on their own souls, on their own thoughts, on their own conduct, and this in a manner so as to transform themselves, modify themselves, and to attain a certain state of perfection, of happiness, of purity, of supernatural power, and so on. (2005: 214)

In a simple sense, care of the self is the work we do to know ourselves, to constitute ourselves as subjects in relation to what one understands as the truth (Foucault 1997: 271). In such a truth, Indigenous people are vulnerable and care is performed through acts of benevolence that welcome Indigenous people into an already determined future. I am arguing that a contemporary practice of self-seeking—*care of the self*—is the activity of knowing who I am in relation to Indigenous issues and intercultural relations, which offers self-certainty. Of course, these activities do not produce an authentic self, but a certain kind of subjectivity that does particular work in the world, reproducing colonial relations of authority and vulnerability. These are, as Foucault argues:

> not something invented by the individual himself. They are models that he finds in his culture and are proposed, suggested, imposed upon him by his culture, his society, and his social group. (1997: 291)

Foucault's concern, as is mine, is that the attitude to the cultivation of the self is governed by claiming a self-knowledge or 'truth', which will then tell us how to behave in given situations but not intervene in and transform politics. To do so, we need different models. But first, I will map some aspects of the sociocultural formation that produce the *good* white settler and their much-needed companion, the so-called *vulnerable* blackfella.

Witnessing and the Shamed Nation

It is easy to forget that over the last 30 to 40 years, Australia's cultural memory has been fundamentally reconfigured. Indigenous memory and testimony, revisionist historiography, land rights, and native title and the reconciliation movement, just to name a few, reformed the public sphere. Multiple and contested alternative histories disrupted the dominant and benign narratives of Australian settlement and the white nation, which was the bedrock of national identity and foundation of white belonging (Butler 2013: 4). It might seem strange now, but well into the 1990s the statement that Australia was colonized was for many radical and divisive. With the handing down of the *Bringing Them Home* and *Deaths in Custody* Reports (Johnstone 1991; Wilson 1997), and the proliferation of stories—novels, film, autobiography, public debate, academic work, media—a deeply unsettling image of white Australia came into frame. The systematic violence of colonialism, and most notably, the Protection and Assimilation eras,[2] became public knowledge, and it hurt.

Mainstream Australians became witness to a history of institutional abuse of Indigenous people. Former Prime Minister, Kevin Rudd's National Apology (and to a lesser extent but perhaps more remarkable for its time, Paul Keating's Redfern Speech) was an act of collective witnessing of and response to, as Kelly Jean Butler writes, Indigenous peoples' testimony of historic injustices and suffering. The challenge of testimony to public figures, academics, and ordinary citizens alike, as Butler argues is:

> to reimagine a vision of good citizenship against the revelation that Australia is not only a nation founded on dispossession, but also one which actively perpetuates the disadvantage of a range of sociocultural groups. (2013: 5)

In opposition to former Prime Minister John Howard's (and conservative commentators') refusal to bear witness, Kevin Rudd understood reconciliation as a core Australian value—*the fair go*—and as Ahmed writes, the very ideal of civility (2005: 78). The act of bearing witness, affirming the voices of Indigenous people, and empathizing became the role and vision of good citizenship; the answer to the challenge posed by the revelation of the horrors of colonialism. Witnessing, as Butler writes, was yoked to notions of good citizenship (2013: 2), with the so-called core value of the 'fair go' recuperated and repurposed "to forge a national community founded on respect for and attentiveness to the testimony of the socially and politically marginalized" (Butler 2013: 9). The 'fair go' functioned as a style of care. Arguably, the vision (although not necessarily the practice) of the 'fair go' has always been linked to the downtrodden, but what changed was the image of the dispossessed. In the public imagination, Indigenous peoples shifted from strangers in the modern nation to a vulnerable population, who needed to be enfolded within the now safe arms of settler Australia. Notably, this imagery positions settlers as performing the welcoming embrace, with this appeal to Australian values providing a self-conscious formation of a newly imagined ethical community; witnessing *became* a civic virtue.

Good white Australians know that colonialism was racist and violent and that systemic injustice and cruelty reached well into the 20th century. Good white people are most deeply saddened and shamed by the removal of children from their families and communities. It could be said that Indigenous people have moved from the socially dead to perceptible in the settler field of vision. Following Judith Butler, Ian Buchanan (2012) argues that the 'frames' in which our lives are situated condition "how we respond to the world, the kinds of moral and ethical choices we make" (116). Like Bourdieu's habitus, Butler's 'frame' is a social and cultural formation that subjects unconsciously internalize. The frame allocates recognizability of certain figures, in this case Indigenous people (Buchanan 2012: 116). Now settlers can perceive Indigenous people, but what is being recognized? What is brought into frame? Or as Buchanan asks, "what makes Indigenous people alive to settlers in their world?" (2012: 116). My answer: as victims of colonization, vulnerability and suffering are brought into frame. Indigenous life has become grieveable, or rather a particular perception of Indigenous people is recognized and mourned—a life that invokes settler pity.

Collective witnessing demands of me to empathize with the pain of such violences as forced child removal, so graphically portrayed in the film *Rabbit Proof Fence* (Noyce 2002), and captured in Rudd's national apology.[3] Good white citizens listen to the pain and suffering of Indigenous people, against a crowded backdrop of ignorance and brutality. To be a good citizen one must contribute to the collective national project of confronting the past, which in turn should produce shame and guilt in the white subject (Butler 2013: 43). "Bad white people" do not feel properly shamed by racism, colonial violence, and ongoing injustice. Notably, everyday racism is often deflected onto socioeconomically marginalized white people. It is the "bad white people", with their racist views and thoughtlessness, that continue to perpetuate racism and injustice in 'our' progressive society. Thus, guilt and shame enable good white people to distinguish themselves from "bad white people" (Sullivan 2014: 5; also see Hage 2002). The sign of a good white person is the performance of compassion, an outcome of which is self-satisfied moralizing. Bearing witness and empathizing renews and remakes the subject position of the progressive Australian. The good white subject becomes a normative character on the stage of white Australia, so essential to the reproduction of power relations (Svirsky 2014). But does she desire social justice or moral redemption?

Good white people feel bad. She feels guilty about racism and her white privilege. To fix the problem of racial injustice, the good white subject works on herself: she imagines that her reason, care, and will can enable her to give up her privilege (Kruks 2005: 182). She is anxious to do so. But such a practice assumes that privilege is a personal possession, rather than historical and structural, and one's capacity to relinquish racial power is tied to one's capacity for self-awareness, rather than social transformation. Audre Lorde (1984) and bell hooks (1989) warn, white guilt can function as a form of self-centeredness, turning the white subject "back into" herself: it is *her* feelings that matter (Ahmed 2005: 82). Their concern is that this further blocks the capacity to hear the claims of others. White worrying, or as I'd prefer, *anxiety*, becomes a substitute for genuine listening. There is a failure to listen or respond to the material conditions, values, and aspirations of Indigenous people, and like the critiques of colonial feminism, good white citizens assume the role of rescuing and recuperating Aboriginal women (and children) into mainstream life—a loss of voice for Aboriginal women (Watson 2005: 26). For all the good intentions, one can be driven by unacknowledged self-interest, and perpetuate racism by attending to the values and aspirations of settlers (Dreher 2009). This is not a commitment to change, but instead the affirmation of a positive white identity and the overcoming of bad feelings (Ahmed, 2005: 82). Indigenous people continue to be a means by which white people *improve* themselves. The black body is still at the service of settler colonialism.

Indigenous people are persistently characterized as vulnerable and in need of settler generosity and benevolence (Veracini 2010: 108). However, there is very little engagement with, what Povinelli refers to as, the imperatives of Aboriginal testimony (2002: 42). As Irene Watson asks, "[i]s there no possibility of a political space to be heard on the concerns we hold as Aboriginal people?" (2007: 36). Notably, there is strong support for the processes of reconciliation. But what appears to be a commitment to alleviating ongoing injustice and restoring Indigenous sovereignty, as Povinelli argues, is "inflected by the conditional" (2002: 17). As long as economic resources are not at stake, then progressive settler sympathy and desire for reconciliation continue. This might be no more evident than in middle class support for policies that do not in any way impinge on their own lives. In no real sense do most progressives have to encounter Indigenous sovereignty. If Indigenous sovereignty is recognized at all, it is largely figured as impractical, impossible, or dangerous (Nicoll 2002: 9). There is little room for an engagement with incommensurability and Indigenous agency, for encountering Aboriginal people on their own terms.

Good white settlers care. I do not doubt that: I am not questioning individuals. It is the radical depersonalisation of settler anxiety that interests me. Good white people can see the gaps, the bad statistics, but can we recognize Indigenous agency? Good white people take responsibility for past injustices, face up to colonial history and the ongoing destruction and marginalization often by feeling guilty and pitying Indigenous people, or empathizing. We want to make amends. I am arguing that these are practices of the anxious subject—forms of biopolitical morality, which reproduce the 'truths' of settler colonial care. Good white people's role is to guide Indigenous people out of the past and into the present and predetermined future. My concern is that this particular style of care prevents settlers taking Indigenous people seriously, and engaging with the imperatives of Aboriginal testimony (Povinelli 2002: 42). As noted, it maintains colonial relationships of authority and vulnerability.

But anxiety also interrupts and disturbs the taken-for-grantedness of the world. For Heidegger, anxiety is significant because it brings us closer to an understanding of human existence. In our everyday lives we are immersed and caught up in the world, absorbed by things and people. In anxiety we experience the world as slipping or drawing away: one feels separate from the world. The world that is so familiar to us becomes uncanny and strange. We are burdened by the meaningless of our existence. Heidegger argues we flee from the nothingness of the world by filling our lives with people and things (1973). My claim is that settlers' normative emotional engagement with Indigeneity—the worry, pity, guilt—is a form of fleeing. After all, we are enmeshed in the world through modes of care. Our everyday existence is interrupted, and there is no longer a common sense, self-evident world that we are caught up in. Heidegger argues that one is thrown back upon him- or herself, questioning the world and who am I. The moment before fleeing or falling back into the world is when everything has disappeared, and I am alone. I am no longer attached to a particular understanding of the world or myself:

> [I]n anxiety there lies the possibility of a disclosure which is quite distinctive; for anxiety individualises. This individualisation brings Dasein back from its falling, and makes manifest to it that authenticity and inauthenticity are possibilities of its Being.
> (Heidegger 1973: 235)

Heidegger is not referring to an individual essence—essential self—but singularity. However to be singular, according to Heidegger, is to not be at home in the world, to take up the choice to change my ordinary life (1973). Following Heidegger, my interest is the moment when the good white settler questions herself but does not flee into the world, but rather her role, her ability to perform normative ethical belonging, biopolitical morality, is disturbed. The good white settler is lost.

Here is a place for cultural studies. With its concern for the everyday— with the ordinary interactions peoples have with structures that marginalize and constrain—cultural studies is well placed to respond to questions of biopolitical morality. Cultural studies is a discipline of care, and of caring about the lot of others and the self. *The pedagogy of cultural studies seeks to understand the world as strange and estranging.*

Care in a Multirealist World

There is an old caring story, which goes a bit like this: caring is instinctual, emotional, and thus feminized, and a personal activity between individuals. Until relatively recently, care was not considered worthy of serious thought. Of course the state has long taken an interest in care, policing who cares for whom and how, with this form of care historically witnessed in numerous manifestations: state interventions such as child removal policies, the valorization of hetero-normativity, or ignorance toward domestic violence or more generally violence against women. Before feminist interventions caring was largely depoliticized, marginalized and neglected as significant knowledge. Care was sidelined as a public good. As we know only too well, there are not neat divisions between the private and public. Personal lives are deeply affected by what societies define is of relevance and value (Puig de la Bellacasa 2010). Feminist scholars of ethics of care have worked hard to demonstrate that practices of everyday care are vital for the maintenance of relationships, social worlds, and the production of citizens (Puig de la Bellacasa 2011; Tronto 1993). The political theorist of care, Joan Tronto, has long argued for care as being conceived as a part of the work of citizens, and that we need to take seriously a collective commitment to care (1993: 5). Feminists have demonstrated that care is life sustaining and necessary, and have affirmed the centrality of particular practices that have been historically associated with women, and the most marginalized (Carrasco 2001, cited in Puig de la Bellacasa 2010). Care matters, a lot.

But care is hard work. It is a material, affective, and ethical practice (Puig de la Bellacasa 2012: 197). Importantly, as Tronto (2006) argues, we need to recognize the power relationships in care, and how social norms are perpetuated through the caring practices. How health or vulnerability is imagined and who is categorized accordingly, differently configures the capacities of citizens and political voices (Tronto 2006: 3). I am following a feminist ethics of care that perceives of the social as a weave of interdependencies, whereby we are all carers and cared for, vulnerable and healthy, and reject the notion of care as private and individualized (Puig de la Bellacasa 2010, 2012). Useful here is Joan Tronto and Berenice Fischer's generic notion of caring:

> [care is] ... everything that we do to maintain, continue and repair 'our world' so that we can live in it as well as possible. That world includes our bodies, our selves, and our environment, all that we seek to interweave in a complex, life sustaining web.
> (Tronto 1993, cited in Puig de la Bellacasa 2012: 198)

Albeit too personalized and human centered, as Puig de la Bellacasa notes, we need to insist on this 'interweaving' in order to be able to think how care holds together the world as we know it and how it perpetuates, and negates, power relationships (2012: 198). In turn, as feminist scholars advocate, we need to repoliticize care—it should not be conceived of as the benevolent toil of the good or kind. However, I want to push this definition a little further by questioning what, or whose, world care holds together? If Western Liberals claim the future, as Elizabeth Povinelli argues, and 'others' the past, then forms of care are about bringing others into an already imagined future (2010: 25). What, or whose, histories are being lived and projected into the imagined future? Povinelli writes:

> To care is not a socially divested action. To care is to make a claim; it is a small theoretical gesture. To care is to make an argument about what a good life is and how such a good life comes into being. Thus the arts of caring for others always emerge from and are a reflection on broader historical material conditions and institutional arrangements. The point is not, therefore, to argue that someone really cares or doesn't really care ... In the first instance, the question is what do we believe care to consist of such that when we experience forms of relating to one another socially, we experience that form of relating as a form of caring for others. (2010: 19–20)

To care is to make a claim on life. What life do you care for? Feminist scholarship is committed to making visible neglected, marginalized and undervalued experiences (Harding 1991; see Puig de la Bellacasa 2010). So if care holds the world together as we know it and allows its perpetuation, then the question that follows is, what world? Instead of the good white settler asking, *what can we do?* I think the question should be, *what have we been caring for?*

To care is to relate. To create a just and sustainable world, we need to relate differently. The methods through which one comes to know and produce particular relations to things can direct for what and how we care. Importantly, social interests are not just added to the nonhuman world but rather, as Puig de la Bellacasa, drawing upon Barad, writes, "interests and other affectively animated forces—such as concern and care—are intimately entangled in the ongoing material remaking of the world" (2011: 87; Barad 2007). How does one practice care in a multirealist world? Puig de la Bellacasa argues for extending feminist ethics of care toward *nature cultures*, which contributes to an ethics that decenters the human subject, and traces the complex articulations of agency of the more-than-human. The human and more-than-human world are interdependent, reliant, and vulnerable (Puig de la Bellacasa 2010: 198). As noted, I am arguing for the importance of drawing upon alternative genealogies and archives of care for generating new political practices, and remaking relations of care. To do so, I want to bring Aboriginal cosmology into relation with feminist politics of care and more-than-human praxis, in the hope of doing more justice to the forms of coexistence that makes the world inhabitable (Hinchliffe et al. 2005).

Jane Bennett's call for (largely non-Indigenous) scholars to take seriously the vitality of nonhuman bodies might be no better evidenced and tested than by Aboriginal cosmology (2010). The more-than-human needs to address a sentient multidimensional country, which has agency, law, and spirit. More so, it is vital that those who have always inhabited and taken seriously the agency and vitality of country are our guides. Creating new political practices requires attentiveness to multiple associations, alliances, coexistence, and inhabitation. Country is multidimensional and has an interdependent web of relations: including people, animal, plants, Dreamings, air, water, minerals, plants, and soils (Rose 1996). Laklak Burarrwanga explains the concept of country:

> Country has many layers of meaning. It incorporates people, animals, plants, water and land. But Country is more than just people and things, it is also what connects them to each other and to multiple spiritual and symbolic realms. It relates to Laws, custom, movement, song, knowledges, relationships, histories, presents, futures and spirit beings. Country can be talked to, it can be known, it can itself communicate, feel and take action. Country for us is alive with story, Law, power and kinship relations that join not only people to each other but link people, ancestors, place, animals, rocks, plants, stories and songs within land and sea. So you see knowledge about Country is important because it's about how and where you fit within the world and how you connect to others and to place.
> (Wright et al. 2012: 54)

The human and more-than-human are entwined in social relationships, and the world is continually co-created by human and nonhuman agents (Wright 2012). A political response that engages with the vitality and agency of Indigenous culture must be attentive to and comprehensive of non-Western modes of interconnection with the more-than-human world as modes of caring for self and others (Slater 2013).

By insisting that country is an active participant, I want to take seriously the diversity of life that country sustains and reproduces. However, I want to make it clear that I am not suggesting reducing and conflating the diversity of contemporary Aboriginal cultural practices with (what is often considered as) *traditionalist* connections to country. Indeed it is worth remembering how the acceptance and institutionalization of the centrality of territorial connections have worked to effectively dispossess many Aboriginal people (Merlan 2009: 306; also see Povinelli 2002). It is necessary to not just think *about* care, Puig de la Bellacasa (2012) advocates, but to think *with* care. If care is a material practice, the work "needed to create, hold together and sustain life's essential heterogeneity" then valuing different modes of existence requires a curiosity and alertness to multiple attachments and affective associations (including one's own) (Puig de la Bellacasa 2012: 198). Caring is always specific: practices of care are created in an interrelationship with the particularities and complexities of the place (Puig de la Bellacasa 2010: 162). What needs to be held in mind, as Puig de la Bellacasa cautions, is that "a way of caring over here could kill over there ... We need to ask 'how to care' in each situation" (2011: 100).

Thus care requires taking a deep interest in another's world. It is the interest of Stenger and Deutscher (2000) that interests me. Instead of containing ourselves to epistemological adjudications, Stengers urges us to encompass a more affective approach to epistemology: "what if we interested ourselves in the ways and in what our 'subjects' are interested in?" (2000: 48). To take up her proposition, I want to think along with Vinciane Despret (2004), who writes about experimenters who live and work with animals. In this case, a man and a goose. To create new articulations of care, the experimenter asks what matters in the goose's world?:

> The experimenter, far from keeping himself in the background, involves himself: he involves his body, he involves his knowledge, his responsibility and his future. The practice of knowing has become a practice of caring. And because he cares for his young goose, he learns what, in a world inhabited by humans and geese, may produce relations.
> (Despret 2004: 130)

By asking what matters in the goose's world, the goose becomes a subject, not an object of study: "a subject of passion, a subject producing passions; a subject of questions, a subject producing questions" (Despret 2004: 131). By passion Despret does not mean some sweet story of love, rather it is an effort to become interested, and to immerse oneself in the multitude of problems presented by the goose. In short, it means to care about the goose's world. What passions teach the experimenter, or in our case the student or scholar, is that *learning* how to address the other—human or more-than-human—is not the end result of the research but the very condition of understanding (Despret 2004: 131). This is not to say one 'knows' the goose, or indeed a peoples, in the sense of old-school anthropology, but rather one is working to create new relations, articulations, and practices of care that help sustain a multirealist world.

Care, practiced as a deep interest in another's life, is not easy. By this I mean that care is not just intellectually hard work and time consuming but also troubling; but as Haraway suggests we need to stay with the trouble (Haraway 2010). The trouble with caring for a multirealist world is that there is no easy avoidance of multiplicity and complexity. There is not a neat, harmonious world. Care is not mere empathy or smoothing out conflicts. It seems to me that good white people need to think carefully about their interest in Aboriginal issues, peoples, and culture. Too often care, however inadvertent and well intentioned, becomes self-interest. If we follow Stengers (2000) and Despret's (2004) practices of interest, then we are less at risk of mistaking politics for making 'good representations' of Aboriginal people, reassuring one's self that the politics is settled and one knows how to proceed. To do so is to fuel the liberal fallacy, as Hinchliffe et al. (2005) contend, that all that is needed is to include the previously excluded or become educated about the issue rather than transform political practices. I am arguing that caring in a multirealist world makes the world strange, and anxiety haunts us. If we engage with anxiety as a potential political good (not a personal failing) because it disturbs one's common-sense world, then to care is to stay with the trouble. There is always the option to flee into a ready-made morality that provides one with self-certainty and the rules and procedures for engagement. But social justice fit for the postcolony demands much more, as disturbing as that might be.

Notes

1. Foucault writes, "techniques which permit one to determine the conduct of individuals, to impose certain wills on them, and to submit them to certain ends or objectives" (2005: 213).
2. The Protection era ran from approximately 1890 to 1950. State and Territory governments introduced laws, known as Protection Acts, which regulated Aboriginal and Torres Strait Islanders peoples' lives and controlled their relations with other Australians. These laws were implemented by government officers, known as protectors, and protection boards and native affairs departments and were used to segregate and control most of the Indigenous population. The Assimilation era was approximately 1940s to the 1960s. In 1937 the federal government held a national conference on Aboriginal Affairs, which was concerned with the growing 'Aboriginal problem': the number of Aboriginal people of 'mixed blood'. The solution was to 'absorb' or 'assimilate' Aboriginal people of mixed heritage into the wider population, with the aim of making Aboriginality 'disappear'. Assimilation practices included the forced removal of Indigenous children from families and communities and placing them in institutions or white foster families, known as the Stolen Generation. Protection and assimilation policies were severe and destructive, and included separate education for Aboriginal children, town curfews, alcohol bans, low or no wages, State

guardianship of all Aboriginal children, and laws that segregated Indigenous people from non-Indigenous people, mainly on special reserves on the edge of towns or in remote areas (see, http://www.workingwithatsi.info/content/history6.htm; Wilson 1997).
3. On February 13, 2008, the Prime Minister, Kevin Rudd, delivered an apology to Australia's Indigenous peoples for the Stolen Generations. It was an historic and moving speech, which 'stopped' the nation. The Stolen Generations were the children of Australian Aboriginal and Torres Strait Islander descent who were, largely, forcibly removed—from approximately 1905 to 1970—from their families by the state and federal government agencies and church missions, under Protection and Assimilation acts (see endnote 2).

References

Ahmed, S. (2005). The politics of bad feelings. *Australian Critical Race and Whiteness Studies Association Journal*, 1: 72–85.
Barad, K. (2007). *Meeting the universe halfway: quantum physics and the entanglement of matter and meaning*. Durham, Duke University Press.
Bennett, J. (2010). *Vibrant materialism: a political ecology of things*. Durham, Duke University Press.
Birch, T. (2014). 'I'm not sure how to begin it': the welcome uncertainties of doing history. In Neale, T., McKinnon, C., and Vincent, E. (eds). *History, power, text: cultural studies and Indigenous studies* (pp. 39–49). Sydney, UTS Press.
Buchanan, I. (2012). Symptomatology and racial politics in Australia. *Rivista Internazionale di Filosofia e Psicologia*, 3: 110–24.
Butler, K. J. (2013). *Witnessing Australian stories: history, testimony, and memory in contemporary culture*. New Brunswick, Transaction Publishers.
Cowlishaw, G. (2013). Reproducing criminality: how cure enhances cause. In Carrington, K., Ball, M., O'Brien, E. and Tauri, J. (eds). *Crime, justice and social democracy: international perspectives* (pp. 234–47). Basingstoke, Palgrave Macmillan.
Despret, V. (2004). The body we care for: figures of anthropo-zoo-genesis. *Body and Society*, 10: 111–34.
Dreher, T. (2009). Eavesdropping with permission: the politics of listening for safer speaking spaces. *borderlands ejournal*, 8: 1–21.
Foucault, M. (1997). *Ethics, subjectivity, and truth. Essential works of Foucault, 1954–1984*. New York, New Press.
Foucault, M. (2005). About the beginnings of the hermeneutics of the self: two lectures at Dartmouth. In Atkins, K. (ed). *Self and subjectivity* (pp. 198–227). Oxford, Wiley-Blackwell.
Gelder, K., and Jacobs, J. (1998). *Uncanny Australia*. Melbourne, Melbourne University Publishing.
Hage, G. (2002). Citizenship and honourability: belonging to Australia today. In Hage, G. (ed). *Arab-Australians today: citizenship and belonging* (pp. 1–15). Melbourne, Melbourne University Press.
Haraway, D. (1988). Situated knowledges: the science question in feminism and the privilege of partial perspective. *Feminist Studies*, 14: 575–99.
Haraway, D. (2008). *When species meet*. Minneapolis, University of Minnesota Press.

Haraway, D. (2010). When species meet: staying with the trouble. *Environment and Planning D: Society and Space*, 28: 53–55.
Harding, S. (1991). *Whose science? Whose knowledge? Thinking from women's lives*, Ithaca, Cornell University Press.
Heidegger, M. (1973). *Being and time*. Oxford, Basil Blackwell.
Hinchcliffe, S., Kearnes, M. B., Degeb and M., Whatmore, S. (2005). Urban wild things: a cosmopolitical experiment, *Environment and Planning D: Society and Space*. 23: 643–658.
Hooks, b. (1989). *Talking back: thinking feminist, thinking black*. London, Sheba Feminist Publishers.
Johnstone, E. (1991). *Royal commission into Aboriginal deaths in custody: national report, overview and recommendations*. Canberra, AGPS.
Kruks, S. (2005). Simone de Beauvoir and the politics of privilege. *Hypatia*, 20: 178–205.
Lorde, A. (1984). *Sister outside: essays and speeches*. New York, Crossing Press.
Merlan, F. (2009). Indigeneity: global and local. *Current Anthropology*, 50: 303–33.
Nicoll, F. (2002). Defacing Terra Nullius and facing the public secret of Indigenous sovereignty in Australia. *borderlands e-journal*, 1: 1–13.
Noyce, P. (Director). (2002). *Rabbit-Proof Fence*, Australia: Magna Pacific Video.
Povinelli, E. (2002). *The cunning of recognition: Indigenous alterities and the making of Australian multiculturalism*. Durham, Duke University Press.
Povinelli, E. (2010). Indigenous politics in late liberalism. In Altman, J. and Hinkson, M. (ed). *Culture crisis* (pp. 17–31). Sydney, UNSW Press.
Puig de la Bellacasa, M. (2010). Ethical doings in naturecultures. *Ethics, Place and Environment: A Journal of Philosophy and Geography*, 13: 151–69.
Puig de la Bellacasa, M. (2011). Matters of care in technoscience: assembling neglected things. *Social Studies of Science*, 41: 85–106.
Puig de la Bellacasa, M. (2012). 'Nothing comes without its world': thinking with care. *Sociological Review*, 60: 197–216.
Rose, D. B. (1996). *Nourishing terrains: Australian Aboriginal views of landscape and wilderness*. Canberra, Australian Heritage Commission.
Slater, L. (2013). 'Wild rivers, wild ideas': emerging political ecologies of Cape York Wild Rivers. *Environment and Planning D: Society and Space*, 31: 763–78.
Stengers, I., and Deutscher, P. (2000). Another look: relearning to laugh. *Hypatia*, 15: 41–52.
Sullivan, S. (2014). *Good white people: the problem with middle-class white anti-racism*. Albany, SUNY Press.
Svirsky, M. (2014). *After Israel: towards cultural transformation*. London, Zed Books.
Tronto, J. (1993). *Moral boundaries: a political argument for an ethic of care*. New York, Routledge.
Tronto, J. (2006). Vicious circles of privatized caring. In Hamington, M., and Miller, D.C. (eds). *Socializing care: feminist ethics and public issues* (pp. 3–26). Oxford, Rowman and Littlefield.
Veracini, L. (2010). *Settler colonialism: a theoretical overview*. New York, Palgrave Macmillan.
Watson, I. (2005). Illusionists and hunters: being Aboriginal in this occupied space. *Australian Feminist Law Journal*, 2: 15–28.
Watson, I. (2007). Aboriginal sovereignties: past, present and future (im)possibilities. In Perera, S. (ed). *Our patch* (pp. 23–43). Curtin: Network Books.

Wilson, R. (1997). *Bringing them home: report of the national inquiry into the separation of Aboriginal and Torres Strait Islander children from their families.* Sydney, Human Rights and Equal Opportunity Commission.

Wright, S., Lloyd, K., Suchet-Pearson, S., Burarrwanga, L., and Tofa, M., (2012). Telling stories in, through and with country: engaging with Indigenous and more-than-human methodologies at Bawaka, North East Australia. *Journal of Cultural Geography*, 29: 39–60.

Section III
The Sites of Cultural Studies Pedagogy

8 Cultural Studies, Pedagogy and Reimagining Multicultural Education

Working with Teachers to Effect Change in Schools

Megan Watkins

Introduction

Multicultural education has operated in Australian schools in one form or another since the late 1960s. Beginning with a pilot program providing English as a Second Language (ESL) support to students as part of the then *Child Migrant Education Program* in nine schools in New South Wales (NSW) (Inglis 2009), it has grown to encompass a range of programs including not only ESL, community engagement and refugee support to students and their families with a language background other than English (LBOTE), but also programs around antiracism and intercultural understanding designed for all students no matter what their cultural and linguistic background. Such a wide range of programs demonstrates that multicultural education has a broader remit than providing assistance to children of migrants to ensure they acquire the requisite resources to participate effectively at school and that their parents are welcomed and supported within school communities. Multicultural education also performs the important roles of promoting a particular ethic around cultural difference, countering racism and engendering social harmony.

While these aims have long underpinned multicultural education, given the changing nature of Australia's cultural diversity, schools may now need to rethink long-established practice in this area. Early policies of multiculturalism were premised on notions of distinct and cohesive ethnic communities, a view that has similarly influenced their application within schooling. Intergenerational change, cultural adaptation, increasing globalization, and mass migration, however, have led to a questioning of such bounded and static notions of culture and for the need to consider, not only more hybrid forms of identity but multiple senses of belonging that are no longer so narrowly aligned with that of the nation. Teachers, therefore, require the necessary resources to make sense of this complexity to allow them to move beyond the cultural essentialism so characteristic of much policy and practice in this area (Tellez 2007; Watkins 2015a). Drawing on recent research which involved training teachers to undertake this task in the form of site-specific action research, this chapter explores their receptiveness toward rethinking categories of culture and identity and engaging with the intellectual skepticism that cultural studies promotes—a pedagogic mode designed to encourage a questioning of the normative assumptions that can frame our view of the social world. While examining the responses of teachers in a number of schools, it focuses on those two in particular and the degree to which they were able to apply these understandings in the process of reimagining how multicultural education is practiced in their schools.

Background to the Study

The action research informing this chapter, and its related teacher training comprised the final stage of an Australian Research Council (ARC) Linkage project, *Rethinking Multiculturalism/Reassessing Multicultural Education* (RMRME), conducted with the NSW Department of Education and Communities (DEC), and the Board of Studies, Teaching and Educational Standards (BOSTES). This last component of the project was preceded by a state-wide survey of all NSW DEC teachers (Watkins et al. 2013) together with focus groups with parents, teachers, and students in the 14 project schools around attitudes and understandings related to multicultural education and multiculturalism more broadly (Noble and Watkins 2013). The project schools, in which the focus groups and action research were conducted, were a mix of urban and rural, primary and secondary schools from across NSW with student populations that were of either a high or low LBOTE and of a high or low socioeconomic status (SES).[1]

As already indicated, multicultural education is not only designed for those schools with high LBOTE student populations. Programs around antiracism and intercultural understanding are required to be implemented in all NSW public schools and in fact are mandated by NSW DEC policy (NSW DEC, 2005). Yet, while this may be a requirement, the ways in which schools implement this policy and the degree of priority it is assigned—particularly given their differing demographics—vary considerably. There is also considerable variation in the expertise of teachers in terms of understanding how increasing cultural complexity impacts not only upon schools and their communities, but upon Australia as part of the broader global community. Education policy at all levels requires schools to promote ideas of global citizenship and an openness toward cultural diversity (Australian Curriculum, Assessment and Reporting Authority [ACARA] 2015; Ministerial Council on Education, Employment, Training and Youth Affairs [MCEETYA] 2008), but how these ideas translate in practice is largely dependent upon teachers themselves, many of whom have little or no training in this area. The state-wide survey of NSW DEC teachers, which comprised the initial stage of RMRME, provided important insights in this regard. It revealed that, while 69.2% of early career teachers of less than 6 years of experience had some knowledge of multicultural education from their preservice training, this fell away sharply for those with longer years of service to the extent that only half of those with 15 to 25 years of experience had received this training prior to service and only 33.3% of those with over 25 years in the profession (Watkins et al. 2013). More worrying, however, was the amount of professional learning that teachers had undertaken during the course of their career with the survey indicating that over one in five had never received any professional learning in multicultural education at any time since commencing in the profession.

With recent changes implemented in NSW aimed at improving the professional knowledge of teachers, all are now required to undertake 100 hours of professional learning every 5 years to remain accredited (BOSTES, 2015). While in some respects this is a pleasing development, with this learning linked to professional standards at a national level (Education Services Australia, 2011),[2] these changes will take time to have an effect. Yet, even with this regulation, it is uncertain the degree to which issues around multicultural education will figure in a teacher's professional learning. The standard with direct relevance to this area requires teachers to possess the necessary professional knowledge for teaching "students with diverse, linguistic, cultural, religious and socio-economic backgrounds" (Education Services Australia 2011: 8). There is no stipulation regarding the need for a broader sociocultural knowledge that would assist teachers in ensuring all students develop the necessary capacities for understanding how processes of globalization and transnationalism affect their world and for engendering forms of reflexive civility so essential for functioning within it. Instead, the focus is on developing the requisite knowledge for teaching the 'Other', identified in terms of having diverse linguistic, cultural, religious, and socio-economic backgrounds. Of course it is necessary for teachers to cater for the learning needs of their students, whatever their background, but here 'diverse' seems to operate as a signifier for 'different' from those who are Anglo, English-speaking, Christian, and middle class with the assumption that their learning needs may differ as well. While this may be the case—many LBOTE students, for example, require additional support with English, especially English for academic purposes—there is a huge difference, between identifying a student's individual learning needs from assuming those needs derive from a perceived cultural difference. Culture, in this sense, is narrowly understood as ethnicity and used as an explanatory category for a student's performance at school, often resulting in ill-conceived, if well-intentioned, teaching programs (Watkins and Noble 2013). A number of teachers who participated in the RMRME training that preceded the action research commented on this problematic interpretation of culture and the essentializing it tended to encourage. Amy from Graham's Point High School, in a Sydney suburb with a high LBOTE/high SES student population, remarked:

> [I]f a kid is not working or not doing homework it may be because of their cultural background. You are told to sort of identify what is behind it, which theoretically is based on their cultural background

and I was thinking well maybe then professional development around that needs to be more focused on looking at individual students rather than looking at culture, it's about the whole student and possibly the background of the student.

A colleague, also from Graham's Point. added, "it's maybe a shorthand way of saying things rather than saying, you know this boy did this and this boy did that, they find it easier or more appropriate just to put people in groups in schools: the Islander boys, the Middle Eastern kids".

In such cases ethnicity is treated as the defining feature of a student's identity, rather than simply one of a number of contributing factors. But, together with this, it is assumed that ethnicity then determines a student's behavior, which, of course, is never considered a factor in relation to students of Anglo-Australian background where class or individual family experience is seen to play the major role. A more complex engagement with notions of culture would equip teachers with the understanding to better meet their students' individual learning needs and to counter the essentializing tendencies that much practice around multicultural education has tended to encourage.

While the *Australian Professional Standards for Teachers* makes no explicit reference to this important aspect of professional knowledge, it could be argued that the intercultural understanding general capability within the Australian National Curriculum makes up for this shortfall (ACARA 2015). Intended as a competence that students should acquire in the course of their schooling, this, however, is also reliant upon the professional capacities of teachers and their interpretation of what intercultural understanding might mean. While the materials made available to schools appear to encourage a more fluid and processual conception of culture and, unlike multicultural education, are inclusive of Indigenous culture, the term itself may present problems. 'Inter' seems to suggest boundaries to be crossed, and so the immutability of culture, and 'understanding' could signify both an intellectual engagement—understanding how identities are shaped—and an ethical stance—involving empathy and an unreflexive valuing of cultural difference (Watkins 2015b). If intercultural understanding within the Australian National Curriculum intends to foreground the former and avoid any slippage from an ethical stance into the moralizing of which multiculturalism is often accused, it is not only greater clarification of its intent that is needed but the effective training of teachers responsible for its implementation.

Yet, it is not simply the impact of globalization, mass migration, and intergenerational change that necessitates a more complex engagement with notions of culture, ethnicity, and identity; hybrid notions of culture, and identity as a more shifting and contingent phenomenon, are simply a more accurate reflection of reality. As Donald (2007) remarks, "communities and cultures are never hermetic" (292). To see them as such is simply a function of the persistence of what are largely outmoded understandings fed, in particular, by late 19th and early 20th century anthropology that sought the identification of different cultures and the so-called systematic relations that characterized them. Such understandings have long since been critiqued within anthropology (Barth 1994) as they have within cultural studies which, from its beginnings, sought a more nuanced engagement with how culture is understood beyond its anthropological reification (Bennett and Frow 2008). Yet while these ideas may be commonplace within academe, they seem to have had limited impact in schools. The recognition of this is what led to RMRME and, in particular, its emphasis on teacher-led action research.

Theory Practice and Action Research

As indicated, RMRME was a multifaceted project. Through its state-wide survey of teachers and focus groups with parents, teachers, and students in its 14 project schools, its intention was to gather data on current understandings and practices around multicultural education. The aim of the action research was to then draw on this data to allow teachers to identify an area of need in their school and to rethink their approach to multicultural education in addressing this. In each of the 14 project schools, research teams of up to five members were appointed from staff who had expressed an interest in participating. These teams were composed of at least one executive member, classroom, and/or ESL teachers—depending on a school's demographics and staffing—and, in one case, there was also two parents. Each of the school project teams attended a 2-day training course, a week apart, delivered by the academics and partner investigators from the NSW DEC and BOSTES in the RMRME project team. Together with this, each school research team was allocated a NSW DEC Multicultural Education consultant,[3] who had undertaken their own specific training in advance to enable them to assist the school to which they had been assigned in the design and implementation of their action research. The training that the research teams received involved an overview of the research process; sessions on culture, identity, and multiculturalism; and a presentation on the RMRME state-wide survey. In addition to this, there was discussion of the RMRME approach to action research and a range of relevant data collection techniques, relevant resources including those available through the project website, and a teacher portal where research teams had access to a discussion board for posting queries and seeking advice from other teams. Explanation was also provided on how to access the University of Western Sydney University Library for wider reading given all participants were granted a year's borrowing rights and, finally, information regarding the project implementation, timeline, and in-school support. Content was delivered in various formats including lectures by members of the RMRME project team, small group tutorials focused on specific readings, and various group-based activities.

The approach to action research utilized within RMRME was quite specifically framed, or at least the training encouraged a particular process. Approaches to action research vary enormously depending, it seems, on whether emphasis is given to *action* or *research* and on the way in which research itself is understood. The origins of action research can be found in the work of Kurt Lewin who, in the late 1930s, introduced participatory research methods into workplaces in the United States to improve the conditions of marginalized workers (Adelman 1993). Together with its participatory focus, Lewin drew on the research methods of the social sciences to encourage a systematic approach to data collection in gauging the effectiveness of workplace practices. His ideas were later adopted in education in the United States and United Kingdom during the 1950s and 1960s where action research was refashioned as a tool for teachers to improve their classroom practice (Silver and Silver 1991) and now has quite broad application as a form of research-based practitioner enquiry (Macintyre 2000; McNiff and Whitehead 2006). Stemming from Lewin's early approach, however, action research tends to place little emphasis on the theoretical. It typically involves the identification of a problem or issue, devising an action to address it, collecting data to assess its effectiveness, and then reflecting upon the findings, followed in many cases by the repetition of this cycle to monitor practice in an ongoing way. Indeed, Brown University's manual on action research in education points out that "[r]ather than dealing with the theoretical, action research allows practitioners to address those concerns that are closest to them, ones over which they can exhibit some influence and make change" (Ferrance 2000: Introduction).

Rather than excising the theoretical, the RMRME approach to action research placed it squarely at the forefront stressing the necessity for teachers to engage with particular theoretical perspectives drawn from critical and cultural theory around cultural identification, globalization, transnationalism, and hybridity. In many respects it was an approach guided by the insights of Stuart Hall (1990) that emphasized that "[t]he gap between theory and practice is only overcome in developing a practice in its own right. It is a practice to bring together theory and practice" (18). While this was the intent of the theoretically informed approach to action research that the training encouraged, there was a realization that this needed to be broached as a pedagogic process. Teachers needed to be supported in their learning as they encountered new knowledge and were then required to apply it *in practice* in the context of their own school, hence the ongoing support of the DEC consultants and that provided by their peers via the project website. The RMRME project team also considered that the theory itself possessed a pedagogic dimension in its contestation of any certainty regarding categories such as 'culture', 'identity', and 'multiculturalism', prompting debate during the training over the inherent complexity of these terms and the implications that particular understandings might have for practice. Teachers were encouraged to conceive of their role much in the way that Connell (2009) envisaged it:

> Interpreting the world for others, and doing it well, requires not just a skill set but also a knowledge of how interpretation is done, of the cultural field in which it is done, and of the possibilities of interpretation that surround one's own. This requirement helps to define teaching as intellectual labour and teachers as a group of intellectual workers. (224)

The degree to which teachers involved in the research took up this challenge was variable. The outcomes of any pedagogic encounter are always contingent on numerous factors. In this case these included each teacher's commitment to the project, that of their team's, their experience in teaching and multicultural education, and the particular demographics of their own school. What proved most important, however, was the professional ethos that guided their practice, whether or not they engaged with the intellectual nature of the profession, as Connell defined it, or if their focus was simply on the practicalities of teachers' work with little interest in the way in which theory might impact upon this.

While taking a major role in the training of the school teams, following this, the focus of the RMRME academic investigators was to then conduct a macroanalysis of each of the action research projects. Though providing feedback on the initial drafts of each team's research plan, teachers were then left to implement their projects with the support of their DEC consultant. In a pilot project to RMRME, the academic investigators had also acted as mentors for school teams in the conduct of their research. Performing both these roles—as mentor and researcher—however, had at times led to conflicts of interest. As a result, within RMRME, the academic investigators did not intervene to assist school teams in the carriage of their projects. This gave a sharper focus to how each grappled with the ideas presented in the training, their uptake of the approach to action research, and their ability to effect change within an area of multicultural education in their school. To gauge this, the macroanalysis involved interviews with the principal and focus groups with the research teams in each school before the project commenced[4] and on its completion. Observations were also conducted of the actions that each project team was undertaking and additional data, such as each school's research plan, final report, and any other relevant documentary material, were also collected and analyzed. Questions during the interviews and focus groups did not only relate to matters such as the rationale for each project, research design, and project implementation, but to perspectives on the training, the ideas given focus, and the extent to which these were applied within the projects that the teams devised. Before examining two of these projects, teachers' reactions to the training are considered and, in particular, their view of the theory that framed it.

Engaging With Theory, Enhancing Professional Practice

Many of the teachers who attended the training found it intellectually stimulating but challenging. Daphne from Barnett, a high school in rural NSW with a low LBOTE/low SES student population, pointed out that it "took me back basically to my college days. I hadn't really been exposed to anything like that at that level for a long time". This was a view echoed by Lena from Thurston, a small Sydney primary school with a high LBOTE/low SES population: "I think that's probably why it has been overwhelming for us because we have—it's a long time since I've been at uni". The team at Getty Road, a Sydney primary school with a high LBOTE/high SES student population, were pleased at the level of theoretical engagement in the training with one member commenting,

> Sorcha and I were talking about, as teachers, you are often in your classroom and you don't get to go back and do things and talk to adults about intellectual things. You know, use your brain.

Others, however, were less comfortable with the theoretical dimension of the training. One team member from Wollami Lakes, a primary school in rural NSW with a growing LBOTE population, found,

> the first one difficult to sit through because it was so academic. The second one was good because it gave us a sense of, all right now we know what we have to do; we are not just talking intellectual stuff. ...

To the RMRME Project team, however, the "intellectual stuff", was crucial for reconceiving the way multicultural education is approached in schools. Yet, Marta from Addington, a low LBOTE/low SES high school in outer western Sydney, saw little need for this: "you could have condensed that day, introduction, here it is, off with your teams, here's your paperwork you've got to fill in, how are you going to do it, just let people work together". In other words, Marta saw the 2 days of training as a time when her team, released from face-to-face teaching, could plan their project with little need for further input.

Many teachers took a different view. Gillian at Wellington Heights, a high LBOTE/high SES primary school, valued the intellectual input and time for reflecting on different conceptions of culture:

> I think having a really in-depth look at that really made me start to think there was a little bit more to the way I was thinking and it kind of turned my thinking around to point in the direction of equity and I think that all the things that we did ... I think the first day in particular was really like, wow, I need to have another think about this.

Isaac, her colleague on the research team, added "thinking about what is culture, I found that quite powerful". The training had a similar impact on Sybilla at Thurston Primary School, who began to make use of some of the concepts in an everyday sense:

> What's that word again? Essentialised. I've been using that on my husband quite a bit ... you don't realise how much you do it until I guess that first week made me think OK you do do it.

Julie, from high LBOTE/mid SES Harringvale HS, summed it up in the following way:

> Yeah, I think if we didn't have the professional learning that our definition of multicultural education and any action to address it would be very limited.

These comments from many involved in the training are suggestive of two quite distinct professional cultures among the participating teachers: one with a narrow pragmatic focus in which professional learning serves a purely instrumental function, the other having a broader intellectual orientation more akin to how Connell (2009) sees a teacher's role in which professional learning melds theory and practice and, effecting change, is dependent on a capacity for critical thought. While teachers need to be mindful of the immediate concerns of the day-to-day teaching of students in classrooms, the extent to which this is divorced from any intellectual engagement is the point of differentiation being made here. Each team's capacity to engage with and apply the understandings from the training seemed reliant upon the professional capacities of those involved and the degree to which their professional identities were formed by these quite divergent cultures of teaching. The pedagogic effect of the training and the knowledge the teachers encountered, however, is best understood in terms of each team's ability to apply it. Two of the 14 projects are now examined to illustrate this point, both from primary schools in suburban Sydney. The first of these is Binto Valley Primary School where teachers had difficulty challenging more traditional notions of multiculturalism around empathy and cultural recognition in the project they devised. This is compared to the project at Getty Road Primary School where the research team fully embraced their task and sought to rethink their school's approach to multicultural education.

Putting Theory Into Practice: From Reproducing to Reimagining Multicultural Education

Binto Valley Primary School is located in the affluent eastern suburbs of Sydney. It has a small student population with only 22% having a LBOTE. Of these, the vast majority are French speaking with increasing numbers having Japanese, Mandarin, and Cantonese. Many of the parents of these students are on temporary visas—highly paid professionals who are resident in Australia for 2 or 3 years before moving elsewhere given the transitory and transnational nature of their employment. The school research team, led by the principal, was keen to increase the involvement of these and other LBOTE parents in the school. There was also some concern about racism at the school, particularly toward the increasing number of children from various Asian backgrounds who, in comparison to those of European backgrounds, were treated by some as a less acceptable 'difference' within the school community. While, ostensibly, the aim of the school's project was to increase the participation of LBOTE parents, it was felt that lifting their profile in the school would have payoffs in terms of countering this racism. The research team decided that the course of action they would take would be to hold what they referred to as 'Multicultural Cafes' at the school, which proved to be a more sophisticated take on the multicultural day. In effect it involved all classes from Years 3 to 6 choosing a country and investigating its 'culture' including such things as aspects of language, traditional dress, music, history, various customs, and especially food. This was incorporated into the curriculum over two terms and, as the principal explained, "I want to generate an understanding, an appreciation of the different cultures … I want them to appreciate the multiple sort of diversity that would be in every child's heritage". This seemed an attempt to engage with ideas around cultural hybridity but understood as a patchwork of different cultures.

On the day itself each of the Years 3 to 6 classes set up a café in their room serving food and conducting activities related to aspects of the culture of the country they had investigated: China, France, Spain, Italy, Australia, England, and the United States (though actually Hawaii). The audience for these activities, and the 'customers' in the cafes, were K–2 students who moved from class (country) to class (country) complete with a passport that had to be stamped on entry to each. Parents had been notified well in advance of the day and some attended, assisting students and teachers in preparing and serving food. This constituted their involvement. In the 'China' classroom, for example, one mother of Chinese background was busy steaming dumplings and passing them to the 'Chinese' students to serve. In discussion with the research team following the event, it was considered "a positive start" and a "success", because "the kids were immersed in that culture". It was unclear, however, the extent to which the event—and the data the team collected from student surveys and parent focus groups (to which few attended) in evaluating it—had shifted teachers' understandings of culture and, even more importantly, those of their students and the parents they had hoped to involve. Culture, it seemed, was still very much perceived as bounded and static, with activities on the day simply reinforcing this view.

It is interesting, therefore, that this was the type of 'action' that the team chose to research. Despite these limitations, the day had in fact presented plenty of opportunities for a more nuanced examination of culture with students as did, no doubt, the lessons conducted in advance. In the 'China' room, for example, one of the activities for the K–2 students, while eating their dumplings, was to watch excerpts from the Walt Disney animated movie *Mulan*, replete with the Chinese characters speaking in American accents. Rather than simply presenting this as a depiction of 'Chinese culture', it could have acted as a useful stimulus for young children to discuss globalization, hybrid identities, and more fluid conceptions of culture with questions being posed such as: Where was this movie made? What type of accents do the characters have? Who are the actors who are voicing the

Cultural Studies, Pedagogy and Reimagining Multicultural Education 143

characters? (Eddie Murphy, an African American actor and Pat Morita, a Japanese American actor both voice characters). Is this a Chinese or an American movie? Do you think people of other nationalities were involved in its making? What's the difference between nationality and culture? What is similar/different in culture between China, as depicted in the film, and China today? What connections do we have with China today and in the past? What aspects of culture do we share? What do travel, technology, and migration do to culture? Yet such questioning did not eventuate. Instead, as students were in the 'China' room, this was presented as an example of 'Chinese culture'. Perhaps because of the age of the students, teachers thought ideas around cultural hybridity and globalization were far too complex—as they would be if discussed in this way—but the profession of teaching requires practitioners to translate these ideas. It would have been possible to skillfully inflect their pedagogy with understandings, such as those drawn from the training, but made more readily accessible for younger students. This, however, requires engagement with these ideas to begin with. Despite the enthusiasm of the principal heading the Binto Valley team, she explained there was 'massive resistance' from the team especially in relation to reading. Consequently, they made little headway in their approach to rethinking multicultural education with one team member on the completion of their project commenting that, "I don't really know what an action research project is. A lot of that kind of high-brow stuff was lost on me because it's years since I've been at uni".

The age of students did not prove a problem for the teachers at Getty Road Primary School in terms of having them engage with the ideas presented in the training. Compared to Binto Valley, Getty Road is a much larger school with a much larger LBOTE population of 79%. The main languages spoken at the school are Arabic, Vietnamese, Mandarin, and Cantonese. Located in Sydney's less affluent western suburbs, the principal still considered the school to be in a "comfortable soci-economic area". It also had opportunity classes for gifted students in Years 5 and 6 and was recognized as academically high achieving. Multicultural education was given considerable emphasis at the school, but the principal and the research team were dissatisfied with the way it has been approached in the past and saw the RMRME project as an opportunity for rethinking their practice in this area. As the principal explained,

> [W]e've had multicultural lunches and we've had multicultural dances and we've had the kids come in dressed in multicultural costumes and we've had the multicultural concert which is fine and all that's great as long as its coupled with more in-depth understanding.

For this reason the research team, who taught across the four stages of the primary school curriculum,[5] decided to take a very different approach and devised an action research project around critical literacy. Prior to completing their research plan and implementing their project, the Getty Rd team decided to survey relevant literature. Sayuri commented on how,

> [W]e looked at fairly—material that was related to critical literacy, looking at ways that a reading program, however, it was delivered, could impact on children, their thinking, so that was the material mostly that we looked at to support our project because we wanted to know if we were going on the right track.

The team drew on these understandings from their readings, together with those from the training, in their design of the critical literacy units. Despite working with young students they wanted to challenge them by engaging with some complex ideas. Sorcha explained,

> [T]he concept of culture is so ambiguous and difficult, so we found that the older grades grasped on to it quite quickly and you know, I mean even adults have trouble defining that, but they were giving it a go and they were really you know hitting some good concepts.

It was the students' conceptual understanding and their development of critical capacities in examining issues around multiculturalism and cultural diversity that the team sought to promote in their teaching, with Sorcha adding,

> because I think if you take the superficial take on it, like at the beginning of the unit the kids are, especially if they are clever, they are pre-programmed to say what the teachers want to hear. Is multiculturalism good? Oh yeah multiculturalism is great, oh yes it's about accepting each other and blah, blah, blah … but I felt the critical literacy meant people were speaking honestly and it wasn't superficial, yes let's all hold hands and be friendly.

What Sorcha and her colleagues were aiming for here was to move beyond the kind of unreflexive civility that she felt characterized some forms of multicultural education—"let's all hold hands and be friendly"—blandly prizing cultural diversity without interrogating the challenges it poses. Developing skills around critical literacy, informed by the cultural theory their teachers had met in their training together with their own professional reading, enabled the students to approach such issues as an analytic exercise rather than one that was emotive and moralizing. Students spent a lot of time examining texts, "analysing articles, we were looking for emotive language, what is the aim of this journalist, what are they doing?" Sorcha detailed one particular lesson with her Year 5/6 class:

> [T]he kids were writing interviews, a media interview where they were interviewing a refugee and they had to make it very clear whether or

not they were going to have a negative slant on the interview or a positive slant on the interview and they did it all in the language, like you know, oh in these traumatic circumstances, you know, really loaded words and we looked at different stories, and they started to realise when they were being persuaded and you know, just to take it on facts and it was great, well it wasn't great, but the riots in Hyde Park happened right then when we were teaching it and I remember I heard it on the weekend oh God, oh God, I'm teaching this!

Rather than avoid classroom discussion of this contentious event, Sorcha decided to make use of it in class: "we tried to get as much information as we could about it, we tried to get rid of all the crap and just find out what happened". To Sorcha's surprise it resulted in some interesting discussions between students and their parents. She recounted how one girl questioned her father's take on the event with her mother then supporting her daughter's stance:

Mum came to tell me, [I was] talking to parents and Mum thought it was brilliant especially that kid because Dad was a refugee and she said I don't get it either, he's a refugee, but it's different because they are different, and Samantha launched into him about that.

What ensued was a lively family debate with Samantha being able to make a strong argument based on a detailed understanding of the event. While such anecdotes attest to the impact of the work at Getty Road, this was also borne out by the data they collected from focus groups and work samples. While the units of work had greatest impact in the senior class, the team could see that such work in the earlier years would be useful for providing the necessary foundation for examining these issues in later years. Sorcha summed up the teams' efforts in the following way:

I think it is more than scratching the surface, and I know it is very difficult with multiculturalism to do something meaningful, and it's awkward and you don't want to offend anybody and it's hard, but I really do think that we've done something quite good.

Conclusion

While it may be the case, as the acting principal at Getty Road remarked, that "teaching is a hard gig!", it seems greater emphasis needs to be placed on developing the professional capacities of teachers to effect change in schools. Rethinking multicultural education requires the development of a richer sociocultural knowledge to guard against the simple reproduction of multicultural education as it is traditionally understood where emphasis is placed on the promotion of empathetic understanding and limited forms of cultural recognition that tend to essentialize the assumed ethnicity of students. Such approaches generally have a narrow national frame, often encouraging little more than a kind of unreflexive civility; a tolerance of difference but little meaningful dialogue that is robust enough to weather the challenges increasing cultural complexity now poses.

In the process of rethinking multicultural education, an alternate perspective is required that enables the development of critical understanding informed by a view of knowledge that is comfortable with the uncertainties of cultural dynamism and its resultant complexities. Such a perspective is also alert to reductive forms of cultural recognition, tending more toward what could be termed 'cultural acknowledgement' that enables individuals to be recognized in the fullness of their humanity rather than simply foregrounding ethnicity as the single defining feature of identity (Noble 2009). Such understandings engender a productive engagement with the global, and promote forms of reflexive civility (Kalantzis 2011) that allow individuals to more effectively negotiate the culturally complex world in which we all now live. Such a move, however, is reliant upon the professional capacities of teachers, which can be enhanced through the pedagogic possibilities of the knowledge practices that cultural studies can engender. RMRME provided the opportunity for some teachers to undertake this task and, while there were those that had difficulty rising to the challenge, others embraced the opportunity with transformative results not only for themselves as professionals but for their students and their broader school community.

Acknowledgment

The research upon which this chapter is based was funded by an Australian Research Council Linkage Project with the New South Wales Department of Education and Communities and Board of Studies Teaching and Education Standards. I wish to acknowledge the generous support of each body and also the assistance of my co-investigators Greg Noble and Kevin Dunn from the University of Western Sydney.

Notes

1. The SES of each school was determined by its ICSEA or Index of Community Socio-Educational Advantage. This is a scale used by ACARA based on the occupation and level of education of all parents in each Australian school.
2. There are some quite valid critiques of the use of national standards to regulate the teaching profession. Rather than seeing it as a move to improve the professional status of teaching, Gannon (2012), for example, views the standards as an example of neoliberal managerialism that may obscure elements of what constitutes good teaching.
3. At the time the NSW DEC employed a number of consultants with expertise in ESL and multicultural education to support schools across NSW. With the move

to a new resource allocation model for schools in 2014, these positions were axed leaving schools to source expertise in this area themselves.
4. Each of the research projects were undertaken during 2012. In a number of schools the projects are ongoing, reevaluated in line with the principles of action research.
5. The primary years of schooling in NSW are organized in terms of four stages: Early Stage 1—Kindergarten, Stage 1—Year 1 and 2, Stage 2—Years 3 and 4, and Stage 4—Years 5 and 6.

References

Adelman, C. (1993). Kurt Lewin and the origins of action research. *Educational Action Research*, 1 (1): 7–24.

Australian Curriculum, Assessment and Reporting Authority (ACARA). (2013). *General capabilities in the Australian Curriculum.* Accessed July 2015, http://www.australiancurriculum.edu.au/GeneralCapabilities/Pdf/Overview.

Barth, F. (1994). Enduring and emerging issues in the analysis of ethnicity. In Vermeulen, H., and Govers, C. (eds). *The anthropology of ethnicity: beyond 'ethnic groups and boundaries'* (pp. 11–32). The Hague, Martinus Nijhoff.

Bennett, T., and Frow, J. (2008). Introduction: vocabularies of culture. In Bennett, T., and Frow, J. (eds). *The Sage handbook of cultural analysis* (pp. 1–15). London, Sage.

Board of Studies, Teaching and Educational Standards, NSW. (2015). Accessed July 2015, http://www.nswteachers.nsw.edu.au/great-teaching-inspired-learning/blueprint-for-action/develop-and-maintain-professional-practice/.

Connell, R. (2009). Good teachers on dangerous ground: towards a new view of teacher quality and professionalism. *Critical Studies in Education*, 50 (3): 213–29.

Donald, J. (2007). Internationalisation, diversity and the humanities curriculum: cosmopolitanism and multiculturalism revisited. *Journal of Philosophy of Education*, 41 (3): 289–308.

Education Services Australia. (2011). *Australian professional standards for teachers.* Carlton South, Education Services Australia.

Ferrance, E. (2000). *Themes in education: action research.* Providence, Brown University.

Gannon, S. (2012). Changing lives and standardising teachers: the possibilities and limits of professional standards. *English Teaching: Practice and Critique.* 11 (3): 59–77.

Hall, S. (1990). The emergence of cultural studies and the crisis of the humanities. *October*, 53, 11–23.

Inglis, C. (2009). Multicultural education in Australia: Two generations of evolution. In Banks, J. (ed). *The Routledge international companion to multicultural education* (pp. 109–20). New York and London, Routledge.

Kalantzis, M. (2011). Some insights on Australian and US multiculturalism and multicultural education. In *Rethinking Multiculturalism/Reassessing Multicultural Education Project Report Number 1: International Symposium Report* (pp. 31–32). Penrith South, University of Western Sydney.

Macintyre, C. (2000). *The art of action research in the classroom.* London, David Fulton.

McNiff, J., and Whitehead, J. (2006). *All you need to know about action research.* London, Sage.

Ministerial Council on Education, Employment, Training and Youth Affairs (MCEETYA). (2008). *Melbourne declaration on educational goals for young Australians*. Canberra, MCEETYA.

New South Wales Department of Education and Communities. (2005). *Multicultural education policy*. Sydney, New South Wales Department of Education and Communities.

New South Wales Department of Education and Communities. (2013). *Great teaching, inspired learning: a blueprint for action*. Sydney, New South Wales Department of Education and Communities.

Noble, G. (2009). Countless acts of recognition: young men, ethnicity and the messiness of identities in everyday life. *Social and Cultural Geography*, 10 (8): 875–892.

Noble, G., and Watkins, M. (2013). *Rethinking Multiculturalism/Reassessing Multicultural Education Project Report Number 2: Perspectives on Multicultural Education*. Penrith South, University of Western Sydney.

Silver, H., and Silver, P. (1991). *An educational war on poverty: American and British policy-making, 1960–1980*. Cambridge, Cambridge University Press.

Tellez, K. (2007). Have conceptual reforms (and one anti-reform) in preservice teacher education improved the education of multicultural, multilingual children and youth? *Teachers and Teaching*, 13 (6), 543–64.

Watkins, M., Lean, G., Noble, G., and Dunn, K. (2013). *Rethinking Multiculturalism/Reassessing Multicultural Education Project Report Number 1: Surveying NSW Public School Teachers*. Penrith South, University of Western Sydney.

Watkins, M. (2015a). Multicultural education: contemporary heresy or simply another doxa. In Proctor, H., Freebody, P., and Brownlee, P. (eds). *New and enduring controversies in education: orthodoxy and heresy in policy and practice* (pp. 129–37). New York, Springer.

Watkins, M. (2015b). Culture, hybridity and globalisation: rethinking multicultural education in schools. In Ferfolja, T., Jones-Diaz, C., and Ullman, J. (eds). *Understanding sociological theory for educational practices* (pp. 146–62). Cambridge, Cambridge University Press.

Watkins, M., and Noble, G. (2013). *Disposed to learn: schooling, ethnicity and the scholarly habitus*. London, Bloomsbury.

9 Cultural Studies, DIY Pedagogies, and Storytelling

Gregory Martin and Andrew Hickey

The crisis faced by cultural studies is not one of simply (pre)figuring new methods for countering the effects characteristic of this period of late capitalism (Mandel 1975). This challenge is not solely concerned with the pragmatic mobilization of cultural studies as a critical viewpoint for considering marginalizing social formations, unsustainable consumption, or inequitable distributions of wealth, power, and governance. The real challenge of contemporary cultural studies is in confronting the crisis of the political *imagination* inherent to cultural studies' purpose and motivation (Ang 2006). Cultural studies' impetus grew from the deep interest in the everyday politics of 'ordinary' lives and under the influence of the Birmingham Centre for Contemporary Cultural Studies (and other, equally significant early expressions of organized, 'institutional' formations of cultural studies as detailed by Turner 1990) ushered in a paradigmatic shift in the humanities' treatment of popular culture and the 'texts' of everyday life. Cultural studies fractured existing structures of knowledge production and challenged orthodox accounts of the world produced by established disciplinary formations (most markedly those of literature, history, and sociology) through its applications of 'bottom-up' approaches to material, or lived, cultures. Cultural studies sought to transgress established distinctions between 'high' and 'low' culture and the disciplinary and pedagogical norms that supported these (Agger 1992: 84). Hebdige (2015) suggests that cultural studies opened up the academy to "the something nasty down below" (37), and it has been with this emphasis on the quotidian experiences of lives lived that a defining feature of cultural studies' has been positioned. As a project of disruption and rearticulation, cultural studies' focus on the "*now*" of everyday life (Hebdige, 2015: 37) situated culture as an intensified battleground and site for challenging hegemonic forms of knowledge, education, and learning. This was an imaginative project, and one that drew on new formulations of method and practice to present its case.

What cultural studies has and continues to offer is an opportunity to explore otherwise ignored topics (and subjects) of scholarly scrutiny, to open these "cultural products, social practices, even institutions, *as* 'texts'" (Turner 1990: 71, emphasis added). The opportunity to look again and re-read the "very material of our daily lives, the bricks and mortar of our most commonplace understandings" (Willis in Turner 1990: 1) provides a useful orienting purpose—a central project—for enabling meaningful change in the world. Yet it remains that cultural studies has struggled to maintain its momentum, to continue to speak for those from 'down below', and to effectively respond to and shape such change. Rapid transformations of those publics from which cultural studies sought to locate its objects of inquiry, changes in the higher education systems that support cultural studies, and (perhaps as the most challenging problem inherent in this dynamic) a looming stasis in the practice of the institutional(ized) articulations of the discipline have conspired to leave cultural studies somewhat fractured in itself. This is a problem centered on the discipline's capacity to *imagine* new worlds through modes of inquiry that remain inventive and drawn from the material realities of the settings it seeks to report from.

That 'cultural studies' is not a unified project in itself is also significant to this argument, with different projects operating under the name 'cultural studies' corresponding to various modes of inquiry, objects of study, and national formulations that mark cultural studies as arguably fractured (Ang 2006). The problem facing cultural studies is how to reimagine itself as active and interventionist but also heterogeneous, dynamic, and flexible enough to correspond to local interventions and idiosyncratic application as the sites of cultural studies' encounters prescribe (Ang 2006). In a world that is now markedly different to the one confronted by the Centre for Contemporary Cultural Studies, the question stands, *what is now possible for cultural studies?* How might cultural studies (re)imagine itself and its projects in these fractured times?

Foundational Characteristics

It carries, however, that with this concern for the everyday and the quotidian aspects of lives-lived that a common core for cultural studies, in all its formations, remains as recognizable. Cultural studies' declaration that "every aspect of human life is ... cultural and is part of a larger cultural totality" (Donbasch 2015: 130) provides a touchstone for not only marking cultural studies' presence but also for defining its futures. This is a project interested in, however broadly this might materialize in practice, the questioning of the political implications of the everyday *as* culture (and cultural). Even in terms of the plurality and hybridity possible in the application of cultural studies, this prevailing concern for the everyday and the commensurate assemblage of methods of analysis that correspond to this specificity provides a reference point—a prompt toward a common epistemology—for cultural studies as a useful basis from which to reimagine its continuing presence.

Indeed, a new wave of scholars increasingly frustrated with reformations of the academic status quo have begun to explore DIY (do-it-yourself) culture as a possibility for pedagogical reenchantment of the political *and* the pedagogical (Giroux 2004; Ratto et al. 2014; Sandlin and Milam 2008).

We count ourselves as part of this group. Inspired by Giroux's (1992) work on "border pedagogy" and "border crossing", our interest in DIY activist pedagogies traverses both critical education and cultural studies. It is motivated by a growing disillusionment with formal politics and the capability present *within* social institutions (primarily the university) as sites for social change, as well as the seemingly elitist, fragmented, and isolated nature of academic work (Halfacree 1999). We suggest that cultural studies has much to offer but also much to learn from the emergence of such counterpedagogical approaches to scholarship. The possibility for critically accounting for Self and Other, questioning the ontological bases of scholarly intervention in-the-world and decentering the politics of knowledge production and claims to authority that academic work sometimes speak from are broached by DIY as sites for productive, creative, and critically attuned modes of scholarly engagement (Halfacree 1999).

For DIY, scholarship is dialogical and performative and encompasses a broad range of connections, multiplicities, and accountabilities extant within the act of scholarship. Accounts of the world produced as DIY interventions are necessarily also multiple and dis/connected in complex ways from other recognized and 'formal' scholarly accounts, accounts that Apple (2000: xvi) characterizes as "official" views of the world and its structure. Such imaginative and enacted ways of knowing provide insight into how "critical performative pedagogy" (Denzin 2003: 31), or rather *pedagogies*, offer to reconfigure the geopolitics of contemporary knowledge production (Alexander et al. 2005a). For DIY, the production of understanding and knowledge is always contingent and for cultural studies in particular this provides a freedom to move beyond existing ways of doing things—different ways of knowing and producing knowledge—to reclaim a space for the authentic consideration of what Anna Hickey-Moody (2015: 117) refers to as "little publics"—everyday spaces of experience and inhabitance that carry their own specificity and logics. This deep consideration of the specificity of modes of inquiry built upon a consideration of and respect for *the ways things are done* in these 'local' settings serves as a reminder of cultural studies' prevailing concerns and a point of opportunity for thinking again about how it is that accounts from the field are produced, disseminated, and used to frame knowledge.

With this in mind, this chapter explores the potential of "critical performative pedagogies" to broach a DIY ethic for cultural studies (Denzin 2003: 31; see also Alexander et al. 2005a). Critical performative pedagogies are grounded in embodied forms of 'doing', learning, and knowing that facilitate a multiplicity of connections, including those that function between and through theory-to-practice and the interactions that researchers and researched (Alexander et al. 2005b: 2; see also Denzin 2003; Lather 1997) might enact. Critical performative pedagogies also ask questions of the role of formal articulations of knowledge produced from the interactions of universities, their scholars, and communities

(Alexander et al. 2005a; Denzin 2003; Giroux 2001; hooks 1994; McLaren 1993). As a form of "culture-making practice" that academics can shape, performative approaches to cultural studies scholarship suggest something disruptive to educational orthodoxies (Slottje 2015). Specifically, we argue that the storytelling core to critical performative pedagogies and the re/telling of experiences of place, in all of its complex and even contradictory manifestations, has pedagogical/political potential for the development of what has been referred to as "participatory-cultural studies" (Burgess 2006; Delwiche and Henderson 2012: 4). Rather than seeking to establish dichotomous 'inside-outside' binary relationships between community and scholarship, the point is to reconfigure the relationship of scholarship and everyday life. Within DIY, informed as it might be by critical performative pedagogy, the scholarly act is not centered on the extraction of 'data' from informed sectors of 'the community', but instead is situated as a generative act performed *within* community. This coconstructed view of scholarship seeks to establish formulations of knowledge that remain as meaningful and grounded in the concerns of community. Knowledge is produced relationally and authentically within community for the purposes of community. This is a necessarily situated form of knowing that seeks to relocate from the authorial precincts of the ivory tower a more participatory form of cultural studies, shaped by and respondent to the conditions of those diverse "counter-publics" (Fraser 1990: 61) encountered in the performative pedagogy of DIY scholarship.

Cultural Studies and Critical Pedagogies

The so-called "project" of cultural studies has never been a static, unified, or coherent body of scholarship (Stacey 2015: 47). Despite efforts to maintain or establish a cohesive canon, cultural studies is constantly evolving with contested variations (Barker 2003; Stacey 2015). As a response to moves in the academy for 'critically' invested and oriented scholarship, cultural studies emerged as fundamentally political in its pedagogical orientation, and like other disciplines that drew closely on critical theory for their theoretical prompts (critical pedagogy is most closely linked to cultural studies in the terms of this chapter), it is this same critical orientation that prompts new forms of scholarship, objects of study, and interdisciplinary relationships that are in constant formation and evolution.

The disciplining of cultural studies is far from complete in this regard, and while this *un*disciplined feature of cultural studies has stood as representative of its dynamism (Ang 2006: 184), it is also this feature of cultural studies that has caused some to critique its political/pedagogical potential as little more than a set of esoteric practices that achieve little more than inaccessible critiques of culture as 'text' (Diamond 1996; Grossberg 1997, 2014; Katz 2000). Even within cultural studies, criticisms regarding the *disconnection*—both politically and pedagogically—from meaningful engagement with the cultural production of actual people in actual settings are prominent (Ang 2006; Grossberg 2014). Cultural studies tendency for 'abstraction' and the complication of the cultural texts of everyday life (Farred 2009: 149; Katz 2000) often seems in contrast to its concern for "lived experience, and the articulated relationship between texts and everyday life" (Denzin and Lincoln 2011: 93). The danger for cultural studies lies in this perception, that it is (currently) engaged in little more than "self-serving and elitist" (Jensen 2002: 24) theorizing, with Jensen (2002) echoing a widely shared sentiment that cultural studies has become reduced to "impotent social criticism" (24).

If these criticisms hold any currency, and it seems that they do, it would appear that reclaiming praxis—the "*doing* of cultural studies" (Johnson et al. 2004: 94)—stands as a vital orientation from which cultural studies might reclaim its utility. A central concern here is how to reassert the institutional legitimacy of cultural studies (Ang 2006), while at the same time regenerating the "civic role" (190) it might speak from and through. Ang (2006) refers to the latter as "questions from the outside"—points of concern that sit "beyond the academy" (189). Here, knowledge production has political relevance to the everyday contexts of lived or embodied relationships existing beyond the academy, in the *wilds* of community.

To achieve this effectively, Ang (2006) suggests that cultural studies must open itself to "dialogue and exchange" with other disciplinary spaces and public arenas (188) and in doing so provides a clarion for her concern regarding reasserting the institutional legitimacy of cultural studies. Far from looking inward and to itself for cues and points of reference, a legitimate, reasserted cultural studies would offer the possibility for "innovation and renewal" (Ang 2006: 188) by seeking collaboration and shared production of knowledge that transcends disciplinary boundaries. It is in this sense, and as one example of how this ethic for collaboration might continue, that she suggests the term "cultural research" as more appropriate and "less parochial" than "cultural studies". Ang's concerns center on building an approach to scholarship that presents openness to disciplinary interactions and border crossing between academic and public realms as core to its practice.

Drawing from a similar spirit, Giroux (2004) has placed an explicit focus on the pedagogical aspects of everyday or popular culture, but in doing so by arguing for the active crossing of "borders" in an effort to generate new ways of knowing. For Giroux (2004), cultural studies offers an opportunity for engagement in-the-world and the potential for deepened critical insight and expanded possibilities for political agency that authentic and collaborative engagement in community *with* publics prescribes. He cites Raymond Williams to remind us of the "deepest impulse [informing cultural studies] was the desire to make learning part of the process of social change itself" (Giroux 2004). For this reason, Giroux (2004) suggests pedagogy "is not merely about deconstructing texts, but is also about situating politics itself within a broader set of relations that address what it might mean to create modes of individual and social agency that enable rather than shut down democratic values, practices, and social relations" (84). Consequently, Giroux (1994) argues for a more expansive definition of cultural studies, one in which the focus is on "making the political more pedagogical" (499) (and concomitantly, the pedagogical more political). In keeping with this, he has also argued for cultural studies to embrace the pedagogical as a "performative act" (Giroux 2001).

This explicit connection between pedagogy and cultural studies, drawn as it is within Ang (2006) and Giroux's (2004) articulations of an engaged cultural studies practice, provides a useful reference point for considering a DIY scholarship for cultural studies. It is with concern for the active participation in the world *and* the assertion of legitimacy that cultural studies might claim as a discipline able to speak from and for those publics from which it conducts its work that Ang's (2006) suggestions provide a useful reference for cultural studies. Equally significant, however, are Giroux's (2004) suggestions that these engagements with publics are pedagogical encounters, where publics might speak to the academy and the academy to publics. DIY scholarship draws on these reference points in framing its practice as scholarship that is done *in* and *for* publics, using the structure of the academy and the formal codes of knowledge production that this proclaims to give further weight to these accounts.

Critical Pedagogy

Spanning a range of approaches and issues, including environmental and multicultural education, critical accounts of race and ethnicity, scholarship in whiteness and settler studies, the theorization of queer identities through the consideration of gender and sexualities, as well as concerns for globalized economic structures, marginalization, and disenfranchised populations, critical pedagogy is often represented as a "big tent" coalition (Lather 1998: 487). Ideally animated by its situated and participatory contexts, critical pedagogy is sensitive to the inherently power-laden nature of identity and knowledge construction. For this reason, critical pedagogy often rejects the assumptions, rationales, and "official knowledge[s]" used to buttress authority of the status quo (Apple 2014: xvi). Through access to a broad range of resources and affordances, critical pedagogy facilitates the coconstruction of alternative worldviews and practices (Martin and Te Riele 2011).

Yet, and much like cultural studies, the field of critical pedagogy is marked by perpetual critique and conflict (Martin and Te Riele 2011). For example, despite its "noble sentiments" (Yoon 2005: 717), critical pedagogy is variously critiqued for its elitism, paternalism, and deep internal divisions (Ellsworth 1989; Pinar 2009). Instead of offering lofty prescriptions, Martin and Brown (2013) suggest that the relationship between theory and praxis ought to be recalibrated with an emphasis on how critical pedagogy is embodied, practiced, or performed through a broad range of everyday practices, and not solely within the formal classroom. This calls for consideration of not only the sites and practices through which critical pedagogy might be practiced, but also the embodied and performative dimensions of *doing* critical pedagogy (Alexander et al. 2005b: 2). Nonetheless, and also like cultural studies, the existing literature remains somewhat abstract, fragmented, and/or episodic on exactly how this might be achieved.

With multiple perspectives and on-the-ground variations, critical performative pedagogies must be "made and remade" to fit unique and imperfect institutional arrangements (Freire 1972: 33). Indeed, critical performative pedagogies are performed "against the grain" of the educational status quo in ways that are typically contingent and context specific (Simon 1992). No blueprints or recipe books exist. Nor can critical performative pedagogies be sustained in isolation. Critical performative pedagogies are informed by geographies of power and counterpublics that transcend institutional and disciplinary boundaries. In this context, we suggest that the pedagogical/political renewal of cultural studies might be enriched methodologically through the "relocation" of learning around a broad range of contemporary spaces, issues, and connections that a critical pedagogical orientation prescribes (Erni 2011: 180).

This implies that cultural studies ought to become more pedagogically *and* politically expansive and accountable (Ang 2006) by functioning in-the-field, with community. Nonetheless, the so-called 'activism gap' that materializes between well-meaning but ultimately constrained academic pursuits is difficult to negotiate for many reasons, with accounts of the realities of neo-liberal performativity in contemporary university settings highlighting the institutional restrictions and pressures placed upon academics and academic incursions into-the-world (Ball 2003). Discourses of 'professionalism' make it exceedingly difficult to envision and enact futures that are not caught up with some "neo-liberal imaginary" (Ball 2012: 2). More pragmatically, the gold-standard of academic work, the journal article, runs short in offering a meaningful incursion into the world (especially when consideration of who comes to read these works is given; rarely do those beyond the academy engage with such work). Membership within the academy, achieved through supposed neutrality of "expert" status demarcated in narrowly defined terms often runs counter to the immediate, *practical* concerns of community (Ang 2006; Behm et al. 2014). Such conditions translate as being less about meaningful, useful knowledge production and genuine engagement with communities and sites outside the university than they are the reification of established hierarchies of prestige or 'quality', defined as these are by simplistic relationships between academic knowledge production and the potential for commercialization or 'industry adaptability' this knowledge might have (Ang 2006).

Despite attempts to preserve the social contexts that make scholar-activism possible, the current (re)formulations of the "corporate university"

(Marginson 1993) often relegate community-focused modes of scholarly practice to the background. Active, scholarly participation in the world typically does not 'count' as 'measurable', or worse, is counter to the political concerns of the corporate university. In this context, some scholars have reasserted the potential of the classroom as a site of political action (Heyman 2007), and while other academics continue to work at the borders, interstices, or margins of multiple borders that are available for scholar-activism, the restructuring, deskilling, and casualization of employment in higher education have forced others to abandon it. How can academics—particularly those in cultural studies—disenfranchised with these production practices, reconnect with publics and demonstrate their value?

Within the regime of "competitive performativity" characteristic of the contemporary university (Ball 2003: 219), the uneven and often contradictory politics of higher education have induced recurring bouts of self-examination, angst, and self-doubt among activist-academics about the "relevance" they hold (Hodkinson 2009: 463). This is particularly evident within the field of cultural studies (Ang 2006); however, the plight of cultural studies is not unique. The transformation of the university into an *enterprise* has "virtually squeezed out" (Hill 2007: 214) the spaces available for critical and creative forms of intellectual work across the suite of disciplines that take their cue from the critical interventions into the world, critical pedagogy and cultural studies among these. There is a rich and storied tradition of scholar-activism in the sector that due to its limitations (both conceptual and practical) continues to shift and change (Chatterton et al. 2010). Informed by diverse intellectual traditions and approaches, academic-activists have sought to redefine their disciplines as well as both the shape and meaning of activism. Activism, it turns out, is practiced in a number of different ways (Barker et al. 2009; Martin and Brown 2013). In spite of the perennial problems of most insider/outsider research, knowledge production is recast in these situations as politically motivated and participatory, but also deeply reflexive and cognizant of the realities that resistant practice provokes.

DIY and Counter-Pedagogies/Publics

One hallmark of the current condition of higher education and critical scholarly practice is the turn to performative and collaborative methods such as storytelling (Haseman 2006). Although notions of performativity draw upon diverse and contested traditions (Alexander et al. 2005b), a central tenet of performative methodologies can be found in the relational and participatory occurrences of *doing* that these methods prescribe. Here, the relationship between the teacher/researcher/performer and audience is blurred. Such an approach is in keeping with the 'spirit' of cultural studies, with "relationality" (Grossberg 2014: 6) and participation "valorized" even if such discourses are embraced or affirmed uncritically (Driscoll and Gregg 2011: 567).

Storytelling as an approach for mobilizing a critical performative pedagogy provides opportunities for an authentic engagement with community (Canning and Reinsborough 2010; Stone-Mediatore 2003). Through the capacity cultural studies scholars have for engaging with others in the coconstruction that cultural studies methods allow, storytelling provides powerful performative potential for evoking points of view, senses of place, emotion, knowledge, and scale (Bell 2010; Stone-Mediatore 2003). Importantly, the authority of storytelling deployed by other sectors of the cultural industry will stand in contrast to the storytelling of cultural studies. The critical performative pedagogy of cultural studies' storytelling exposes counternarratives that refute the dominant articulations of other sectors of the cultural industry to inform what Carey (1989) refers to as "the conversation society has with itself" (in Deuze 2008). In this sense, storytelling is an important site for mobilizing participatory cultures that are generated by diverse audiences (Jenkins 2006); however, it remains that the purposes to which these stories are put and the motivations that give rise to them stand as crucial in terms of the ultimate ends they might hope to meet (Canning and Reinsborough 2010).

This is in keeping with bottom-up focus of cultural studies. Cultural studies offers an interdisciplinary insight into the possibilities of emergent spaces meaningful to the "little publics" (Hickey-Moody 2015: 117) the cultural studies scholar encounters. In this context, activists of DIY culture are not mere consumers, spectators, or victims of culture but rather active participants in its creation or making, with storytelling the mechanism for elaborating accounts that will brush-up against, resist, actively contradict, and provide weight to other representations of experience drawn from community. Through this process, DIY scholarly practice is concerned with eliciting stories of community, in all their diversity, in an attempt to build a culture of knowledge sharing that sets the basis for new forms of learning, interaction, and agency. As a slogan, 'do-it-yourself' infuses critical participatory pedagogies of storytelling with a more nondogmatic and autonomous conception of political power. Whether explicitly political or not, participation through collaboration is valorized as a way to trigger creativity, innovation/invention, participation and engagement, and (perhaps most markedly) democratic political change. DIY, enacted through storytelling, stands as less a producer of objects and more a coproducer of situations and relational or dialogical practices (Kester 2004, 2011). This approach to the telling of stories—as diverse accounts of experience—stand in contrast to notions of the passive audience/spectator. Storytelling is active and an agentic demonstration of one's awareness of Self in community (Canning and Reinsborough 2010; Stone-Mediatore 2003).

The point here is that storytelling offers possibilities for a critical public pedagogy of resistance that raises questions, poses problems, and presents alternative visions and models for participation (Sandlin et al. 2010; Stone-Mediatore 2003). Indeed, bell hooks (2015) makes reference to the historical character of storytelling as a kind of "talking back" (9). Counterstories made possible through the performative critical pedagogy of storytelling challenge the "stock stories" or the "common-sense" mainstream narratives of the dominant culture (Bell 2010: 29). In particular, counter-storytelling that draws upon nonprofessional or subjugated knowledges is central to what Canning and Reinsborough (2010) refer to as the "battle of the story" (46). Here, participation is important to interrogating the "culture of silence" (Freire 1985: 73) that nourishes and sustains the legitimacy of mainstream discourses or stories as well as the recrafting of "a new story" (Canning and Reinsborough 2010: 46). In this context, the "battle of the story" is connected to "the larger struggle to determine whose stories are told, how they are framed, how widely these stories are heard, and how deeply they impact the dominant discourse" (2010: 46).

What is important here is that we, as academics, have become increasingly dissatisfied with the stories we (are required to) tell about our research or scholar-activism. In practice, a strong push exists to conform to the language of academia for elite consumption (Ang 2006). There is an irony in this, given that the elitism of universities is critiqued in many different forums. Academics, including those situated in cultural studies, have long been criticized for failing to make their research understandable to a lay audience (Ang 2006; Behm et al. 2014). Yet, it remains that this mode of critique is a *conservative* critique.

Drawing upon insights from Canning and Reinsborough (2010), we suggest that changing both the content and form of critical intellectual engagement can amplify the power of our own stories by making them more accessible and likely to "stick" (see Heath and Heath 2007: 8), but at the same time opening for accessibility the stories we encounter and produce as scholars when working with community. This extends beyond demonstrating the "relevance" of academic research or ideas, or indeed, simply reporting on the 'findings' drawn from engagement with the field, but stands as a marked attempt to use the format and authority that academic works still carry to bring to light submerged stories and counternarratives.

What we want to argue is that storytelling offers potential for a relational and participatory cultural studies marked by a more critical, creative, and imaginative activism (Burgess 2006; Canning and Reinsborough 2010). Agger (1992) suggests that cultural studies is "an activity of critical theory that directly decodes the hegemonising messages of the culture industry permeating every nook and cranny of lived experiences, from entertainment to education" (5). Rey and Nabizadeh (2011) define cultural studies "as a study of and engagement with culture" (54). Yet, questions remain at this moment around how it is that cultural studies *does* its critique and how it might perform its engagement with culture. For this reason, Larry Grossberg has called repeatedly for a "relocation" of cultural studies (Erni 2011: 180). What we argue for is the relocating of the *doing* of cultural studies through more embodied and reciprocal engagements *with* community *through* storytelling.

The remapping and repurposing of storytelling within cultural studies has the capacity to shift its focus from textual critique to a more dialogical and embodied form of pedagogical and storied social action (Hancox 2011). The subjectivity of storytelling as we imagine it moves cultural studies outside the domain of formalized institutionalized rules of engagement. Writing in the 1920 and 1930s, Walter Benjamin warned about the threat of the loss of the public intellectual with the decline of the art of storytelling due to the rise of mass communications and the focus on information processing (Garoian and Gaudelius 2008: 107–8). As a site of collective invention, storytelling then offers academics the opportunity to remake themselves as what Giroux (2011) and others refer to as "public intellectuals" (see also Ang 2006). In the moment of storytelling, both the storyteller and the audience are potentially participants (Bruner 1991; Polletta 1998). For Giroux (2011), public intellectuals ought to "connect critical ideas, traditions, disciplines, and values to the public realm of everyday life" (186), with storytelling central to such an approach for opening for dialogue alternative, submerged and marginalized accounts of the world. The role of the cultural studies scholars in this regard translates as one of both critical interlocutor and active participant—the embedded scholar working *in* the wilds of community.

Storytellers using the tools of critical, participatory storytelling can weave narratives and critiques from both inside and outside of the academy to challenge the legitimizing myths and ideologies of the dominant culture. Here, communities are not passive receptacles into which 'expert' knowledge is poured. Instead, the ethics of the kind of storytelling we suggest here corresponds with the recent 'participatory turn' of cultural analysis by placing a focus on emergent collaborative processes and practices including non-professional and *vernacular* production. Storytelling offers to rearticulate the relationship between cultural studies and the field, the researcher and the researched, through dialogue, the coproduction knowledge, and other performative dimensions including trust (Stone-Mediatore 2003).

This is not to naively ignore or downplay critiques of narrative and experience (Stone-Mediatore 2003). Yet, as Sharon Stone-Mediatore (2003) argues, the tendency to dismiss "experience-based narratives as mere ideological artefacts ... reinforce[s] the disempowerment of people who have been excluded from official knowledge production" (2). In other words, it has a pernicious political effect. What's more, as critical race theorists, feminist theorists, and others engaged in the explanation of subaltern positionality point out, peoples' narration of their experience is never entirely determined by dominant discourses or power relations (Bell 2010; Stone-Mediatore 2003). In her justly praised book *Reading Across Borders: Storytelling and Knowledges of Resistance*, Shari Stone-Mediatore (2003) argues "everyday experiences can also react against, register the contradictions of, and ultimately constitute the motivation for intervening in ideological processes" (2).

With this in mind, effective counterstories are stories that critique or bring attention to the contested nature of dominant narratives by amplifying voices, forcing listeners to question, and motivating them to act (Bell 2010; Canning and Reinsborough 2010). Importantly, Ganz (2001) points to the emotional work of stories and how they can motivate or inspire action. In this context, storytelling is not just a powerful methodological tool, it is also an important pedagogical and political practice. Utilizing hybrid forms of multimedia and narrative, storytelling can cross borders to facilitate participatory analysis, learning, and agency (Benmayor 2008; Solorzano and Yosso 2002). Counterstorytelling is a field of cultural practice, a site of relations, enacted to amplify voice, forge identification, and inspire social action.

Conclusion

Cultural studies currently lacks both ethical and political force. Its practice needs to undergo some sort of metamorphosis. However, it is important to not equate reinventing with *remembering*—that is, making recourse to nostalgia and resorting to how things were in the jaundiced view of a reconstructed past. For this reason, as a political project, cultural studies needs to move beyond itself, to cast off the binds of its past and begin interacting with other sites and agendas. Cultural studies requires an intellectual and political orientation that is more expansive. Storytelling embedded in processes that are dialogical and participatory is one way a reconstructed and rearticulated cultural studies might begin to reclaim its imaginaries and publics.

Stuart Hall (1990) noted that in the early days "nobody knew what cultural studies was ... we had to go on as if we were all making it up together" (15). In this current uncertain context, cultural studies will have to engage in the difficult work of unlearning its disciplinary attachments to reimagine and remake its possibilities (Grossberg 2014). Cultural studies might do well to again do what Hall has suggested—to *make it up*. But rather than hark back to some sepia myth, Hebdige (2015: 37) suggests that "contemporizing" is key to reworking the fatalism that surrounds such institutional developments that cultural studies now finds itself. He puts it like this: "The point is not to analyse culture for its own sake but to produce compelling and persuasive analysis of issues pressing contemporary concern that can connect to and become meaningful for broader, more dispersed constituencies outside the academy" (2014: 37). We suggest here that at this moment, marked as it is by uncertainty in the world at large and the discipline more specifically, that taking stock of what it is that cultural studies does well and reconfiguring the discipline's purpose in terms of the (counter)stories it might tell, that a renewed vigour and prospect for cultural studies' imagination might be found.

References

Agger, B. (1992). *Cultural studies as critical theory*. London, Falmer Press.
Alexander, B.K., Anderson, G.L., and Gallegos, B. (eds). (2005a). *Performance theories in education: power, pedagogy, and the politics of identity*. New York, Routledge.

Alexander, B., Anderson, G., and Gallegos, B. (eds). (2005b). Introduction: performance in education. In Alexander, B., Anderson, G., and Gallegos, B. (eds), *Performance theories in education: power, pedagogy, and the politics of identity* (pp. 1–14). New York, Routledge.

Ang, I. (2006). From cultural studies to cultural research: engaged scholarship in the twenty-first century. *Cultural Studies Review*, 12 (2): 183–97.

Apple, M. (2000). *Official knowledge: democratic education in a conservative age.* New York, Routledge.

Ball, S. (2003). The teacher's soul and the terrors of performativity. *Journal of Education Policy*, 18 (2): 215–28.

Ball, S. (2012). *Global education inc.: new policy networks and the neo-liberal imaginary.* New York, Routledge.

Barker, C. (2003). *Cultural studies: theory and practice.* London, Sage.

Barker, J., Kraftl, P., Horton, J., and Tucker, F. (2009). The road less travelled? New directions in children's mobility. *Mobilities*, 4: 1–10.

Behm, N., Rankins-Robertson, S., and Roen, D. (2014). The case for academics as public intellectuals. *Academe*, 100 (1): 12–13.

Bell, L.A. (2010). *Storytelling for social justice: connecting narrative and the arts in antiracist teaching.* New York, Routledge.

Benmayor, R. (2008). Digital storytelling as a signature pedagogy for the new humanities. *Arts and Humanities in Higher Education*, 7 (2): 188–204.

Bruner, J. (1991). The narrative construction of reality. *Critical Inquiry*, 18 (1): 1–21.

Burgess, J. (2006). Hearing ordinary voices: cultural studies, vernacular creativity and digital storytelling. *Continuum: Journal of Media and Cultural Studies*, 20 (2): 201–14.

Canning, D., and Reinsborough, P. (2010). *Re:imagining change: an introduction to story-based strategy.* Portland, PM Press Verlag.

Canning, D., and Reinsborough, P. (2010). *Re: Imagining change: How to use story-based strategy to win campaigns, build movements, and change the world.* Chicago: PM Press.

Carey, J. (1989). *Communication as culture: essays on media and society.* London, Unwin.

Chatterton, P., Hodkinson, S., and Pickerill, J. (2010). Beyond scholar activism: making strategic interventions inside and outside the neoliberal university. *Acme: An International e-Journal for Critical Geographies*, 9 (2): 245–75.

Delwiche, A., and Henderson, J.J. (eds). (2012). *The participatory cultures handbook.* New York, Routledge.

Denzin, N. (2003). *Performance ethnography: critical pedagogy and the politics of culture.* Thousand Oaks, Sage.

Denzin, N., and Lincoln, Y. (eds). (2011). *The SAGE handbook of qualitative research* (4th ed.). Thousand Oaks, Sage.

Deuze, M. (2008). The changing context of news work: liquid journalism and monitorial citizenship. *International Journal of Communication*, 2: 848–65.

Diamond, E. (1996). Introduction. *Performance and cultural politics.* New York, Routledge.

Donbasch, W. (2015). *The concise encyclopedia of communication.* Chichester, Wiley.

Driscoll, C., and Gregg, M. (2011). Convergence culture and the legacy of feminist cultural studies. *Cultural Studies*, 25(4–5): 566–84.

Ellsworth, E. (1989). Why doesn't this feel empowering? Working through the repressive myths of critical pedagogy. *Harvard Educational Review*, 59 (3): 297–325.

Erni, J.N. (ed). (2011). *Cultural studies of rights: critical articulations.* New York, Routledge.
Farred, G. (2009). Out of context: thinking cultural studies diasporically. *Cultural Studies Review,* 15 (1): 130–50.
Fraser, N. (1990). Rethinking the public sphere: a contribution to the critique of actually existing democracy. *Social Text,* 25/26: 56–80.
Freire, P. (1972). *Pedagogy of the oppressed.* Harmondsworth, Penguin.
Freire, P. (1985). *The politics of education: culture, power and liberation.* Massachusetts, Bergin & Garvey.
Ganz, M. (2001). The power of story in social movements. Paper presented to Annual Meeting of the American Sociological Association, August, Anaheim, California.
Garaoian, C.R., and Gaudelius, Y.M. (2008). *Spectacle pedagogy: art, politics and visual culture.* New York, State University of New York Press.
Giroux, H.A. (1992). *Border crossings: cultural workers and the politics of education.* New York, Psychology Press.
Giroux, H.A. (1994). *Disturbing pleasures: learning popular culture.* New York, Routledge.
Giroux, H.A. (2001). Cultural studies as performative politics. *Cultural Studies-Critical Methodologies,* 1 (1): 5–23.
Giroux, H.A. (2004). Cultural studies and the politics of public pedagogy: making the political more pedagogical. *Parallax,* 10 (2–3): 494–503.
Giroux, H.A. (2011). *On critical pedagogy.* New York, Bloomsbury.
Grossberg, L. (1997). *Bringing it all back home: essays on cultural studies.* Durham, Duke University Press.
Grossberg, L. (2014). *We gotta get out of this place: popular conservatism and postmodern culture.* New York, Routledge.
Halfacree, K. (1999). Anarchy doesn't work unless you think about it: one intellectual interpretation and DIY culture. *Area,* 31 (3): 209–20.
Hall, S. (1990). The emergence of cultural studies and the crisis of the humanities. *October,* 53: 11–23.
Hancox, D. (ed). (2011). *Fight back! A reader on the winter of protest.* OpenDemocracy. Accessed from http://felixcohen.co.uk/fightback.pdf.
Haseman, B. (2006). A manifesto for performative research. *Media International Australia, Incorporating Culture and Policy,* 118: 98–106.
Heath, C., & Heath, D. (2007). *Made to stick: why some ideas survive and others die.* New York, Random House.
Hebdige, D. (2014). Contemporizing subculture: 30 years to life. *Journal of European Cultural Studies,* 15 (3): 399–424.
Hebdige, D. (2015). The worldliness of cultural studies. *Cultural Studies,* 29 (1): 32–42.
Heyman, R. (2007). "Who's going to man the factories and be the sexual slaves if we all get PhDs?" Democratizing knowledge production, pedagogy, and the Detroit Geographical Expedition and Institute. *Antipode,* 39 (1): 99–120.
Hickey-Moody, A. (2015). Little publics and youth arts as a cultural pedagogy. In Watkins, M., Noble, G., and Driscoll, C. (eds). *Cultural pedagogies and human conduct* (pp. 78–91). New York, Routledge.
Hill, D. (2007). Critical teacher education, new labour, and the global project of neoliberal capital. *Policy Futures in Education,* 5 (2): 204–25.
Hodkinson, S. 2009. Teaching what we (preach and) practice: The MA in Activism and Social Change. *ACME* 8 (3): 462– 73.

hooks, b. (1994). *Outlaw culture: Resisting representations*. New York, Routledge.
hooks, b. (2015). *Talking back: thinking feminist, thinking black*. New York, Routledge.
Jenkins, H. (2006). *Fans, bloggers, and gamers: exploring participatory culture*. New York, New York University Press.
Jensen, J. (2002). Arts, intellectuals and the public: the legacies and limits of American cultural criticism, 1910–1950. In Warren, C.A., and Varvus, M.D. (eds). *American cultural studies* (pp. 23–54). Urbana, University of Illinois Press.
Johnson, R., Chambers, D., Raghuram, P., and Tincknell, E. 2004. *The practice of cultural studies*. Thousand Oaks, Sage.
Katz, A. (2000). *Postmodernism and the politics of "culture"*. Boulder, Westview Press.
Kester, G.H. (2004). *Conversation pieces: community and communication in modern art*. Berkeley, University of California Press.
Kester, G.H. (2011). *The one and the many: contemporary collaborative art in a global context*. Durham, Duke University Press.
Lather, P. (1997). Drawing the line at angels: working the ruins of feminist ethnography. *International Journal of Qualitative Studies in Education*, 10 (3): 285–304.
Lather, P. (1998). Critical pedagogy and its complicities: a praxis of stuck places. *Educational Theory*, 48 (4): 487–97.
Mandel, E. (1975). *Late capitalism*. London, Humanities Press.
Marginson, S. (1993). *Education and public policy in Australia*. Melbourne, Cambridge University Press.
Martin, G., & Brown, T. (2013). Out of the box: making space for everyday critical pedagogies. *The Canadian Geographer/Le Géographe canadien*, 57 (3): 381–88.
Martin, G., and Te Riele, K. (2011). A place-based critical pedagogy in turbulent times. In Malott, C. S., and Porfilio, B. (eds). *Critical pedagogy in the twenty-first century: a new generation of scholars* (pp. 23–52). Charlotte, IAP.
McLaren, P. (1993). Multiculturalism and the postmodern critique: towards a pedagogy of resistance and transformation. *Cultural Studies*, 7 (1): 118–46.
Pinar, W. (2009). The unaddressed 'I' of ideology critique. *Power and Education*, 1 (2): 189–200.
Polletta, F. (1998). Contending stories: narrative in social movements. *Qualitative Sociology*, 21 (4): 419–46.
Ratto, M., Boler, M., and Deibert, R. (eds). (2014). *DIY citizenship: Critical making and social media*. Cambridge, MIT Press.
Rey, R., and Nabizadeh, G. (2011). Going places: Praxis and pedagogy in Australian cultural studies. *Cultural Studies Review*, 17 (2): 49–70.
Sandlin, J., and Milam, J. (2008). "Mixing pop (culture) and politics": cultural resistance, culture jamming, and anti-consumption activism as critical public pedagogy. *Curriculum Inquiry*, 38 (3): 323–50.
Sandlin, J., Schultz, B., and Burdick, J. (eds). (2010). *Handbook of public pedagogy: education and learning beyond schooling*. New York, Routledge.
Simon, R. (1992). *Teaching against the grain: essays towards a pedagogy of possibility*. Boston, Bergin and Garvey.
Slottje, E. E. (2015). Stories tell culture, connecting identity with place: Australian cultural policy and collective creativity. *Journal of Economic and Social Policy*, 17 (1): 7.

Solorzano, D. G., and Yosso, T. J. (2002). Critical race methodology: counter-storytelling as an analytical framework for education research. *Qualitative Inquiry*, 8 (1): 23–44.

Stacey, J. (2015). The unfinished conversations of cultural studies. *Cultural Studies*, 29 (1): 43–50.

Stone-Mediatore, S. (2003). *Reading across borders: storytelling and knowledges of resistance*. London, Palgrave-Macmillan.

Turner, G. (1990). *British cultural studies: an introduction*. New York, Routledge.

Yoon, K. H. (2005). Affecting the transformative intellectual: questioning "noble" sentiments in critical pedagogy and composition. *JAC*, 25 (4): 717–59.

10 Lessons from the Site
Catastrophe and Cultural Studies

Katrina Schlunke

Cultural studies is all about practices. Those practices include signifying practices, theory as a discursive practice, and everyday practices. And they can be seen in the world through how we work, how we relate to and with the world, and how we, as teachers and students, become sets of performative practices that are assembled through the organizing structures of gender, race, and class (to name only the fewest). This is not meant to suggest that my students will come to name their own experiences and everyday practices in exactly those same terms but suggests the terrains that practices produce.

Discovering what matters to our students, taking their concerns seriously and providing the conceptual tools for them to include those experiences within learning and research is an assumed part of 'doing' cultural studies (Anderson and Schlunke 2008; Turner 2009). This approach reproduces students' experiences as potential sites for political transformation and/or sites of intervention with the thinking they are being introduced to. Creating one's life as a site of pedagogical experimentation is one of the modes of practice that keeps cultural studies as an affecting and evolving force. It is also axiomatic that we as cultural studies teachers would in turn learn from our students and practice what we teach—self-reflection and situated use of conceptual tools to make new knowledge.

The School of Life is an organization cum franchise that originated in London and has now opened in Melbourne and other places across the world. It describes itself as "devoted to developing emotional intelligence through the help of culture" (http://www.theschooloflife.com). They publish a series of accessible guides to philosophers. These are framed about the idea of different historical thinkers offering particular 'life lessons' so that the guide to Freud, for example, is called; *Life Lessons From Freud*. Their other book series, billed as the "Toolkit for Life", is made up of sets of 'how to' guides. Titles include *How to find fulfilling work*, *How to stay sane*, *How to think more about sex*, and so on. These two series with their therapeutic, philosophical, reader-centered DIY ethos echo something of what cultural studies also aspires to albeit in very different educational settings. Where university-based cultural studies would emphasize the rigorous training in the frameworks and methodologies of cultural studies which would lead to ethical investigations, *The School of Life* appears to focus upon reinterpretations of key humanities thinkers using simple self-help formulas. But their approach also throws up a heuristic challenge to the cultural studies researcher, to me, to translate some of what cultural studies offers for a generalized life, to a potential student, to the ordinary person. So using that organisation of 'life lessons' and 'how to' guides, one take on cultural studies would look like this:

Life lessons from cultural studies:
- How to recognize you are raced, sexed, and classed (among many other possibilities) and exist in a particular cultural and historical context
- How to understand how the 'everyday' is produced
- How to understand your experience as connected to the experience of others (both human and nonhuman)
- How to create a 'networked' sense of self
- How to use key conceptual tools emerging from theory and philosophy

But perhaps unlike the ever optimistic and more directly self-help tone of The School of Life, cultural studies recognizes that learning about oneself and ones experience with and through theory is not always a simple 'good'. Ruth Barcan in her search for the joy in critical theory and the effects of teaching theory to undergraduates notes the liberatory effects and positive affect of the cultural studies learning experience but also records the sense of loss experienced by some students. As Barcan (2002) notes:

> [t]his sense of loss can result from a perceived assault on religious belief (all the more powerful for being almost always tacit), or on ideals (like truth or authenticity or consensus), or on identity itself (especially the notion of an essential self). I have actually heard students waiting for a lecture turn to the current week's topic and say, 'Oh, don't tell me they're going to take that away from us too'. (345)

So perhaps we need to list some further life lessons from cultural studies that might also arise:

- How to feel uncomfortable about being 'you'
- How to lose confidence in the idea that anything about you is 'natural', 'real', or 'true'
- How to practice an intellectually rewarded scepticism of everyone and everything
- How to learn to complicate everything (even television shows you really love)

This second list may not be a wholly negative one. 'Complication' and even loss of a 'true' self might also imply renewed appreciation and the embrace of new subjectivities and cultural identities. But it might not.

The focus on the contemporary moment and knowing how you fit into it and why this moment is the way it is, is indicative of both the contemporary focus of cultural studies and its association with the past. This goes hand in hand with the constant testing of whether what we call cultural studies can continue to respond to the conditions of the contemporary moment. John Frow (2005) summed that up as, 'beyond that [*historical self-reflection*] they are questions of social purpose: does cultural studies, in Australia as elsewhere, have the capacity to articulate a 'history of the present' to which it could respond in ways that would be at once intellectually and politically productive?' (15). Frow situates that question within a particular concern with the historicization and theorization of and by cultural studies, but I would like to extend that query back into the 'history of the present'.

The 'history of the present' was the expression used by Foucault to describe his genealogical approach and the ways in which it differed from a simple interest in the past. He finishes the first chapter of *Discipline and Punish* with the flourish: 'Why [write a history of the prison]? Simply because I am interested in the past? No, if one means by that writing a history of the past in terms of the present. Yes, if one means writing the history of the present' (Foucault 1995: 31). This attention to the ways in which the present was itself a production of diverse and contingent forces also meant that we ourselves as teachers and researchers were also without a certain continuity. As Foucault wrote in his essay *Nietzsche, Genealogy, History*; "Nothing in man—not even his body is sufficiently stable to serve as the basis for self-recognition or for understanding other men" (153). And later in the same essay; "History becomes 'effective' to the degree that it introduces discontinuity into our very being—as it divides our emotions, dramatizes our instincts, multiplies our body and sets it against itself" (154). In this way the possible discomforts induced by cultural studies might be indicative of practices that will reveal the "implicit systems which determine our most familiar behavior without our knowing it" (Foucault in Simon 1971: 201).

The practices of cultural studies that will teach us about our world, cannot but also include 'ourselves' as figures produced within the same orders of discontinuities as its organizing discourses. In this way the teaching of cultural studies is a simultaneous diagnosis of 'self' and 'society' within a particular historicized moment. In this sense nothing as certain as a 'Life Lesson' might be found, but the process of doing, of practicing the 'how to' could produce not just new ideas about 'ourselves' but a deeper appreciation of the constraints and freedoms of the contemporary context.

But what are these diagnostic practices? How do we come to understand the contemporary context we are within? One summary of a cultural studies approach could be

- Identify the site and situation that you are within and some of the key words and behaviors that arise from it. (*Write the cultural setting.*)
- Recognize that that situation has other interpretations of it particularly as they pertain to histories of race, colonialism, sex, environment, and capital. (*Contextualise and connect to the means by which power and knowledge is practiced and produced.*)
- Assess your place in the world using key thinkers, not to privilege that thinking alone but to establish both the limits of your own experience and its singular possibilities. (*What existing theories does this situation call up as good to work with?*)
- Through an awareness of those contextualizing tales begin to produce your own stories that enable connections with others and new considerations of 'self'. (*What new knowledge or additions to existing knowledge emerge?*)

So if we have now established the 'why' of cultural studies and the 'how'—what does it actually look like in practice? Does it 'work'? Does it produce both 'effective histories' and 'politically productive' insights into our contemporary world? Is the researcher both undone and productively refigured?

Well aware that 'self' reflection and production involve orders of self-exposure, in what follows I attempt an embodied pedagogical experiment where some of the most taught conceptual tools of cultural studies are put to use within the site of a natural disaster to see if they work 'under duress' and to see if they can and do create new knowledge. In this way I am attempting to enact on the page the very pedagogical practices I teach while all too well aware how on so many occasions in the past my students have done it so much better and will continue to do so in the future. So let's begin.

Everyday Places

The site of this experiment in self and place is the home, my home. In October 2013 my partner's and my home (along with six others in our street in Mt Victoria in the Blue Mountains of New South Wales) was burnt down in the bushfires that engulfed many sites within the mountains and surrounding areas. Suddenly I was in the middle of an event that was a maelstrom of competing and complementary discourses and happenings previously unknown to me at least on the scale in which they were now occurring. I was also challenged to ask whether the kind of approaches outlined above would still work. What kinds of practices, meaning what conceptual tools, work with these eruptions of environmental 'catastrophe' in our everyday world? Would the kinds of approaches I ask students to take—those involving self-reflection, application and adjustment of concepts, and creation of

Lessons from the Site 169

new knowledge—work for me in this situation? Could I take the teaching and walk the talk so to speak?

Strategy 1. Writing the Cultural Setting

Perhaps you know the cover of *Writing Culture* and the picture of Stephen Tyler on the cover? James Clifford (1986) begins the book with a reflection on that image:

> Our frontpiece shows Stephen Tyler, one of this volume's contributors at work in India in 1963. The ethnographer is absorbed in writing—taking dictation? fleshing out an interpretation? recording an important observation? dashing off a poem? Hunched over in the heat, he has draped a wet cloth over his glasses. His expression is obscured. An interlocutor looks over his shoulder—with boredom? patience? amusement? (1)

Clifford goes on to say how this image of the 'hand that writes' is not the usual one for ethnography accustomed to laughing children and listening anthropologists. George Marcus also briefly referred to this image in a talk given in Australia 2014 and noted the way the ethnographer has his or her back to the informants and suggested that ethnography is now, usually, never depicted like this. Figure 10.1 shows myself writing in the mess of my home the week after it was engulfed by bushfire.

Figure 10.1 Writing on. Photograph Katrina Schlunke.

Like Stephen Tyler I am absorbed and I am hunched over, not in the heat but in the out-of-season cold that rushed over the upper mountains in the week following the fires—as if the weather after such high hot winds met our longing to be cool again. But in the aftermath of fire the interlocutors are not bored, amused locals, but melted water heaters fallen through the ceiling, twisted metal from the roof, unidentifiable stuff, and everywhere ash. The familiar made irrevocably strange. If in 1963 the writing of culture arose from listening to and translating others, perhaps the writing of culture today arises from listening with and translating between things, storms, animals, assemblages of people, and stuff that are violently thrown together and banally and incrementally sifted into each other through global capital, changing weather, and delicate webs of communication. This is the anthropocene. We are already being asked to write about very different cultural actors including the clearly nonhuman and yet their organization within the media still seems a vital thing to explore to appreciate why we think the way we do.

In the hands of the media always looking for the human interest story, bushfire becomes a story only about humans. Those who fight it, those who suffer it, and all those who are supposedly organized and governed by its unpredictable 'natural' force. For the streets of homes that the fire travels through, it is not a bushfire but a massive flame wall turned into individual house fires that wipe out our street life, our ordinary neighborliness, and yet leave some homes untouched and in our case the beginnings and end of the street unharmed, where only the middle is missing.

The obvious, ordinary, and ongoing connection between climate change and the frequency and ferocity of fires is made unsayable by this human-centered focus. To speak of that connection was according to the Australian Federal Government's Minister for Environment, Greg Hunt: "an attempt by some to misuse tragedy and suffering and hardship and nobody should do that" (Lauder 2013). Nobody. And yet, the 'some' Hunt was referring to included Professor Will Steffen of the Australian Government's defunded Climate Commission[1] who Lauder reported as saying:

> [T]o deny the influence of climate change in areas of Australia with extreme bushfires places people and property at risk. To deny and say that nothing is happening and we don't need to change anything, actually would increase risk for people and property. (Lauder 2013)

So how should one write of the climate culture produced through these representations and alongside the experience of a bushfire that was rated as 'catastrophic'; a fire having a *Fire Danger Rating* of 100+?

Cultural studies has used ethnography to think *with*, rather than *against* the subcultures of young people and minorities that had been stigmatized through successive moral panics driven by escalations in media attention. Cultural studies critiqued but also learned alongside anthropologists to seek out thick descriptions, specific use of languages, and key rituals that might be performed through dress and style to reveal the dense cultural life of overlooked groups. This culture writing would simultaneously problematize the role of the media in spectacularizing these cultures while ignoring the politics of their resistance. Can cultural studies do the same here, in this situation of fires and climate change? Can I speak with the animals and with the drying soil? Can I write the climate culture connections between the polar bears driven from their melting homes and the mostly middle-class Australians waiting in 'Disaster Recovery Centres' for their losses to be properly recorded by government agencies? No media takes up this story of shared homelessness—one forever, one temporary. Already, in the first stages of writing the cultural context of this event, the limits of its public representations can be noted as can the emergent need for a style of communication that can account for global effects and local intensities. At the same time the emplaced process of stopping and recording provides both the means of creating a bearable story of an event that is partially unspeakable and a way of recreating routines and everyday narratives that quite directly allow for an 'ordinary' life to be rebuilt. Learning from this new site requires first a way of writing this site, and in my mimetic reproduction of Stephen Tyler I find both the limits and the unexpectedly affecting force of 'writing culture'.

Strategy 2. Contextualize and Connect to the Means by Which Power and Knowledge Is Practiced and Produced

The common language associated with this event is that of 'disaster', 'emergency', and increasingly 'catastrophe'. A 'State of Emergency' was declared by the New South Wales Premier which, among many other things, allows firefighters to evict residents and demolish fire-affected buildings if necessary. 'Disaster Assistance' was made available by the federal government which includes payments to $1000) to individuals, concessional loans to small businesses, and financial assistance to local and government authorities (Australian Government Disaster Assist 2011).

With a Fire Danger Rating listed as 'catastrophic'—a category that organizes the various emergency response groups, particularly the fire services and police into ways of acting in this context—forms of action take specific shape. One example of this would be that under 'catastrophic' conditions there is an emphasis on evacuation over assistance, among other things. Catastrophe is also a term the insurance agencies use: "Catastrophe events are large natural or man-made disasters that cause a significant number of claims in a region" (Insurance Council of Australia 2015).

As one part of the response to the fire, which almost always was referred to as 'coordinated', several charities came into play, most obviously the Red Cross and the Salvation Army. The Salvation Army and the Blue Mountains City Council launched public appeals and money from people right across Australia was collected. The Mayoral Fund raised over $3 million and the

Salvation Army over $11 million and each of these distributed those funds according to their own formulas. It was a sudden and shocking shift in subjectivity to be asked whether we would like something from the charities that we might usually have given to rather than taken from. And many people did not accept the offers knowing that their insurance would eventually come through. There were also incredible gifts of love and money from friends and strangers that were of inestimable assistance, psychologically and financially, and that simultaneously restored a space to become 'ordinary' again. But in between the work of the large appeals and the actions of friends a category of public charity that organizes life in unexpected and penetrating ways emerged.

We were in the city, away from our neighbors' place where we were staying when the Johnson & Johnson care package was delivered to each house and/or wherever a fire victim was said to be living. Inside this large box are band aids, tampons, baby powder, soap, facial and body products, and tissues and skin cleaning rounds. We were also absent when 10 boxes of Mt Franklin spring water were delivered. Bottled water. Bottled water—that magical object that simultaneously saves lives and kills waterways. Bottled water for whom? *Where?* Weeks later people in the Philippines struck by Typhoon Yolanda will hold up signs asking for food and water. While here, in a country with a strong infrastructure, I am shocked that they, whoever they are, think we might be living without water. Or is it a strange kind of advertising—*catastrophe capitalism*?

Then bags from Penrith City Council come. Ten packs of Maggi Noodles and long-life milk. Perhaps this is not charity but an emergency response ration. How do these things differ or stay the same when one is a ration and the other a gift? And just before Christmas we got hampers. Celebratory hampers. The difference between a hamper and a ration is the inclusion of cheezels and candy canes and long-life fruitcake. The hampers are the worst actually. By Christmas we have a kind of local caseworker who works out of the 'Bushfire Response Office' and he tells us that one hamper filled with very bad food was 'hand packed' for us. Looking down at the beans and noodles is a horrible confrontation with one's own class and taste snobberies. Can't he see we are two queer gourmands? Couldn't they? And somehow this food has been put together by companies and individual donations and then 'hand packed' for us. Of course we back down from our efforts to refuse.

Stuck with this excess we are told about the charity assisting refugees who are living on the notorious 'bridging visas' (which means living without access to any form of social security and are unable in most situations to take work). The organizer of that charity assures us that they would welcome foodstuffs and any other household or clothing items. And so we become one link in a circle of stuff that we hope eventually finds a proper place for these emotionally freighted, banal foods. And what does it mean for us to be handing our charity on to another charity? We simultaneously feel fraudulent for failing to be so needy that beans and noodles are not needed, and failures for refusing this potential moment of deeper connection with those who do regularly live on beans and noodles. And given we are miserable anyway, we feel an even stronger need for good wine. No one donates alcohol and yet everyone we speak to who has lost their home talks of the absolute need of it.

Somewhere some folk have heard that there are two 'ladies' and so we are sent more specific kinds of pamper kits. Kits with essential oils and kits called 'Tender Love' with hair product and specialized moisturizers including one for the neck and one that helps your cuticles. There is even an alternative deodorant made from ash which really doesn't work very well if you associate cleanliness with being able to see the usual color of your skin. We could of course walk back to the site of our home and scoop up as much ash as we wish, but we do not feel inclined. We also receive manicure sets, in pink. We keep one and pass the other on. These are semipublic charity gifts. Gifts with enough gender specificity to qualify as personal rather than corporate or government, and these are small companies that are kind. And they are fun. They bring a kind of ridiculousness to the occasion and an order of comforting, sensual pleasure. But to sustain this kind of attention we have to be particular kind of lady, and a particular kind of victim. Our order of docility arises as Foucault said it would, from partitioned space in this case a combination of media spectacle and literal enclosure. We keep asking as do our neighbors and friends in other sorts of way; *'Who have we become in this space?'* For the first time in my life I have become imagined as a 'lady'. A lady who manicures, uses excessive personal products, and has a deep concern for personal hygiene. Or at least a glance at my bathroom might now suggest that.

Spatially we become an exclusive neighbourhood. Months after the fire we still have signs asking (nicely) "Local Residents only please". This is to ward off the voyeurs. Already Winnmalee (where the biggest fires have hit) has reported that two busloads have been seen and stopped, and 'Marjorie' up our street has seen one bus come along our street to which she made rude signs. She showed me these rude signs but 'Marjorie' being an older woman may have looked as if she was encouraging the bus or perhaps sending the sign that we were all ok as her 'rude sign' were two emphatic thumbs going sideways—something even with my vast cultural studies training I could not translate. We cannot even walk our usual tracks, the usual reason for living in the mountains in its tangled geography with forest reserves and national parks. It becomes a fineable offence to walk even the very well established old road tracks which are in fact clearer and safer than ever before. But someone somewhere has said there could be a risk and so there is. A risk from a tree, from something the bushfire left behind that hasn't yet been spotted but could occur.

One of the "Local Residents Only" signs sits below a roadside sign warning of kangaroos. This juxtaposition of kangaroo and local heaves into view the space of Indigenous sovereignty and Indigenous histories of care and transformation of bush where fire was the key productive medium. What would the fire say? What do we say the fire is—local or outsider? And I think about the 'intervention'[2] in the Northern Territory and the huge, "WARNING—Prescribed Area" signs erected outside Indigenous communities and of course they could have used signs like that for us but of course they didn't. We are mostly white-ish, mostly middle class victims—innocent. We are already or about to become 'battlers' (in the romanticized Australian sense), and most of all *recovered*. We are in recovery almost before we have been frightened. And yet for many the fear was not the fire but the prolonged engagement with loss that continued long after the fire itself. Loss of surety, loss of the stuff that enables one to be middle class, write, make music, run a backyard coffee shop—whatever people did in our street until that moment. And this major unsettlement perhaps recalls the first 'settlement'. This sign asking where are the 'real' locals? Where *are* the Gunungurra and Dharug peoples? In an immediate experience organised around the 'protection' of us shown in the delivery of assorted 'stuff' and the warding off of unauthorized visitors I also catch a glimpse of the power of state and private 'goodness' to effect an intimate emotional organization of us. Who benefits from our docility? What kinds of subjects have we become in this charitable discourse and with what effects?

Strategy 3. What Existing Theories Does This Situation Call Up as Good to Work With?

What thinking does a site of confused stuff evoke? I notice the ways in which old and new stuff, natured and cultured stuff have become amalgams of each other. Some are embedded, growing things, like the aluminum fragment from the louvre window frames that has blown out to land on a nearby ironbark and is growing into the tree while the new shoots of that burnt tree are growing out around it. Others are more the observed rearrangements between elements. The collapsed chimney that has been burned into the color scheme of the surrounding bush—an orange and black natured culture.

Other things have formed new objects. Two of my mother's 'best cups' are recognizable but have been supplemented by melted glass from the wine glasses they once sat next to, to become neither cup nor glass but some new event. The cups were part of my share of her possessions when they were split up 'among the girls' when she died. Best cups were what country mothers kept in something called a china cabinet and bought out for afternoon tea when visitors came. And now they are cracked and a black ash has been burned into the glaze and a solid lump of shiny glass sticks to the side of one looking like a block of iceberg. Together wine glass and teacup, dinner and afternoon tea, mother's thing and my thing, her tea drinking, my wine drinking have become another order of being. Looking at it I know I am one form of being among many. And I see Bryant's (2014) wilderness ontology where nature and culture are undivided and the "rogue object", that is the fire in this case, modifies the usual relations of assemblages, to forge new kinds of relations and new kinds of imaginings (210). His work reminds me of other thinking that reorders the place of the human in the environment and revivifies the material. That thinking seems like simple description in this setting.

After the fire, after we saw what was left, after we went down and came back again, and after our friends invited us to stay in their studio down the end of our street, I had time to be with what remained of our house, our home. The first week was beautiful weather. Weather is always beautiful when you have nothing left to be threatened by. The fourth consecutive month without rain, or the unseasonable heat and the high winds were nothing to me for a moment and it was so quiet in our street. The four houses immediately in front of ours, our three neighbors, and a weekender whom we didn't know, had been burnt to the ground. A neighbor four houses along on our side had also been burnt out and in between are homes untouched by fire and yet surrounded by the blackened bush. We are all cast into the eerie quietness of a street without its dogs, humans, or cars. No one had died in our street, no humans at least, but it has lost its verticality. The whole landscape looks winded as if punched from above with roofs and walls flattened or puffed out in strange places, everything vulnerable or implacably ruined. The day after the fire there was a report of looting or perhaps it is standard practice but no one was allowed into the street who didn't have direct business here, and so we became for a week or so a 'gated community'. We were protected from the voyeurs and they were protected from the sight of our silence.

Did I say it was beautiful weather? Sitting in a ruined home writing may sound strange but it wasn't. And writing does something to us at the level of physiology. It seems to organize the nervous system and quietens the adrenals that pound away. Our house had always been about what you could see through it. The tree, the bush, the kangaroos that were just outside the windows, and could be heard through walls and doors as they went about their business at night. So sitting in a ruined room without windows, with light ash falling from the breeze doesn't seem that strange. Outside was often inside our home. The breeze picks up and I wonder about the roof iron falling in further but then I think of the heat, that incredible heat that melted the windows and that we felt for only about an hour in reality and then so intensely on our final run out to the fire truck and I am sure there are only two states—ash that flies away and molten forms that will never, ever move again. A kookaburra is making its prelaugh gurgle but no cackle comes forth. Nobody to warn off, and no ordinary life of the bush to declare to us humans. Fragments of book pages occasionally lift up and for a moment I think it is an animal but in all of this house I have only seen a small ant that stayed for a moment on this small fold-up table. I look across to where the bookshelves were on both sides of this room and wonder what books were what. Even their approximate positions are now lost in the heaps of ash—no poetic single pages, no words at all. When I pull back a clump the pages are always white, slates wiped clean. What chemical reaction explains this? Is text more volatile than paper? The kookaburra has flown into view but still that strangled gurgling, no laugh. Tony, another neighbor, is back on his block below ours, continuing to build his house, the beginnings of which were untouched by the fire. And a train is moving along the ridge as ever.

These acts of descriptions, this very ordinary kind of writing has a new intention in relation to a world where the weather and things need to be accounted for along with the human. A way into that world and its systems and histories and interconnected stuff and more stuff might be by seeing it, describing it, and going on describing it more and more. The flat ontology of new materialism suggests humans and objects can be as important as each other. Or in Bryant's (2011) words—we are all objects and all "entangled objects" (16). Decentering the human was already done here. Instead the alliance between electricity, weather, and environment that we call bushfire exposed and expunged the place of the human. The fire figured the human as a generalized creator of climate extremities and as such was both centered and dismissed. The other objects in the house with me are now either to be nostalgically recalled to their rightful place as things that gained their meaning in relation to what my partner and I had done to them, their use, their provenance, their capacity to evoke in us love, remembrance, laughter—and they could be their changed selves. Their capacity to inspire difference, to become unrecognizable, to figure in a life well beyond my representations seemed so very obvious. But how do we give those things beyond representation their representational due? Asking that question then leads me to ask of some new materialism more broadly—how do we write post-representationally? Write not as a human but as a one aspect of a cup-cum-glass? Perhaps it is simply important to signal the intention. This is after all an attempt to try out the "how to" of cultural studies where our own situation is one of the sites we learn from through description and theoretical techniques and so make of a situation a pedagogical experiment. And this experiment has arrived at a point requiring both material and semiotic tools as so many sites have before, whether they are memorials, youth cultures, or regional communities.

The Pedagogical Practice

The sites from which we will teach will change. The sites that teach us will change. Taking account of the environment in extremis and through the more than human might challenge what we have traditionally seen as the great pedagogical strength of cultural studies—to take seriously the 'ordinary' as revealed through the qualitative studies, the groundbreaking ethnographies of urban, immigrant, and youthful lives. But it is probably worth remembering that those Birmingham School studies began with dismissed lives that were also spectacularized lives. In a related but nonetheless different way, our means of considering global climate change, forces like the weather, and the human and more than human will also need to think about the moments in which climate is spectacularized as well as its everyday banalities. Perhaps I was always going to say this, but I think the practices of cultural studies allow us to teach accounts of emerging worlds, or realities coming into being. Even a very simplified version of a cultural studies practice, vis, *write the cultural setting, identify the ways in which power and knowledge is produced there, consider what existing theories and thinking are good to work with*, and finally, *think how your site which is also your experience might change that existent thinking*; will provide a way to act with the world. These practices can still account for the 'history of the present'. In just the same way, what we teach changes with the experiences our students bring into the tutorial room because to teach is to translate existing knowledge and see it transformed in its new relation with others. So we remain in play with the new conditions producing us in this moment.

The model of teaching I am imagining here still assumes the capacity to create a tutorial space where an order of trust is developed between students and where there is time and space to practice the collaborative, usually text-based, critical readings of concepts so that everyone can see how differently particular concepts work within peoples' lives. This is best done face-to-face and best done over a sustained period of time. In my current institution the shift has been toward shorter and shorter semesters and with face-to-face time replaced with online stimuli and online surveys of what the student have encountered. That teaching is an embodied and affective experience, could once be assumed and if that changes entirely then very different ideas of what we could ask of students and ourselves as teachers will have to emerge.

My attempt in this piece was to conspicuously perform the kinds of cultural studies practices I teach. I wanted to offer a basic 'how to' do cultural studies example. You will see that in my case the writing in many instances became the description which I hope also became the explanation of my cultural moment. I know others would have done this differently, as of course this site shared by so many, will give rise to multiple ways of thinking. Cultural studies is attuned to the diverse conditions that produce every new site while appreciating some continuing and intractable politics.

Some of the biggest global challenges are those that emerge from considerations of environmental change and human relations organized around the manufacture and exchange of 'stuff', material and emotional. This chapter attempted to talk with fire and burnt remains, to translate key cultural studies research methods and to rethink ideas of charity and suffering as potential social collaborators. The exercise of writing this chapter taught me all over again that cultural studies pedagogy is not just a practice that enables the writing of the present but is always a practice of the Self.

Notes

1. The Australian Government Climate Commission was formed in 2011 under former Gillard Labour government, and was abolished in 2013 under the then new Abbott conservative Liberal government. Following this, the Commission relaunched as the Climate Council as an independent, not-for-profit organization funded through public donation.
2. Formally known as the Northern Territory National Emergency Response, the Intervention was a response from the then Howard conservative Liberal government in 2007 to claims of widespread sexual abuse of children in Aboriginal communities. The 'intervention' involved the formation of a military operation, Operation Outreach, and the deployment of 600 Australian Defence Force personnel. The Intervention has been heavily criticized, not least for racial vilification, including criticism from the United Nations for the subsequent suspension of the Racial Discrimination Act that the Intervention provoked.

References

Anderson, N., and Schlunke, K. (eds). (2008). *Cultural theory in everyday practice*. London, Oxford University Press.
Barcan, R. (2002). Problems without solutions: teaching theory and the politics of hope. *Continuum: Journal of Media and Cultural Studies*, 16 (3): 343–56.
Bryant, L. (2011). *The democracy of objects*. Ann Arbor, Open Humanities Press.
Bryant, L. (2014). *Onto-cartography: an ontology of machines and media*. Edinburgh, Edinburgh University Press.
Commonwealth of Australia. (2011). *Australian Government disaster assist*. Accessed June 2015, http://www.disasterassist.gov.au/Pages/default.aspx.
Clifford, J., and Marcus, G. (1986). *Writing culture: the poetics and politics of ethnography*. Berkeley, University of California Press.
Foucault, M. (1971). *Nietzsche, genealogy, history*. Paris, Presses Universitaires de France.
Foucault, M. (1995). *Discipline and punish*. New York, Vintage Books.
Frow, J. (2005). Australian cultural studies: theory, story, history. *Australian Humanities Review*, 37: 15.
Insurance Council of Australia. (2015). *Catastrophe events and the community*. Accessed June 2015, http://www.insurancecouncil.com.au/issue-submissions/issues/catastrophe-events.
Lauder, S. (2013). *Climate Council links NSW bushfires to climate change. The World Today*. Australian Broadcasting Commission, October 25. Accessed June 2015, http://www.abc.net.au/news/2013-10-25/climate-council-links-bushfires-to-climate-change/5046164.
Simon, A. (1971). A conversation with Michel Foucault. Partisan Review, 38 (2): 192–201.
Turner, G. (2009). Cultural studies 101: canonical, mystificatory and elitist?' *Cultural Studies Review*, 15 (1): 175–87.

11 Women Who Surf
Female Difference, Intersecting Subjectivities and Cultural Pedagogies

Rebecca Olive

Surfing has shifted from the margins to the mainstream, with millions of people now participating at organized and recreational levels globally (Booth 2004; McGloin 2005; Surfing Australia 2012; Waitt 2008). This widespread participation includes a growing number of women who paddle out into surfbreaks. However, despite women's participation as surfers becoming increasingly visible, the cultural representation and participation of women is often downplayed or cast in highly sexualized ways. Particularly at a competitive level, women's achievements and skills as surfers remain largely defined in terms of existing performative and cultural understandings attached to male surfers (Ford and Brown 2006; Olive, McCuaig and Phillips 2015). The continued marginalization and sexualization of women who surf is well documented by scholars in Australia, Britain, New Zealand, the United States, and Brazil (Booth 2001; Comer 2010; Evers 2004, 2010; Henderson 1999, 2001; Heywood 2008; Knijnik, Horton and Cruz 2010; Olive 2013a, 2015; Olive et al. 2015; Roy 2013; Roy and Caudwell 2014; Stedman 1997), although research on women and surfing has tended toward a focus on the representations of women (predominantly in surf media) and how these representations mediate the positions of women who surf within wider surfing culture. This research has argued that while changes in the attitudes of women toward participation in surfing are important, until men include women in their understandings of surfing as an activity, women will continue to struggle for recognition and acceptance (Booth 2001; Ford and Brown 2006; Henderson 1999, 2001; Stedman 1997).

More recent studies have begun to explore gendered power relations operating among everyday surfers *in the surf*, taking into account women's understandings and experiences of the surfing hierarchy (Comer 2010; Fendt and Wilson 2012; Knijnik et al. 2010; Olive 2013a, 2015; Olive et al. 2015; Roy and Caudwell 2014; Spowart, Burrows and Shaw 2010; Waitt 2007, 2008). By focusing on lived experience rather than media representation, these studies have moved away from understanding women as marginalized, to consider the ways that women actively negotiate surfing cultural power relations.

This approach to the consideration of the gendered power relations in surfing culture resonates with the theoretical work of Michel Foucault. Foucault argued that relationships—to people, places, histories, cultures, and contexts—are key to the operation of power, in particular to the ways "in which the individual establishes his relation to the rule and recognizes himself as obliged to put it into practice" (Foucault 1986: 27). Foucault would not be surprised with the recent research showing that relationships among surfers—women *and* men (despite the gendered language applied by Foucault)—are central to understandings and experiences of surfing, as well as how surfers are able to negotiate their individual connections to surfing and to other surfers, in order to make decisions about the kind of surfer they want to be. This approach is different to earlier research in which surfing power relations were largely explained in terms of women being defined by (and against) male-dominated norms—that is, in terms of how men and male norms work to frame women's experiences. More recent research has begun to consider, for instance, how women form culturally significant relationships with other women, and how these relationships intersect with other aspects of female surfing subjectivities (Roy 2013; Spowart et al. 2010).

However, consideration of everyday surfing relationships between men and women beyond theorizations of masculine hegemony remains limited, with little engagement with how women's perspectives and contributions to surfing impact on men who surf and the culture of surfing more broadly. With the significant growth in the numbers of women participating in surfing globally, failing to account for the influence and authority that women possess within surfing culture limits the understandings that might be drawn of surfing as a highly gendered, culturally mediated, and learned activity. In this chapter, I pay attention to the possibility that women who surf not only influence the other women they encounter, but also the men. My argument builds on research about women and surfing that understands power as relational, potential, and productive, complementing existing work to contribute to a fuller understanding of the dynamics within which the woman as surfer operates. In particular, it follows Foucault's suggestion that even marginalized individuals are able to wield power by making individual choices relating to their own behavior and subjectivity (Foucault 1980).

Engaging with processes of relational and embodied pedagogy, this chapter will explore the ways women influence the experience of the surf, including changing normative understandings of women who surf. Using pedagogy as a central concept for explaining this influence, I seek to extend the notion of pedagogical exchange from something that is intentional (Tinning 2010) to a form of teaching and learning that is implicit and occurs as a result of difference and relationships, working to disrupt cultural knowledges and cultural inequality even without meaning to. In this sense, a bodily knowledge is predicated, whereby:

> The body ... becomes a site for the production of knowledge, feelings, emotions and history, all of which are central to subjectivity [yet] the body cannot be thought of as a contained entity; it is in constant contact with others.
>
> (Probyn 2003: 290)

Our understandings and behaviors are learned through the cultural and subjective relationships individuals have with people and contexts (Foucault 1988). My use of Foucault reveals the feminist cultural studies positioning of this discussion, underscored as it is by its focus on the possible effects that relationships to others have on how we each come to be affected and formed as individuals.

Both feminism and cultural studies take this activist position to research, requiring researchers to privilege the lived realities and material conditions of the people they are researching in order to uncover a possibility for something beyond what currently exists. This mode of research also demands that researchers remain active in improving conditions for those whom culture constrains. However, while imagining potential for change at a cultural, subjective, and embodied level is fundamental for this sort of (activist) research, this approach to research—to the practice of feminist cultural studies—remains difficult to enact (Olive In Press; Olive and Thorpe 2011). As a form of research that has at its core the changing of attitudes, behaviors, and ways of knowing for women (and others) at a social and cultural level, this is research that draws on concerns for the practices of subjective and cultural pedagogies. This chapter will argue that the experiences and negotiations of surfbreaks and lineups encountered by women who surf in Byron Bay, on the north coast of New South Wales, Australia, provide an example of how stealthy and 'difficult to argue against' cultural change is possible, and how these experiences present as culturally learned and mediated activities (Heywood 2008; Nealon 2008).

Cultural Power Relations and Female Difference: Thinking Beyond Hegemony in the Surf

This discussion will draw on my research about women who surf in Australia, in which a series of interviews revealed how the subjectivities of a group of women who surf intersect with the subjectivities of various others, as well as cultures and places. The project that provides the basis for this chapter explored how a number of women who surf in a small coastal town in Australia understand, experience, and negotiate the male-dominated culture of surfing. As a woman and a longboard surfer, I had a very different experience of surfing than that I was able to locate in most mainstream media,[1] and so my research responded to the disconnection between the idea that located women as marginalized and sexualized, and my own experiences in the surfbreak, where I felt included and encouraged (Olive 2013a).

Methodologically, I drew on Elspeth Probyn's (1993) suggestion that we "think the social through the self" (3), which allowed me to use my existing identity as a woman who lived and surfed in Byron Bay on the far north coast of New South Wales to take a participatory research approach that focused on 'everyday' surfing culture. To do this, I used three methods: I went surfing as much as I could, and participated in the culture of surfing in Byron Bay; I conducted 18 interviews with 11 local women, whose ideas and insights ended up becoming the core of the project; and I published a blog and participated in the surf blogging community (Olive 2013a, 2013b). My blog had a cultural rather than academic focus in that it was written for surfers in a language and style that encouraged engagement and feedback.

Participatory methods, such as the one I deployed in this project, always have a heightened ethical concern relating to engaging with participants (Olive and Thorpe 2011; Probyn 1993; St. Pierre 1997). These ethical concerns were enhanced by my own subjectivity, which was already implicated in the community and culture I was researching. I was researching with people I already knew and surfed with; these were familiar people, friends and acquaintances I encountered in other aspects of my life around town. Researching using these methods allowed me to think the social through myself by drawing on my subjectivity to access and make sense of surfing culture in my own community while providing tools through which to centralize the experiences and perspectives of others.

Thinking about power relations as always in process, my research about women who surf revealed that while gendered power relations in the surf are certainly male dominated, the women I interviewed felt differentiated but not marginalized, with this providing a range of implications for understanding experiences of surfing (Olive 2013a, In Press; Olive et al. 2015). Women's positioning was not necessarily linked to heterosexual interest in their bodies (although this was certainly a common experience) so much as it was linked to the ways their female-ness was seen as different to the male majority. As is common in many other physical cultures, the women I spoke with felt as though they were seen as 'female surfers', not 'surfers':

GEORGIE: Just like, well it's just that, um, just coming down to that it's not just your surfing. Like, that a girl could surf better than them, but she won't take that natural place in the lineup out there. (…) I s'pose there's guys that would say that, that, that that happens to them out there as well. I'm sure it does. (…) I just think it would probably happen to a girl more.

* * *

RENEE: (…) yeah there's still the less respect anyway, in the surf. 'Cause you could put an amazing, male surfer and a female together and the guy's always gonna get more praise. Like he's gonna get more praise from men. Because obviously [women are] the minority in the water.

Regardless of how amazing a woman is in the surf—of the talent and sophistication of technique she demonstrates—men's surfing remains more highly valued on a cultural level because, obviously, the bodies and presence women are different to the male majority. Often this differentiation results in men excluding women; however, women are active in these processes as well. For example, during our first interview, Skye explained how she avoided surfing in places where the guys were dominant and overbearing in the lineup, yet in the second interview she admitted that she judged other women's surfing performances by criteria already established by men:

SKYE (INTERVIEW 1): (…) I mean I, when I was on my shortboard and I used to surf Tallows and that just turned me off totally. No-one was friendly, no-one talked to you. Just the tension, um, totally went against, what I felt, even at that stage I didn't realise it, what surfing should be. So I almost wonder, like, what it is that these guys do? (…) I really hate it when the ego gets brought into surfing, and when I find myself dragged into that.

SKYE (INTERVIEW 2): (…) I find it kind of weird actually when I see girls surfing really aggressively, 'cause it's such a male trait. But I do think men look at it like, 'Oh yeah. You know, she surfs'. And even I found myself being judgemental if I'm watching a girl shortboarding in a competition thinking, 'Oh, that's not as good as the guys.'

Skye was aware that she does not want to see women surfing 'aggressively' like male surfers, yet she admittedly continued to locate this style as the benchmark for 'good' surfing. Her subjective and cultural understandings and values were complex and contradictory, shifting and changing depending on what aspects of surfing we were discussing, how one should conduct oneself in the water, or how one should perform surfing on a wave. In regulating her own female understandings of 'good' surfing, Skye validates and perpetuates the dominance of the most powerful group—the male/masculine majority—by accepting existing performative norms as the most valid and authentic.

Gordon Tait (2000) argues that existing norms become so entrenched and implicit that those who fit them best are able to manipulate other people—people outside of the norm—to become active and complicit in regulating their own behavior:

> A specific group of individuals … are identified as the target population, and then various sets of knowledges … are brought to bear upon this object, with the intention of both modifying its conduct and recruiting persons into their own self-modification. (145)

Drawing on Tait helps explain how women who surf "are persuaded in various ways … to do work on [themselves], work that can be understood in terms of an array of different practices" (160). In this way, power relations are dynamic, but also difficult to define as dominating or resistant in any given situation. Instead, as Foucault suggests, power should always be considered as a potential and productive relationship between subjects involved (Pringle 2005):

> If power were never anything but repressive, if it never did anything but say no, do you really think one would be brought to obey it? What

makes power so good, what makes it accepted, is simply the fact that it doesn't weigh on us as a force that says no, but that it produces and traverses things, it induces pleasure, forms of knowledge, produces discourses. It needs to be considered as a productive network which runs through the whole social as a body, much more than a negative instance whose focus is repression.

(Foucault 1980: 119)

Foucault (1983) defined a relationship of power as an action designed to guide or direct "the possible field of action of others" (221). Within a relationship of power there is always the potential for resistance, as without the possibility of resistance, there is no power (Markula and Pringle 2006). Such a conception decentralizes power and conceives of it as a kind of network or web with multiple places where freedom may be wielded.

For example, while Sophie recognizes the power relations at play in the surf as 'politics', she chooses her own approach to engaging with these. Even more significantly, she recognizes that power relations are something that all surfers must negotiate, not just women:

SOPHIE: (…) I believe it's politics, always politics. I don't care what anyone says. You can, you can be a new girl off the block, you can be a new guy off the block, and you can get that one surf. But after that, its politics, and its always gonna be politics, and its, how you play the game and, you know if you behave and, um, etcetera, etcetera. Yeah. Its, it's really, it is, no matter what anyone says and I don't like to think about it, it's quite complicated. I'm sure it is, its just, politics. Um, but you know, I, I don't wanna be, I, I'm different now. I don't really wanna be part of any of it anymore. I just, um, I really just want to surf …

This admission from Sophie resonates with suggestions from Nikolas Rose (1996a), that processes of resistance are not necessarily conscious or explicit, but that agency is already always implicit in how we negotiate the never-ceasing intersection of our individual subjectivities with those around us. Also, it implies that we are not necessarily working toward one version of 'self', of being a surfer. Since the decisions surfers make about cultural norms and knowledges have a range of influences outside of surfing culture as well as within it, individual surfers take different approaches to negotiating their responses to the power relations they encountered. In the interviews for this research, I found that while some women sometimes chose to explicitly respond to their differentiation as female surfers, they were also aware that the existing and normative behaviors in surfing are "by no means the only option" (Tait 2000: 167) for becoming a surfer (Olive 2013a, In Press). In this way, relationships were key to the cultural processes of pedagogy and change.

The Pedagogical Potential of Intersecting Subjectivities

To explore the implicit potential of these relationships, I am borrowing the notion of 'intersecting subjectivities' from Nikolas Rose (1996a) who imagines these relationships as ongoing intersections between people who "live their lives in a constant movement across different practices that address them in different ways" (140). With so many different options in everyday lived experiences, Rose highlights the specific and contextual nature of power networks by asking us to consider "in relation to what demands and what forms of authority" do we know the world (139)? Put another way, how do we identify the voices of authority that influence our knowledge, behavior, and choices? Rose explores how and why we identify social and cultural 'problems' (such as the differentiation of women in surfing cultures) by considering the ways that we are governed or constrained in context. Rose argues that those who govern us—those who regulate what is normative, right, or moral—must maintain a performance of their own ideals, which in turn limits their own possibilities for difference and change. Like women, men must become complicit in regulating their own behavior (Tait 2000). Yet Rose (1996a) also highlights that in our daily existence we may encounter a number of these performances, many of which are conflicting and are thus questioned through our own attempts at negotiating the inconsistencies. By thinking about our surfing knowledges only in terms of the specificity of relationships in the surf, it is difficult to account for how we are subjects in a range of contexts every day, all of which contribute to the complexity of our subjectivities and how we know surfing. The diverse and multifaceted nature of our subjectivities helps us identify voices of authority in one context by drawing on our experiences from multiple other contexts.

Let me use the subjective experience of my research process as an example. I am a woman, surfer, researcher, teacher, colleague, writer, sister, daughter, lover, local, stranger, friend, and so on. But the often conflicting histories and requirements of these roles led me to ask questions of some aspects of my cultural worlds—of my female-ness in surfing culture in particular—which has been highlighted by my feminist politics and research, leading me to question why women are treated differently in the surf and beyond. This in turn is tempered by my personal knowledge of and relationships to local men who surf, all of which helps me critique existing research about women and surfing, based on my surfing experiences (Olive and Thorpe 2011). My understandings and experiences of various contexts including the beach, surfbreaks, Byron Bay, Brisbane, my blogging community, my relationships, my research topic, the university campus, conferences, teaching, friends, parties, exhibitions, mainstream media, surf media, and so on, each impact on the ways I make subjective sense of the others. Being aware of all of this helps me locate normalizing voices of authority privileged in each context, and to make choices about how I respond to each of them. In this understanding, negotiations of various power relations are implicit in the ways we navigate daily experiences, and are dependent upon the formation of the context in which we find ourselves.

Thinking about surfing (or any physical culture) as relational is important given that, as Nikolas Rose argues, "people do not exist in the form of thought" (1996a: 140). Instead, we are always moving through and making sense of time, space, and relationships, encountering a range of subjectivities that are very often different than our own. For surfers, being culturally different can be a form of cultural and historical transgression and thus treated as a 'mistake'. Yet contextual and cultural 'mistakes' can be productive pedagogical moments, encouraging subjects into considerations of their own ways of knowing and being. Clifton Evers (2004) argues that surfing experiences include a pedagogy of "fucking up" (35), where surfers learn lessons about surfing culture and performances through feelings of shame, pride, and fear (see also Evers 2006; Probyn 2004). These feelings have largely been incited by historical understandings of normalized and authentic ways of surfing, but it is important to remember that while men are the ones upholding and maintaining the status quo by regulating the surfing behaviors of women, they are also under pressure to uphold and maintain their own participation as surfers (Evers 2004, 2006, 2008). That is, those who are required to regulate and maintain established normative and authentic surfing practices, are "themselves called upon to play their part in the making up of others and to inculcate them into a certain relation to themselves" (Rose 1996a: 139). Men who surf also have to maintain a performance of the ideals they wish to uphold, or face similar cultural differentiation (Booth 2001; Evers 2008; Waitt and Warren 2008).

Of course, this form of pedagogy is different to the intentional pedagogies of a classroom, where processes of teaching and learning find articulation through a teacher (Tinning 2010). Instead embodied, relational pedagogies are implicit and often unintended. For example, while some women sometimes choose to explicitly respond to their differentiation as female surfers by acting like the guys, they are also aware that the existing and normative behaviors in surfing are "by no means the only option" (Tait 2000: 167) for becoming a surfer:

GEORGIE: 'Cause I'd hate to do [something] and then have people go 'Oh, there goes that girl who just keeps, you know, paddling up the inside and blah, blah, blah, and she's so annoying', like, I'd hate to think that I'd turn into one of *those* surfers.

* * *

SOPHIE: (...) Well, you know, you just gotta be determined. You know, just try and stay really calm and be really rational about it and, try not to, you know, cross over to the dark side really. I mean, once, once you, walk those, those steps, once you start to be like them then, you're like them then aren't you.

* * *

NOELLA: ... I think when these guys do and say these stupid things most of the time they are just looking for a reason to talk to you. From now on lets just be flattered and not offended (blog comment, posted under Olive, 2009a).

Georgie, Sophie, and Noella move among the surfing cultural power relations in the surf and online, using their cultural knowledge to negotiate the ways they are differentiated and the kinds of behavior they want to avoid emulating. Yet by taking the approach of 'not wanting to be one of *those* surfers', these women embody new readings of the pedagogies they encounter in the surf. In the surf, women like Georgie and Sophie were not explicitly attempting to change the gendered cultural power relations that surrounded them. Instead they moved among them, using their cultural understandings and experiences to negotiate and respond to the ways that they came to be differentiated, and to the kinds of behavior they wanted to avoid emulating. Like Georgie, Sophie wanted to "try not to, you know, cross over to the dark side really. I mean, once, once you, walk those, those steps, one you start to be like them then, you're like them then aren't you". These women adopted an approach to defining how *not* to behave in the surf by taking a self-determined account of their differentiation. That is, power is a relational process through which it can be maintained and/or transformative (Nealon 2008; Tait 2000).

Strategies such as 'being calm' and 'being flattered and not offended' are important in negotiating the multitude of experiences women have in the surf, acting as a subversive response to increasingly "insidious" (Nealon 2008: 71) processes of power that use resistance against itself, to limit its potential. Jeffrey Nealon (2008) explains that "as power becomes increasingly invested in the minute details of our lives, so too have our modes of resistance become increasingly subtle and intense" (108). The approaches of women who surf that I observed were often considered patient and appropriate to the context of the surfbreak and the power relations operating. While explicitly resistant and disruptive behavior can often lead to the evolution and renewal of the dynamics of power in a given setting, so too can more subtle disruptions: disruptions that are not necessarily recognized as such, but are always in process, always becoming. In understanding these ever-present and evolving relationships in the surf, the women I interviewed were able to draw on the multidimensionality of their identities to make decisions about how and when they responded to instances of differentiation and to how they became surfers, in turn contributing to the culture of surfing at their local breaks.

Subjectivities, Ethics, and Cultural Change

As Rose (1996a) highlights in his discussion of "voices of authority", subjectivities have influence over other subjectivities. Our words and actions are observed and experienced in relation to the subjectivities of the people around us, intersecting with their own understandings, knowledges, and experiences. Historically, the voices of authority at surfbreaks have been consistently masculine, despite (or perhaps because of) the various other social and cultural contexts male surfers pass through each day. This is surfing as "the fantasized last frontier for sometimes anxious men and youths" previously described by Henderson (2001: 329). However, as men in Byron Bay become increasingly invested in long-term, mutual and respectful relationships with women who surf—relationships that are variously performative, loving, frustrating, romantic, fleeting, significant, and respectful—they encounter different possible female ways of being. These 'different' modes of behavior and surfing sometimes ask different questions and present different possibilities, making it increasingly difficult for men who surf to maintain a consistent position in line with historically normalized understandings of women as deserving less respect as surfers. 'Difference' and 'fuck ups' become pedagogical tools for teaching the cultural behavior of others, requiring the requestioning and renegotiation of existing power relations.

As Peta points out, judging others also involves a process of judging ourselves:

PETA: [Talking about these issues in these interviews] really does get me thinking about how I judge other people or, you know, because I think that age old saying of, you know, 'judge someone else, you're really judging yourself'.

In responding to male-dominated sets of cultural power relations, surfers in Byron Bay engage with multiple voices of authority that surround them, all of which influence their embodied and subjective understandings of surfing. That is, what we do and say impacts people around us and thus matters. For example, in response to a blog post I wrote about this issue in terms of the influence of men on women's surfing lives (Olive, 2009b), Toddy reminded me that it works the other way, too:

TODDY: My wife doesn't surf, but she grew up in a family of surfers, at the beach. She has a different take on the whole thing that completely affects my surfing life.

Women's voices are increasingly difficult to ignore in surfing culture (Olive, In Press). I have seen such impacts among local men who surf in Byron Bay, whose experiences and relationships with local women who do (and don't) surf have led to a different set of assumptions about women's surfing abilities and approaches. For example, local male surfers don't question the competency of

Women Who Surf 189

local women, and the larger than usual numbers of women in the surfbreaks around Byron Bay seems to have become a point of pride that men share with other men who surf. Local men tell me stories about male surfers from out of town and how they voice concern about women when the surf gets bigger. My friend John told me one story where his visiting friends had worried about his wife, Nat, who was sitting out the back on a day of solid swell. He kept assuring his friends, 'She's fine. She can handle herself'. Shortly after, Nat paddled into a solid wave and swept past John and his friends, flying along the wave face, capable and strong. His friends were shocked, but John just laughed. He is used to surfing with Nat and other women.

For many men surfing with a woman is highly unusual, leaving their expectations of what women can do as surfers defined by a surf media that has a historically sexist attitude to women. However, men who surf with women regularly are able to see and experience women's approaches to surfing and surfing culture first hand. Through experience, they *know* women can surf. Like John, they know enough to laugh at assumptions that women are collectively weak, lacking in skill, or incapable in the sea.

Drawing on Elspeth Probyn's (2003) work about subjectivities and space, Gordon Waitt (2007) explains that no matter how we understand ourselves, specific aspects of our subjectivities are:

> hailed into existence by a range of ideological systems. Crucially, how subjects experience these multiple and often conflicting subjectivities depends on the site and space of its production. (103)

The context of our subjective relationships accounts for the specificity of what, how, and why we learn (Olive and Thorpe 2011). The experiences we have are specific to our individual subjectivities and cultural contexts, and may reproduce, resist, or disrupt normalized and gendered understandings of culture. Such intersections are key to understanding the pedagogical potential of subjective experiences. Rose (1996b) describes these relations as,

> webs of tension that run across a space that accord human beings capacities and powers to the extent that they catch them up in hybrid assemblages of knowledges, instruments, vocabularies, systems of judgement, and technical devices. (38)

These assemblages and webs of tension are populated by individuals who are constantly in negotiation with multiple knowledges, contexts, and other individuals. Thus, resistance to existing power relations 'requires no theory of agency' (Rose 1996b: 35), because our negotiations of these power relations are implicit in our everyday cultural encounters. Our subjective negotiations of context are already disruptive.

Rose develops the notion of these intersecting subjectivities with Deleuze's extension of Foucault's 'fold'. The fold describes how relationships and interactions between cultures, places, people, and forms of communication are implicitly experienced in exchange with each other—what happens outside of us becomes interiorized as a part of our subjectivity. Rose (1996b) argues that what is inside of us—our subjectivity—'is merely an infolding of an exterior' (37)—the space, time, and cultures that contextualize our knowledge and experiences. Folds blur the lines between inside and outside, place and culture, self and other, body and subjectivity, experience and knowledge, authentic and hypocritical, rendering the borders of these binaries indistinguishable from each other (Deleuze 1988; Rose 1996a; St. Pierre 1997). We can instead imagine these categories as a relational range of possible understandings and experiences that help us make sense of the world. This process of folding highlights the instability of our own ways of knowing:

> For the lines of these folds do not run through a domain coterminous with the fleshy bounds of the human individual. Human being is emplaced, enacted through a regime of devices, gazes, techniques which extend beyond the limits of the flesh into spaces and assemblies.
> (Rose 1996a: 143)

Probyn (2003) takes this even further, explaining that our complex subjectivities, articulated through our bodies, are experienced in a constant process of exchange through relationships, space, and time, to a point where it is almost impossible to 'conceive of ourselves outside of the space we inhabit' (290). For surfers, space itself is not necessarily defining in terms of the cultural possibilities and limitations afforded in the way that a sport field or court is defined. However, surfing spaces are central to the operation and pedagogies of the surfing culture and its subjectivities. That is, it is through subjective experiences of cultural space that pedagogies occur. To be a surfer is to learn to surf and to learn the context of the surfbreak, a process activated through the subjectivity of the self in relationship with others.

We experience our subjectivities in terms of how we are positioned as contextualized subjects, highlighted by the range of voices of authority the context provides, all of whom impact us to varying degrees, depending on our relationships to the people and contexts that surround us (Probyn 2003; Rose 1996a, 1996b). As Probyn (2003) asks,

> How can it be otherwise, given that out bodies and our sense of ourselves are in constant interaction with how and where we are placed? (290)

The conscious process of agency and ethics, which is so often valued as central to changing existing power relations, becomes implicit in the never-ceasing intersections of subjectivities and contexts. In this, bodies and spaces are key to how knowledges and understandings are developed and changed. In my earlier story about Nat, the wave she caught, the conditions she caught it in, and the way she rode it, didn't comply with John's mates' assumptions. Nat was just surfing. She wasn't consciously taking resistant, stealthy, or creative approaches to a patronizing lineup—at the time, Nat didn't even know the conversation was happening—but by catching that wave, on that day, in that context, she was disrupting their assumptions without meaning to. Disruptive experiences in the surf are important in changing attitudes toward women who surf. John's friends will always have seen Nat get that wave. That event is now part of their embodied and subjective knowledge about surfing and women. The incident has become a story that I've heard John proudly tell multiple times, passing along the pedagogy of the experience to others.

Clifton Evers (2005) likens these learning processes to 'wipe-outs', which is the term surfers use to describe what happens when they make a mistake or lose their balance, and are thrown, gracelessly, into the wave:

> It is the wipe-out with its ambiguous and confusing moments that regularly reminds me of the potential to disable claims to fixity, definitions, stable rules, and ordering. ... When I am being tossed about I have to respond to alterity and infinite contestation, unlike [ways of knowing that] favour my familiar mode of belonging. (233–234)

The processes—the wipe-outs—that disrupt our "familiar mode of belonging" (234) are uncertain, risky and "chaotic" (233). As a pedagogical process, wiping-out "tends to come by accident, surprise, and only occasionally is deliberate" (232). Wipe-outs take you out of your comfort zone, and ask you to relinquish control. This contradictory connection—between the unwelcome and disruptive processes of subjective, embodied pedagogy, and the accompanying cultural encouragement to avoid doing so—illustrates the contextual challenges that are faced in engaging in disruptive and reflexive learning.

Evers's evocative description of bodies in a process of contextual pedagogy is useful to centralize bodily experiences in how we understand the world and our place in it. Emphasizing the ever-shifting embodied *and* contextual nature of subjectivity and relationships also reminds us of how we are different from each other, and how that difference matters (Ahmed 1998). Probyn (2003) argues that:

> Instead of plastering over those differences, we need to stop and address them. Sometimes that stopping will result in silence. And that slash between dis/connection should indicate a pause—a moment of non-recognition that may be expressed as simply as 'wow, you really are different than me'. (298)

However, Probyn further reminds us that we "should not stay caught in that moment" (298) and act as though our differences are insurmountable. Instead, we should learn from our differences and find ways to accommodate them. These 'moments' can be the result of unexpected and sudden 'wipe-outs', or longer-term relationships built over time, but either way the productive capacity these moments provide enables a pedagogy of change at a subjective and cultural level. That women continue to paddle out, to catch waves, to surf in male-dominated lineups that are variously hostile, welcome, supportive, and patronizing, is important to the ways the culture of surfing is able to develop in the future, and for how surfers come to understand surfing itself.

Conclusion

As embodied, cultural subjects, how the women involved in this project negotiated the male-dominated culture of surfing has impacts beyond their own individual worlds. Their presence and behavior incite cultural pedagogies, presenting experiences and relationships through which the surfers around them can begin to rethink their assumptions about what surfing is and can look like, and how women can fit into that. I am excited by the changes I see happening in the surf, even in the last few years. Women who surf in Byron Bay are making things better for themselves and in doing so, are making things better for *all* other surfers. There are more women in the surf in Byron Bay now, with several highly visible in surfing media and in local events. This has brought with it a new range of possibilities and ways to negotiate the surf than are represented in the interviews I undertook (Olive, 2015).

However, these new possibilities have not always been met with friendliness. In recent years the women who have arrived in the surf in Byron Bay have brought with them a different attitude and style to those I am familiar with. These women are cute, bikinied, tattooed, and into fashion. With their photogenic looks and style, they have come to dominate the representations of female longboard surfers in local, national, and international media, redefining what it means to be a woman who surfs in Byron Bay, and have thus become a new voice of authority. In many ways they are raising the profile of female surfers and surfing in distinctly female ways, which is to be celebrated. However, they are also doing so in ways that are distinctly feminine, and that possibly exclude women who do not, cannot, or will not fit into this image. My own uneasiness with these new surfers is not easy nor comfortable for me to admit, but I do so to illustrate that there are many different female approaches to surfing in Byron Bay, that surfing culture is changing at a rapid pace, that the direction of this change is conflicted, contentious, and difficult to predict, and that women are increasingly a part of all this.

What we do in our everyday cultural lives matters and affects the people and cultures around us. Thinking about these issues reminds me that I need to consider the effects and impacts of my own embodied understandings of surfing and the ways that I behave in the surf and develop contributions to academia and surf media. I need to reflect on the role of my own relationships and behavior in the operation of power relations in the culture of surfing. Of course, the pace of this kind of change is far from overwhelming. As Gordon Waitt (2008) argues, his (and my) multivocal, contextual, spatialized and embodied female rethinking or reimagining of surfing culture 'does not reveal a gender revolution that breaks the ideology of separate gender spheres' (p. 92), especially when it comes to the responses of men who surf. But in locating embodied experiences and knowledges as a relational process of cultural change, revolution is not really the point. Rather, it is locating processes through which deep, subjective knowledge formation is already in process in surfbreaks around Australia, driven by the presence of the difference that represents the 'problem' itself.

Note

1. Longboarding is a type of surfing that uses surfboards typically 9 feet or longer and with a rounded nose. They can have one or three fins. Shortboarders use surfboards that are generally from 5 to 7 feet long, point-nosed, and have two to four fins. Their performative focus is on power, drive, and maneuverability.

References

Ahmed, S. (1998). *Differences that matter: Feminist theory and postmodernism.* Cambridge, Cambridge University Press.
Booth, D. (2001). From bikinis to boardshorts: *Wahines* and the paradoxes of surfing culture. *Journal of Sporting History,* 28 (1): 3–22.
Booth, D. (2004). Surfing: From one (cultural) extreme to another. In Wheaton, B. (ed). *Understanding lifestyle sports* (pp. 94–109). London, Routledge.
Comer, K. (2010). *Surfer girls in the new world order.* Durham, Duke University Press.
Deleuze, G. (1988). *Foucault.* London, Athlone Press.
Evers, C. (2004). Men who surf. *Cultural Studies Review,* 10 (1): 27–41.
Evers, C. (2005). *Becoming-man, becoming-wave.* Unpublished Doctoral Thesis, University of Sydney, Sydney, Australia. Retrieved from http://ses.library.usyd.edu.au/handle/2123/7082.
Evers, C. (2006). How to surf. *Journal of Sport and Social Issues,* 30 (3): 229–43.
Evers, C. (2008). Queer waves. *Kurungabaa: A Journal of Literature, History and Ideas from the Sea,* July, 1(2): 81–85.
Evers, C. (2010). *Notes for a young surfer.* Carlton, Melbourne University Press.
Fendt, L.S., and Wilson, E. (2012). 'I just push through the barriers because I live for surfing': How women negotiate their constraints to surf tourism. *Annals of Leisure Research,* 15 (1): 4–18.
Foucault, M. (1980). Truth and power. In Gordon, C. (ed). *Power/knowledge: selected interviews and other writings 1972–1977.* New York, Pantheon Books.
Foucault, M. (1983). The subject and power. In Dreyfus, H.L., and Rabinow, P. (eds). *Michel Foucault: Beyond structuralism and heurmenetics* (pp. 208–28). Chicago, University of Chicago Press.
Foucault, M. (1986). *The history of sexuality, volume 2: The uses of pleasure.* New York, Vintage Books.

Foucault, M. (1988). Technologies of the self. In Martin, L.H., Gutman, H., and Hutton, P.H. (eds). *Technologies of the self: A seminar with Michel Foucault* (pp. 16–49). Amherst, University of Massachuasetts Press.

Ford, N., and Brown, D. (2006). *Surfing and social theory: Experience, embodiment, and narrative of the dream glide*. New York, Routledge.

Henderson, M. (1999). Some tales of two mags: Sports magazines as glossy reservoirs of male fantasy. *Journal of Australian Studies*, 62: 64–75.

Henderson, M. (2001). A shifting line up: Men, women and '*Tracks*' surfing magazine. *Continuum: Journal of Media and Cultural Studies*, 15 (3): 319–32.

Heywood, L. (2008). Third-wave feminism, the global economy, and women's surfing: Sport as stealth feminism in girl's surf culture. In Harris, A. (ed). *Next wave cultures: feminism, subcultures, activism* (pp. 63–82). New York, Routledge.

Knijnik, J.D., Horton, P., and Cruz, L.O. (2010). Rhizomatic bodies, gendered waves: transitional femininities in Brazilian surf. *Sport in Society*, 13 (7/8): 1170–1185.

Markula, P., and Pringle, R. (2006). *Foucault, sport and exercise: Power, knowledge and transforming the self*. New York, Routledge.

McGloin, C. (2005). *Surfing nation(s)—Surfing country(s)*. Unpublished Doctoral Thesis, University of Wollongong, Wollongong, Australia.

Nealon, J.T. (2008). *Foucault beyond Foucault: power and its intensifications since 1984*. Stanford, Stanford University Press.

Olive, R. (2009a, July 18), Some days it pays to have a good sense of humour … Posted on *Making friends with the neighbours*, last accessed on April 1, 2013, http://makingfriendswiththeneighbours.blogspot.com/2009/07/some-days-it-pays-to-have-good-sense-of.html.

Olive, R. (2009b, July 10). Women and the waves—film review. Posted on *Making friends with the neighbours*, last accessed April 1, 2013, http://makingfriendswiththeneighbours.blogspot.com.au/2009/07/women-and-waves-film-review.html.

Olive, R, (2013a). *Blurred lines: women, subjectivities and surfing*. Unpublished Doctoral Thesis, The University of Queensland, Brisbane, Australia.

Olive, R. (2013b). Making friends with the neighbours: blogging as a research method. *International Journal of Cultural Studies*, 16 (1): 71–84.

Olive, R. (2015). Reframing surfing: physical culture in online spaces. *Media International Australia, Incorporating Culture and Policy*, 155: 99–107.

Olive, R. (In Press). Going surfing/Doing research: learning how to negotiate cultural politics from women who surf. *Continuum: Journal of Media and Cultural Studies*.

Olive, R., McCuaig, L., and Phillips, M.G. (2015). Women's recreational surfing: A patronizing experience. *Sport, Education and Society*, 20 (2): 258–76.

Olive, R., and Thorpe, H. (2011). Negotiating the 'F-word' in the field: Doing feminist ethnography in action sport cultures. *Sociology of Sport Journal*, 28 (4): 421–40.

Pringle, R. (2005). Masculinities, sport and power: A critical comparison of Gramscian and Foucauldian inspired theoretical tools. *Journal of Sport and Social Issues*, 29 (3): 256–78.

Probyn, E. (1993). *Sexing the self: gendered positions in cultural studies*. London, Routledge.

Probyn, E. (2003). The spatial imperative of subjectivity. In Anderson, K., Domosh, M., Pile, S., and Thrift, N. (eds). *Handbook of Cultural Geography* (pp. 290–99). London, Sage.

Probyn, E. (2004). Everyday shame. *Cultural Studies,* 18 (2–3): 328–49.
Rose, N. (1996a). Identity, genealogy, history. In Hall, S., and Du Gay, P. (eds). *Questions of cultural identity* (pp. 128–49). London, Sage.
Rose, N. (1996b). *Inventing our selves: Psychology, power, and personhood.* Cambridge, Cambridge University Press.
Roy, G. (2013). Women in wetsuits: revolting bodies in lesbian surf culture. *Journal of Lesbian Studies,* 17 (3–4): 329–43.
Roy, G., and Caudwell, J. (2014). Women and surfing spaces in Newquay, UK. In Hargreaves, J., and Anderson, E. (eds). *Routledge handbook of sport, gender and sexuality* (pp. 235–44). Abingdon, Routledge.
Spowart, L., Burrows, L., & Shaw, S. (2010). 'I just eat, sleep and dream of surfing': When surfing meets motherhood. *Sport in Society,* 13 (7/8): 1186–1203.
Stedman, L. (1997). From Gidget to Gonad Man: Surfers, feminists and postmodernisation. *Australian and New Zealand Journal of Sociology,* 33 (1): 75–90.
St. Pierre, E. A. (1997). Methodology in the fold and the interruption of transgressive data. *Qualitative Studies in Education,* 10 (2): 175–89.
Surfing Australia. (2012). Surfing Australia fast facts. *Surfing Australia.* Accessed April 13, 2015, http://www.surfingaustralia.com/statistics.php.
Tait, G. (2000). *Youth, sex, and government.* New York, Peter Lang.
Tinning, R. (2010). *Pedagogy and human movement: Theory, practice, research.* London, Routledge.
Turner, G. (2012). *What's become of cultural studies.* London, Sage.
Waitt, G. (2007). (Hetero)sexy waves: surfing, space, gender and sexuality. In Wellard, I. (ed). *Rethinking gender and youth sport* (pp. 99–115). Abingdon, Routledge.
Waitt, G. (2008). 'Killing waves': Surfing, space and gender. *Social and Cultural Geography,* 9 (1): 75–94.
Waitt, G., & Warren, A. (2008). "Talking shit over a brew after a good session with your mates": Surfing, space and masculinity. *Australian Geographer,* 39 (3): 353–365.

12 Notes Toward a *Signature Pedagogy* for Cultural Studies
Looking Again at Cultural Studies' Disciplinary Boundaries

Andrew Hickey

> *Facing the challenge of the conjuncture, reimagining what our modernity might be, is, then, what cultural studies does.*
>
> (O'Connor 2012: 337)

What would a continuing cultural studies practice look like if we commenced anew, without the reference points and disciplinary baggage that current cultural studies practice invokes? What would cultural studies change about itself and do differently; what would it say in this moment?

To conclude this volume, but to also offer a point of departure for the ideas contained within the preceding chapters, I want to broach for consideration a *signature pedagogy* for cultural studies. Each of the contributions to this volume makes a case for why cultural studies matters, and how the consideration of pedagogy signals an opportunity for the reconsideration of what a cultural studies practice might be. But each also, in its own way, prefaces the point that cultural studies risks being too comfortable with itself and that if meaningful incursions into the world are to continue to come from cultural studies, then a good sense of what this discipline is about, what it can achieve, and how this might be activated requires (re)consideration. This is a concern that asks questions about the very nature of cultural studies, how it presents its modes of inquiry, what it seeks to position as its object/s of study, and how these ways of doing things stand as distinct and different to the ways that other (often similar) disciplines go about approaching their own (often similar) projects. While these questions point to concerns that are by no means new—the boundaries of the discipline have been exhaustively considered in recent years (Grossberg 2010; Rodman 2015; Turner 2012)—what I do seek to offer in this closing contribution is a provocation for understanding cultural studies pedagogically, according to the "personality of this disciplinary field—its values, knowledge, and manner of thinking—almost, perhaps, its total world view" (Calder 2006).

Along with what I regard as cultural studies' *crisis narratives* and its halcyon remembrances of the 1980s and 1990s—themes that have come to feature in more than a few current articulations of the discipline and that have, I argue, come to stand as props for the retelling of the discipline—a third prominent theme to emerge in recent discussions of cultural studies has been with why it *matters*. This dialogue, prefaced as it might be by examples including Miller's (2012) discussion about the role and purpose of the humanities and Rodman's (2015) question of "why cultural studies?", stands as an example of how the place and purpose of cultural studies has come to be considered and talked about. Narratives such as these echo through cultural studies (and the humanities more generally) and conflate themes including the institutional placement of cultural studies (Turner 2012), as well as larger concerns around the role and purpose of university scholarship, and perhaps most significantly, the very purpose of the university itself (Marginson and Considine 2000; Nussbaum 2010). Although these dialogues have been typically good in identifying the lay of the terrain, and in some instances paint a sobering account of what is wrong with the nature of contemporary scholarship (and cultural studies scholarship in particular), less certain is a cohesive sense of what it is that we might now expect from cultural studies. What public good might come of the labor of its practitioners, its intellectual workers? What interventions into the world might it now affect?

What cultural studies might say in *these times* (or as the concerns of Chapter 1 might suggest, *these contexts*) will be determined by the framing that the disciplinary and institutional boundaries of cultural studies will prescribe. The position of the discipline is marked by these contexts of its operation. In the opening chapter for this volume, three principal contexts were considered as central to this understanding of cultural studies: the context of the cultural studies scholar-as-*Self*, the context of the *discipline*, and the context of the *institution*. Each of these contexts necessarily overlaps and intersects at various points of conjuncture. As was suggested in Chapter 1, it follows that each of these contexts should necessarily be read against the other, so much as the *coming-to* cultural studies engaged by the scholar-as-Self will draw on the disciplinary boundaries of cultural studies as an identifiable discipline, set within the context of the university as institution. This again is not to suggest that the practice of cultural studies is rigidly prescribed, but that the shape and flavor of the discipline—the "personality" of the disciplinary field, as recognizable as a discipline—requires from its practitioners those things that stand for and mark the discipline. The discipline is a result of its practitioners undertaking certain practices according to the mandates of the discipline, set as these are within the institutional confines of the university.

The current formulation of this dynamic has been a feature of some of the more problematic aspects of cultural studies. If it is the case that there can be "no guarantee ... that every appearance of cultural studies is valuable or even progressive" (Grossberg 1994: 1), then the question becomes *what does count?* What precisely *is* cultural studies and how should it be done? Paradoxically enough, both the success and failure of cultural studies as disciplinary, but perhaps not quite disciplinary enough, can be read against this question. What is at once a great strength for cultural studies—irreverence toward the constraints of disciplinary boundaries—becomes at the same time an amorphous and groundless context of operation. As Sparks (1996) notes:

> It is extremely difficult to define 'Cultural Studies' with any degree of precision. It is not possible to draw a sharp line and say that on one side of it we can find the proper province of cultural studies. Neither is it possible to point to a unified theory or methodology which are characteristic to it or of it. (14)

Sparks goes on to chart the connections to Marxist theory and the relationship between cultural studies and a radical project of emancipatory intervention into the world, along with suggesting that cultural studies has tended to have a prevailing concern for "a subordinate class, and that this subordination can be something which can be ended" (25). In doing so, Sparks points toward a semblance of what we might call a signature pedagogy; a concern for something beyond a method or set of theoretical constructs. He points here to an ethical concern that mobilizes the practice of the discipline and orients its raison d'etre. Grossberg (2010) too sees this as a prevailing concern of cultural studies, noting that:

> intellectual work matters, that it is a vital component of the struggle to change the world and to make it more humane and just, and that cultural studies, as a particular project, a particular sort of intellectual practice, has something valuable to contribute. (2010: 6)

In affirming and taking seriously "the historical possibilities of transforming people's lived realities and the relations of power within which those realities are constructed" (Grossberg 2010: 8), a central purpose of a project for cultural studies is identified. But without reciting further the (innumerable) articulations of this concern to demonstrate this point, a question remains, *how does cultural studies do this*? How are these noble, perhaps lofty, concerns for "transforming people's lived realities" actually gone about? What is it specifically within the disciplinary confines of cultural studies that enables these transformations to occur?

Broached within these questions is a concern for a flexibility that remains in cultural studies' irreverence for disciplinary protocol, but equally, the sharp realization of where this has failed, and how cultural studies might be recuperated from an orthodoxy of *anything goes*; the downside of the freedom that "mak[ing] it up as you go" (Grossberg 2010: 1) sometimes results in. It may well be argued that cultural studies has in fact done a poor job of achieving these goals, of breaking out of the university in meaningfully sustained ways, and more selfishly, of simply providing a safe space of sustainable employment for its own practitioners to practice. The ideals and the practice oscillate as aporetic in this sense.

Although this again points to some degree to old arguments around *what is cultural studies?*, I do not wish to get caught up within the intricacies of these here. For mine, this 'what is' argument has moved beyond being useful, and has become stuck in a tendency to position cultural studies as either a 'paradise lost'—a moment long gone where things were going well (an articulation of this is found in Rodman's 2015 characterization of "the Sigh")—or, as mired in concerns for a utilitarian practicality; effectively reducing the 'doing' of cultural studies to a series of techniques that are somehow constitutive of 'cultural studies'. This is a mistake I suggest, and posit that it might be better to move productively beyond what *was* and *has been* cultural studies (while acknowledging the foundational narratives these remembrances provide), while also jettisoning attempts to codify too closely what *is*; a *techne* for cultural studies. My concern here is that cultural studies should be viewed as more than a set of rules guarded by a canon of key literature (from whichever tradition one happens to align) and as more than a set of identifiable and instrumental techniques for critically reading the world. I suggest that to productively contemplate the distinct nature of cultural studies at this moment, and as more than a fashionable way to conduct scholarly investigations into 'everyday life', a clear sense of *why* it is we are doing what we do should be grasped, along with a full sense of how it is the cultural studies scholar goes about doing it. In essence what I am arguing for is what Turner (2012) has identified as "a fully developed epistemology" (8) for the discipline, and in this sense, I argue that cultural studies would be well served to identity its "signature pedagogies" (Schulman 2005) as a point of articulation for what this epistemology might consist of. This must commence, as the chapters in this volume suggest, through the consideration of the scholar-as-Self; a practitioner working within and through the disciplinary formulations of cultural studies, set among the institutions that house these sites of cultural studies practice.

Signature Pedagogies and Cultural Studies

Conceptualized by Lee Schulman (2005), signature pedagogies are those "characteristic forms of teaching and learning" that define a profession (52). Schulman expands on this by noting that signature pedagogies contain three major 'structures': the *implicit*, the *deep*, and the *surface*.

The *implicit structure* concerns the "moral dimensions that comprise a set of beliefs about professional attitudes, values, and dispositions" (55), with these providing the ontological orientations of a discipline, including its moral-philosophical bases. For cultural studies, particularly that emerging from British streams, a concern for the minutiae of 'everyday life', the goings-on of ordinary people, and a critical concern for social justice stand as key foundations of the implicit structure of cultural studies. This implicit structure specifies the 'why' of the discipline; why what matters to the discipline actually matters.

The *deep structure* refers to the "core beliefs within a field regarding the best way to educate people in the ways of the craft" (Beck and Eno 2012: 76). Although it might be argued that cultural studies has multiple ways of doing this, depending on which traditions and methods for doing cultural studies one draws upon, it is with the deep structure that the coming-to cultural studies is affected. This does not simply relate to the ways that students of cultural studies are trained, but also the way that established scholars relate to the discipline and each other. The deep structure of cultural studies is, for instance, on show in the modes of address deployed at conferences, in the stylistic and structural formulation of research reportings, the aesthetic of scholarly writing that counts as cultural studies, and so on. In short, the deep structure is what is considered the 'done thing' in cultural studies training—that is, how *what counts* as cultural studies comes to be practiced as such.

The *surface structure* refers to the "actual methods used by teachers to teach" (Beck and Eno 2012: 78). While the performance of cultural studies within university lecture theatres and tutorial rooms (and increasingly, in online spaces), conference halls, scholarly publications, and so on stand as preeminent demonstration of the technique of instruction—the 'expression' of the discipline—so too should less formal engagement with publics, with research participants, and with other scholars be considered an element of the surface structure. Significantly, it is with the *surface structure* that the signature pedagogy finds articulation as practice. Although mobilized and oriented by the *implicit structure* (that is, the underlying ontology through which the discipline is oriented) and the *deep structure* (the epistemic foundations by which the discipline frames how what is known comes to be known), it is with the *surface structure* that the act of doing cultural studies manifests as demonstrable.

For Thomson and Hall (2014) signature pedagogies operate as

> tacit knowledge, which is conveyed as much through the presence of the practitioner and through the way that they orient themselves to questions and tasks, as [to] what they actually say and do. (78)

The important element of this suggestion is the recognition of "presence of the practitioner". This brings back to mind the application in Chapter 1 of Heidegger's suggestions for *Dasein*, and the realization of one's Self through the discipline that coming-to cultural studies provokes. In calling oneself a 'cultural studies scholar' one signs onto the tradition of the discipline—to confront Dasein—and in doing so accepts the alignment with the ontological and epistemological requirements of cultural studies:

> These distinctive practices are intended to do more than inculcate knowledge, they also set out deliberately to teach 'habits of mind', the ways of *thinking* about [a discipline], *doing* [the discipline] and *being* a [practitioner of that discipline].
>
> (Thomson and Hall 2014: 78)

This volume has attempted to identify how the *coming-to* cultural studies might be enacted and realized. In relaying accounts of the practice of cultural studies, each of the contributions contained here identified how the realization of the Self-as-scholar provoked through the coming-to cultural studies gained dimensions *as* pedagogical. The contributions to this volume identify articulations of the surface structure by making apparent encounters with deep structures that mediated these expressions of cultural studies, and the orientations for enacting change in the world that cultural studies' implicit structures suggest.

Elizabeth Ellsworth (2005) draws attention to the dynamics of a signature pedagogy (but without proclaiming such dynamics as a 'signature pedagogy') when noting that practice inculcates:

> the thinking–feeling, the embodied sensation of making sense, the lived experience of our learning selves that make the thing we call knowledge. Thinking and feeling our selves as they *make sense* is more than merely the sensation of knowledge in the making. *It is a sensing of our selves in the making*, and is that not the root of what we call learning?
> (Ellsworth 2005: 1, emphasis added)

In making sense of the discipline, and the institutions out of which it is practiced, we must make sense (of) ourselves. The signature pedagogies of cultural studies suggest how this making-sense should be conducted, and how the application of the discipline might proceed. Via the moral-philosophical declaration of the implicit structure, the *coming-to* of a defined disciplinary practice through the deep structure and cognizance of witnessing the discipline in-action from the surface structure, the conditions for making-sense *through* cultural studies become apparent.

Importantly, and through this activation of coming-to cultural studies, what a signature pedagogy points to are the conditions by which what is known by cultural studies is actually known. This is where the "fully developed epistemology" (Turner 2012: 8) materializes. With the identification of the signature pedagogies of a discipline, a sense of the lay of the land of the discipline is gained—the parameters by which what is known comes to be known, and most significantly, how this comes to be relayed as significant to the discipline through its practitioners. What this broaches is twofold: the 'stuff' of the discipline itself—the form and content of the disciplinary knowledge that provides the terrain of the discipline—but also the means through which this knowledge is translated and enacted into practice by its practitioners. I seek to extrapolate these two points in the following sections of this chapter. To commence, I will start with what I see as the *means* by which cultural studies' signature pedagogies are mediated, moving then to consider what might continue to be central to cultural studies by drawing on pointers taken from the chapters in this volume as prompts.

The Means of Cultural Studies Signature Pedagogies

If, in returning briefly to Sparks' (1996) suggestion that cultural studies is a discipline interested in "subordinate" positionality, then it carries that central to cultural studies' concerns are the explication of regimes of power, the illumination of submerged histories, and chronicling of alternative (to dominant) experiences of the world. It might be suggested in these terms that cultural studies draws upon political interventions into the world to mark its practice, and in light of the Marxist roots that British cultural studies grew from and extended through its radical and anticipative understandings of the public sphere and 'ordinary lives', that the ontological bases of the discipline are written in terms of its critical encounters with marginalization and unequal expressions of power. Read according to the "contexts of possibility" (Grossberg 2010: 57) such critical incursions might illuminate, cultural studies takes as its point of view (if not also its focus) these conditions of marginality as its standpoint.

This is an *emancipatory* calling to borrow loosely from the traditions of Gramscian and Freirean theory/pedagogy that inform cultural studies, with concerns for action via the explication of ordinary and everyday experiences expressed within these traditions carrying a necessarily pedagogical intent. As Freire (2007) argues:

> the object of the investigation is not persons (as if they were anatomical fragments), but rather the thought-language with which men and women refer to reality, the levels with which they perceive that reality, and their view of the world. (97)

The cultural studies scholar's task is in reading the world and experiences had of it; to decode the "thought-language" through which understandings of *how things are* come to be constructed, but also, importantly, how these are taken-on as *learned* undertakings.

These concerns have been largely conveyed in terms of the multiplicity of 'the everyday', albeit often with a stress on the *everyday of the ordinary*. This conceptualization might be more simply prefaced under the centrally important maxim to cultural studies: "the whole way of life" (Williams 1977: 17). But this too has its limitations, and although "the whole way of life" of what might be called 'ordinary culture' has provided a central point of inquiry (if not sole object of study) for cultural studies, the way that configurations of 'culture' in the cultural studies imaginary have been activated offers an insight into the formulations of cultural studies' epistemological core. That is, the way *culture* itself is approached and understood offers a frame within which cultural studies might be interrogated. "The culture concept" (as Tony Bennett (2015) identifies it) reveals the context of cultural studies' focus as something distinctly identifiable. It also reveals the means by which cultural studies goes about enacting its critical project; culture provides the logic underpinning the function of cultural studies itself.

Justin O'Connor (2012) also positions his argument in terms of the treatment cultural studies has given to culture, but does so by querying the (self-imposed) monopoly over the concept:

> [W]hy should cultural studies be the privileged site from which these transformative possibilities might be identified? Do not other disciplines—economics, politics or sociology, for example—have a purchase on the possibilities of the real as much as cultural studies? (338)

These are fair points, and it is the case that the disciplines O'Connor cites (and those beyond) do also take culture seriously as an object of study. So how then is cultural studies' conceptualization different? If the means by which cultural studies' signature pedagogy are realized derive from culture, but a culture that is conceptualized from the standpoint of subordinate positionality and a radical motivation for critical incursion into the world, what then does this say about cultural studies, and more specifically, the world it constructs and responds to? In attempting a response to these questions a sense of cultural studies' signature pedagogies can be determined.

Cultural Studies' Signature Pedagogies

Beyond this epistemological positioning of cultural studies' project, O'Connor (2012) highlights a further problem in terms of cultural studies' turn to empiricism and reification of culture within everyday life. For O'Connor, it is with the ways that cultural studies has been done that an insight into the limits of the cultural studies' imagination materialize. In highlighting what might be characterized as a division between methodological approaches to cultural studies that have, on the one hand applied textual analysis, and on the other, those that use ethnography, Johnson (1986) suggests that such ways of thinking about cultural studies "runs right through" the discipline and takes form according to a dualism:

> On the one side there are those who insist that 'cultures' must be studied as a whole, and in situ, located in their material context ... methodologically they stress the importance of complex, concrete descriptions, which grasps, particularly, the unity or homology of cultural forms and material life ... On the other side, there are those who stress the relative independence or effective autonomy of subjective forms and means of signification ... If the first set of methods are usually derived from sociological, anthropological or socio-historical roots, the second set owe most to literary criticism. ... (86)

Although the problems of suggesting such a seemingly neat split in approaches is ever-present in this suggestion, the broad characterization of approaches identified by Johnson does carry some significance. If the identity crisis of current cultural studies is written in terms of its modes of inquiry and objects of study, framed according to an uneasy sense of what it is that cultural studies might actually *do* with 'culture', then practitioners of cultural studies might be well served to take stock of what these methods for generating understandings of the world can (and cannot) ultimately achieve. It might in this regard be important to do what Angela McRobbie (1994) long ago suggested when noting that cultural studies should encounter "lived experience which breathes life into … inanimate objects [of popular culture]" (27). Here is an opportunity for a *bricolage* that refuses to get bogged down in methodological specificity, that seeks an open and imaginative encounter with the world, and that mobilizes theory and method as a toolkit for explicating experience (and not as a lens for framing it). In short, what I am suggesting here is a pragmatic connection to the everyday, and in building on the first foundational component of a cultural studies signature pedagogy—a critical orientation for illuminating subordination—it emerges that a second foundation might be characterized around this concern for methodological irreverence. This is not to suggest that cultural studies' methods for engaging the world should lack rigor, and that in making a case for 'making it up', I do not at all suggest that cultural studies approaches should be vague, ill-formed, or without a clear sense of explication. What is at stake here, however, is the realization that being too close to method can constrain and limit what it is put in place to uncover. Methodological chauvinism shouldn't be placed ahead of a concern for the application of an array of methods (as bricolage) for understanding the world as complex.

If interested in nothing else, the central concern of cultural studies is placed as a critical-ethical concern for how "everyday lives are articulated by and with culture" (Grossberg 2010: 8). Achieving the intent of these concerns presents as no small feat, but equally, the sentiment expressed by the emancipatory logic of the 'context of possibility' provides a useful starting point for considering what is core to cultural studies and how this should be encountered. That is, by asking what the foundation of this practice of cultural studies might be and how its practitioners might come-to cultural studies accordingly, the identification of cultural studies' signature pedagogies materialize.

Signature Pedagogies and the Lessons from this Volume

The dialogues included throughout this volume point to a speculative sense of the pedagogies of cultural studies. This volume does not present as complete, and instead offers insights into visions of cultural studies suggested by the authors as provocations, as insights into what stands as central to the discipline, in this moment, as experienced by each author. In this sense it is important to remember that cultural studies is not a unified project, that there are multiple versions of cultural studies practiced according to varied theoretical and methodological traditions. However, it should also follow that there are certain underlying concerns that motivate these multiple ways of doing things, and a prevailing concern for the ways "everyday lives are articulated by and with culture" (Grossberg 2010: 8) that identify cultural studies as *a discipline*.

To draw a lead from the chapters contained here, I offer the following points as a move toward the identification of a signature pedagogy for cultural studies. In taking this approach the hope is that something profound about the nature of contemporary cultural studies might be uncovered, but that also, the central concerns of cultural studies might be recognized in terms of the signature pedagogies that specify its disciplinary motivations. What follows is an initial survey of what the signature pedagogies of cultural studies might draw from as their guiding characteristics, extrapolated as these are from the deliberations captured within this volume.

Implicit Structure: The Ontologies of Cultural Studies' Signature Pedagogies

Meaningful Engagement With the 'Culture Concept'

Tony Bennett (2015) argues the point that "there is little doubt that the concept of culture as *a way of life* initially provided the key authorizing concept for cultural studies *as a distinctive intellectual and political practice*" (546, emphasis added). As central as culture is to cultural studies, however, Bennett goes on to highlight that "the cultural studies literature has paid scant attention to … the distinctive intellectual qualities of this concept" (546). Bennett draws attention to the omissions of questions of aesthetics in cultural studies' appraisals of 'culture' and in doing so parallels some of Justin O'Connor's (2012) concerns for the reappraisal of the aesthetic as a fundamental point of contact in the question of culture:

> Maybe cultural studies should not attempt to be a sociology—cultural or otherwise—but engage with the new agenda of the assemblage of cultural possibilities represented by 'cultural economy', actor network theory, and so on. In this it would have to engage again with aesthetics; not just the images, sounds, objects and words but the project of aesthetics itself. If art and culture are sites of governmentality—what do we do about this? If we do not want to give to the state the absolute right—*potentia*—to produce the real, then what kind of counter-production is possible? What is the proper space for 'culture' in this project? Surely this is where art theory—the best of it, including that wrapped up in new media—has been for twenty years or so. If cultural studies no longer wishes to engage with the sensuous particularity of the text, and leaves the field of popular culture to an instrumental creative industries or an encephalous 'entertainment studies', then it should put its wild years in the garage and go out and get a proper job. (339–40)

The important realization within this view is the possibility for 'counter-production'. Here marks a point of differentiation to other disciplinary conceptualizations of culture (namely, cultural sociology in O'Connor's view). The central feature of this vision of practice is in the possibility cultural studies has to not only *report on* the world in order to engage in the mapping of representations of it, but to also activate this production of culture itself. What these views point toward is the serious treatment of the aesthetic capacities of culture as something core to cultural studies and its productive capability. This, in O'Connor's (2012) terms, means embracing the aesthetic as the location at which meaningful engagement with culture might enliven a richer understanding of the ways culture formulates lives and configures the everyday.

In this regard Megan Watkins' contribution to this volume (Chapter 8) provides a starting point for the ways 'the culture concept' might be treated in cultural studies. As Watkins suggests, cultural studies

> [F]rom its beginnings, sought a more nuanced engagment with how culture is understood beyond its anthropological reification (Bennett and Frow 2008). Yet while these ideas may be commonplace within academe, they seem to have had limited impact [outside of the academy].

The important point to be taken from Watkins' discussion identifies the problems inherent in retaining the articulation of culture as an academic pursuit. This concern might be reworked in terms of the question, *what does cultural studies do?* If incursions into the world are core to the differentiation of cultural studies and its guiding capacity to move beyond the mapping of representation, then considering the productive capacity to produce culture should be provided further currency. As Watkins identifies, culture must encounter not only the "commonplace within academe" but marry this to larger questions of how lives come to be configured and the everyday framed as an aesthetic construct. This is an activity of explication and a critical emancipatory project focused not only on the reporting of those material conditions that confront the everyday, but the productive incursions into the world that people enact when making culture; an emancipatory *activation*. In this regard culture becomes both the context upon which cultural studies is done—its object study—but concomitantly the canvas upon which cultural studies might be formulated as a meaningful engagement with (and itself production of) culture. It follows that cultural studies, located as it predominantly is within the academy, might commence to produce more than 'academic reportage' as it goes about this active participation in the production of culture.

Meaningful Engagement With the Material Condition of the Globe

In a telling exchange between social activist Reverend Billy (the alter ego of Bill Talen) and academic and theorist of critical public pedagogy, Jenny

Sandlin, Talen provided the following observation of the use and accessibility of (critical) academic work:

> Why don't you professors stop burrowing farther and farther into your private world? Does that unshareable language make you feel more specific? Or updated? I literally don't understand the upside of creating these walls around a subculture? On the other hand, if I'm not mistaken Savitri and I make our living by being invited into colleges and universities by professors who essentially ask us to translate their essays into common gesture, vernacular talk and popular music. So maybe I should just shut up.
> (Talen in Burdick and Sandlin 2010: 349)

If ours is to remain a discipline of significance, our language must be that of the contexts from which we work. This will require "acts of translation" (Hickey, Reynolds and McDonald 2015) to negotiate the dynamics of the situations we find ourselves within, both public and academic, but should not function to reify a split between academic discourse and knowledge and that of 'the public'. Cultural studies scholars are well-placed to engage in dialogue *with* community and to mediate such incursions into the world. Garbutt's experiences of doing so as detailed in Chapter 2, and Third's articulations of formal university-community engagement in Chapter 6 provide cues as to how this might be done.

As a pointer to the sorts of responses cultural studies might (and is equipped to) make in the world, Satchell, drawing on Serres (2014, 2015), from Chapter 5, notes:

> The conjunction of rapid population expansion, the proliferation of technology in every sphere and the strain of resource exploitation upon biological diversity, calls not only for critical analysis but moreover creative practice.

He goes on by noting:

> This experimental sort of approach to learning is creative and generative of the exchange between the pedagogy of culture and the culture of pedagogy, adaptive to relevant contexts of learning and everyday life issues that matter.

To do cultural studies is to have a meaningful connection with the world as encountered—to read the world as it happens according to where it happens. Continuing the concerns noted above for cultural studies' ongoing consideration of the culture concept, it will be via the production of creative responses to what is confronted in the world that cultural studies will renew its purpose. Satchell's contribution to this volume in particular demonstrates how meaningful connection to concerns for the biodiversity of the globe, the profound changes that mark the Anthropocene and one's own, personal, reflections of a place in the world might be articulated creatively.

Meaningful Connections With Being Human

As Schlunke suggests (Chapter 10), u*sing [a] form*ula of "life lessons" guides the applicability of cultural studies to a generalized life. Although recent considerations of the more than human draw attention to the ways that the affectivity of 'things' (as Whatmore, 2002, and Bennett's, 2010, configurations suggest) repositions a new materialism and its challenges to the exceptionality of being human, it remains that significant questions of experience of humanity in-and-with the world require explication. Cultural studies does this; it enables a critically informed view of the world, an insight into *things*—as a method of inquiry—but does so with an established ethic grounded in the foundations identified above; a concern for subordinate positionality. This resonates with Slater's identification of 'care' (Chapter 7) as both an object of inquiry and ethic for conduct, via the realization of the Self in-the-world that care provokes. As Schlunke continues:

> This is after all an attempt to try out the "how to" of cultural studies where our own situation is one of the sites we learn from through description and theoretical techniques and so make of a situation a pedagogical experiment.
>
> (Schlunke, Chapter 10)

As referred to in Chapter 1, this coming-to cultural studies provides a first context for the pedagogies of cultural studies. But this is always written in terms of the place of the cultural studies scholar in-and-with the world. In this sense, the specific potential of cultural studies is that it takes meaningful account of the work of the cultural studies scholar-as-Self engaged in the explication of worlds encountered.

Meaningful Connections With Colleagues

Satchell (Chapter 5), in his discussion of Delueze and Serres's scholarly relationship, briefly notes that:

> There are some touching connections between Deleuze and Serres as philosophers and friends ... Each acknowledges the other on various occasions. ...

Engaging with each other openly and honestly should be especially central to a pedagogy of cultural studies. Ours is not a discipline of isolated scholarship. Engagement with the world and with each other is central to the project, but when written against 'hard' institutional contexts and higher education landscapes that preface 'measured' competition and personal isolation (whether through exaltation of individual expertise or censure through identifiability), the ethic of caring for each other/caring for the discipline is increasingly difficult to maintain. In laying claim to our competence as scholars within the corporatized university, it is often difficult to sustain a sense of collegiality. Measures of performance and differentiation of one's productivity predispose conditions of individualised competition. As suggested in Chapter 1, the formulation of the context of higher education as it currently stands, celebrates the 'star' academic—that single individual who measures-up well. But this is anathema to good scholarly practice; cultural studies in particular cannot be done individually. How then might we work collaboratively, engaged in the rigorous engagement with each other's ideas and work, but do so with care for each other? This is a space for a pedagogy of love as scholars of critical pedagogy would see it (Darder 2009), aimed distinctly toward each other in the interests of a collegial discipline. This ethic would seem no more needed than at this moment of rampant corporatization of higher education.

Deep Structure: Thinking Through Cultural Studies

Criticism and Critique

I seek to suggest that at core, the deep structure of cultural studies is expressed as *criticality*. With the magnitude of possible angles this characteristic of cultural studies could be examined from keenly in mind, I want to pose for consideration the sort of critique that cultural studies might continue to undertake.

There is a prevailing view circulating currently, in this age of anxiety for the humanities, around making *useful* humanities scholarship. Suggestions such as those that position humanities graduates as creative, as understanding how culture works, and capable of unpicking how it is that people think, are cast according to what this might provide for industry, or government, or ultimately some form of employment, as if this is the only valuable outcome of an education and pursuit of a degree. But this rush to acquiesce—to fall into the rhetoric of the market and attempt to rationalize how the humanities might be made instrumentally *useful*—tends to gloss over one of the major functions of humanities work: its criticality.

To be critical is to be *dangerous*. A very clear expression of this is offered by Raymond Williams (1962) when making the point that:

> One clear way of ensuring a balance between freedom and responsibility is to make sure that as many people as possible are free to reply and criticise. (111)

Here lies an expression of the deep structure for cultural studies and its emancipatory possibilities. To encourage criticality through the motivation of students, research collaborators, members of publics, and others engaged in the doing of cultural studies presents as a core component of a cultural studies signature pedagogy. As Martin and Hickey (Chapter 9) suggest, this aspect of cultural studies' pedagogy is concerned with the relaying of experience and the generation of counternarratives that speak to the manifold encounters that are had in the world.

As an illustration of this approach to criticality drawn from within this volume, Garbutt (Chapter 2) draws attention to the agency of being critical and the formation of a "critically aware counter-cultural current" from his sojourn with community in northern New South Wales. He notes that a productive configuration of cultural studies is:

> [O]ne that is overtly (self-)reflexive whether in terms of local and global concerns, self and others, everyday life and theory, or university and community. There has been a *geophilosophical* (and perhaps what might be called a minor *geopedagogical*) dynamic at work producing this cultural studies configuration.

There is a dialogical nature to this form of criticism. Garbutt continues by noting that this:

> cultural studies pedagogy is decidedly democratic, has the potential to enable personal transformation, and is acknowledged as occurring *within the academy's physical boundaries as well as without*. (emphasis added)

Embracing the critical capacity of cultural studies is central to realizing the "language of possibility and resistance" (Giroux 2004: 76) that Wight discusses (Chapter 3), and that Martin and Hickey (Chapter 9) characterize in terms of DIY and storytelling. Such a criticality enables a position of counterpoint from which to write-back, to explicate culture and (also) inform cultural studies and its disciplinary motivations.

This does, however, juxtapose somewhat Agger's (1992) cautions for falling-into the "plain language" of the vernacular:

> It is not enough (although it is necessary) for cultural studies to conduct itself in the public vernacular lest it lose all political efficacy, particularly with regard to affording readable deconstructive analyses of cultural texts and practices. *The public vernacular itself must change to accommodate new levels of insight and complexity necessary to grasp the social world fully.* (187, emphasis added).

While each of the chapters contained in this volume explore this dynamic, the contributions by Garbutt (Chapter 2), Schlunke (Chapter 10), Third (Chapter 6), and Watkins (Chapter 8) specifically point to the to-and-fro of cultural studies scholarship, and ultimately, to what it might achieve; of the dialogic nature of undertaking scholarly work *in* and *with* publics to explicate the experience of the world, but undertaken in such a way that also illuminates the formulations that cultural studies, as an expression of specialized ways of reading the world, can provide. This is a critical practice that isn't content with merely reporting, but of also writing back to effect change; change that in part involves the transformation of ways things come to be known and enacted within those publics encountered.

Exposure and Conscientization

As a further extension to this consideration of the deep structure of a cultural studies signature pedagogy, the Frierean notion of conscientization (*conscientização*) calls for the unveiling of the social and political contradictions that maintain positionality in an effort to provoke critical consciousness and the realization of one's own 'oppression'. Written in Freire's (2007) deeply Marxist terms, conscientization calls to attention the workings of hegemony and of the unconscious submission to dominant ideology. But read differently, away from the revolutionary intent of a vulgar Marxism and according to an ethic of *care* as a mobilizing point for practice, conscientization can be framed as the realization of relationality and the coming-to of the cultural studies scholar. Slater (Chapter 7) highlights this point:

> To care is to relate. To create a just and sustainable world, we need to relate differently. The methods through which one comes to know and produce particular relations to things can direct for what and how we care.

Caring about what happens in the world is for Slater a process of becoming; of becoming aware, of becoming *critically* aware. This is conscientization as an orientation for the deep structure of cultural studies. To care about one's Self, one's colleagues, one's discipline, and most significantly the world as inhabited, is to realize conscientization.

Conscientization presents as the outcome of the 'radical contextualisation' that Hammer and Kellner (2009) cite. Conscientization in this sense corresponds to "not only changing how people think about themselves, their relationship to others and the world, but also in energising … struggles that further possibilities for living" (Hammer and Kellner 2009: 92). Cultural studies' interest in culture is well placed to respond accordingly.

Surface Structure: The Methods of Cultural Studies

I do not seek to rehearse accounts from the scholarship of cultural studies with a discussion of the various techniques for *doing* cultural studies here.

This is not the orientation a consideration of the surface structure of cultural studies' signature pedagogies should take. There will always be multiple ways of doing things in cultural studies, derived from a variety of techniques for applying method that respond to the requirements of the moment. Bailey and Hall's (1992) suggestion that "different strategies ... are right in different locations and at different moments" carries this intention and speaks to the creative dynamism that might be deployed in the name of cultural studies (in Grossberg 1994: 6). This also brings to mind a more recent assessment from Grossberg (2010):

> Cultural studies [is] something that you make up as you go, as a project that reshapes itself in attempts to respond to new conjunctures as problem-spaces. (1)

Could there be any better orientation toward a cultural studies practice?

The approach to the surface structure suggested here instead looks beyond the technique of enacting a cultural studies practice to ask questions about what comes prior to this. Here is where the deep structure translates into practice—into the surface structure. Methodologically, Elspeth Probyn's (1993) suggestion that we "think the social through [the] self" (3), or of giving credence to doing something but with clear understanding of the intent that drives this doing, provides a useful cue for considering the surface structure. The way that *intent*—as the motivation toward practice—is configured and translated into action carries as an expression of the epistemological conditions of the deep structure.

For cultural studies this involves selecting methods of inquiry as they suit the moment. Rutten, Rodman, Wright, and Soetaert's (2013) discussion of critical literacies articulates this point, as does Ann Gray's (2002) account of ethnography in (and for) cultural studies. Understanding the split between 'method' and 'methodology', or the techniques deployed in the conduct of practice, and the epistemological orientations that prefigure this practice are fundamental to this consideration of how the doing of cultural studies actually comes to be done. But again, regardless of the explicit method applied in the doing of cultural studies, it is with the translation of the epistemological bases articulated through the deep structure into the meaningful practice of the surface structure that demarcates the nature of the signature pedagogy.

There are innumerable ways cultural studies comes to be done, and the point of this book has not been to catalogue these, even if this were considered possible. What is at stake, however, and what this book has hoped to suggest, is that a cognizant cultural studies is one that takes account of itself *through* the cultural studies scholar. The methods of doing cultural studies are hence always contextualized at the point of encounter, mobilized in practice through the cultural studies scholar as the moment declares.

Some Final Remarks

As noted at the outset of this chapter, what I hope this volume has provoked is the consideration of what cultural studies might now orient toward in its contemporary formulations. Set among contexts of dramatic change within publics and higher education, cultural studies is at risk of redundancy at the same time as it is well placed to respond to the challenges these contexts present. Written through the work of its practitioners, and the disciplinary formulations that cultural studies requires, practiced as these are within the context of the institution, the urgency for cultural studies is at present one of understanding not only its place within the dynamics of these contexts, but in also coming to terms with the articulation of its purpose.

Suggested in this chapter, drawing as it has on the earlier chapters, is a consideration of a signature pedagogy for cultural studies. I stress, however, that this remains incomplete in an effort to encourage further consideration of the multiple ways cultural studies comes to be done. But at core, it will remain that there are central provocations that drive cultural studies' purpose/s and certain formulations that define its practice. If accounted for and articulated, it will emerge that cultural studies will be able take stock of its project and the position it seeks to hold in responding to the world.

It is in these terms that I invite readers of this volume to engage with the narratives contained here, to consider the practice that they engage in the name of cultural studies, and to contemplate a renewed project for cultural studies that has at its core a clearly demarcated signature pedagogy.

References

Agger, B. (1992). *Cultural studies as critical theory*. London, Falmer Press.
Bailey, D., and Hall, S. (1992). Critical decade: black British photography in the 80s. *Ten*, 8 (3): 15–23.
Beck, D., & Eno, J. (2012). Signature pedagogy: a literature review of social studies and technology research. *Computers in the Schools*, 29 (1–2), 70–94.
Bennett, J. (2010). *Vibrant matter: a political ecology of things*. Durham, Duke University Press.
Bennett, T. (2015). Cultural studies and the culture concept. *Cultural Studies*, 29 (4): 546–68.
Burdick, J., and Sandlin, J.A. (2010). Inquiry as answerability: toward a methodology of discomfort in researching critical public pedagogies. *Qualitative Inquiry*, 16 (5): 349–60.
Calder, L. (2006). Uncoverage: toward a signature pedagogy for the history survey. *Journal of American History*, 92 (4): 1358–70.
Darder, A. (2009). *Reinventing Paulo Freire: a pedagogy of love*. Boulder, Westview Press.
Ellsworth, E. (2005). *Places of learning: media, architecture, pedagogy*. New York, Routledge.
Freire, P. (2007). *Pedagogy of the oppressed*. New York, Continuum.
Giroux, H.A. (2004). Cultural studies, public pedagogy, and the responsibility of intellectuals. *Communication and Critical/Cultural Studies*. 1 (1): 59–79.

Gray, A. (2002). *Research practice for cultural studies: ethnographic methods and lived cultures*. London, Sage.
Grossberg, L. (1994). Introduction: bringin' it all back home—pedagogy and cultural studies. In Giroux, H.A., and McLaren, P. (eds). *Between borders: pedagogy and the politics of cultural studies* (p. 14). New York, Routledge.
Grossberg, L. (2010). *Cultural studies in a future tense*. Durham, Duke University Press.
Hammer, R., and Kellner, D. (2009). *Media/cultural studies: critical approaches*. New York, Peter Lang.
Hickey, A. and Reynolds, P., and McDonald, L. (2015). Understanding community to engage community: the use of qualitative research techniques in local government community engagement. *Asia Pacific Journal of Public Administration*, 37 (1): 4–17.
Johnson, R. (1986). What is cultural studies anyway? *Social Text*, 16: 38–80.
Marginson, S., and Considine, M. (2000). *The enterprise university: power, governance and reinvention in Australia*. Cambridge, Cambridge University Press.
McRobbie, A. (1994). *Postmodernism and popular culture*. London, Routledge.
Miller, T. (2012). *Blow up the humanities*. Philadelphia, Temple University Press.
Nussbaum, M. (2010). *Not for profit: why democracy needs the humanities*. Princeton, Princeton University Press.
O'Connor, J. (2012). We need to talk about cultural studies. *Cultural Studies Review*, 18 (2): 330–40.
Probyn, E. (1993). *Sexing the self: gendered positions in cultural studies*. New York, Routledge.
Rodman, G. (2015). *Why cultural studies?* Malden, John Wiley and Sons.
Rutten, K., Rodman, G.B., Wright, H.K., and Soetaert, R. (2013). Cultural studies and critical literacies. *International Journal of Cultural Studies*, 16 (5): 443–56.
Schulman, L.S. (2005). Signature pedagogies in the professions. *Daedalus*, 134 (3): 52–59.
Serres, M. (2014). *Times of crisis: what the financial crisis revealed and how to reinvent our lives and futures*. New York, Bloomsbury.
Serres, M. (2015). *Thumbelina: the culture and technology of the millennials*. London, Rowman and Littlefield.
Sparks, C. (1996). The evolution of cultural studies. In Storey, J. *What is cultural studies? A reader* (pp. 14–30). London, Arnold.
Thomson, P., and Hall, C. (2014). The signature pedagogies of creative practitioners. In Westphal, K., Stadler-Altmann, U., Schittler, S., and Lohfield, W. (eds). *Räume kultureller bildung: nationale und transnationale perpsektiven* (pp. 76–91). Weinheim, Juventa.
Turner, G. (2012). *What's become of cultural studies?* London, Sage.
Whatmore, S. (2002). *Hybrid geographies: natures, cultures, spaces*. London, Sage.
Williams, R. (1962). *Communications: Britain in the sixties*. Baltimore, Penguin.
Williams, R. (1977). *Marxism and literature*. Oxford, Oxford University Press.

Contributors

Rob Garbutt is Senior Lecturer in Cultural Studies and Written Communication at Southern Cross University. His research is typically place-based. As a teaching and research scholar, this interest is refracted into a spectrum of projects that consider how ways of belonging, cultural studies pedagogies, and research methods function in practice. Rob's research often includes an element of community engagement. Rob's first book, *The Locals*, was published in 2011. He is also coauthor of *Inside Australian Culture*, published in 2015.

Andrew Hickey is Associate Professor in Communications at the University of Southern Queensland, and President of the Cultural Studies Association of Australasia. Andrew is an ethnographer and has undertaken large-scale projects exploring community, the public pedagogies of place in urban developments, and the enhancement of social harmony with partners including the Canadian Government, Education Queensland, the Toowoomba Regional Council, and a number of community organizations. He is author of *Cities of Signs: Learning the Logic of Urban Spaces* (Peter Lang 2012).

Gregory Martin is Director, Teaching Technologies, Innovation and Support and Core Member, Cosmopolitan Civil Societies Research Centre, University of Technology, Sydney. Gregory has negotiated a number of roles including educator, activist, and researcher in both school- and community-based contexts. He completed his graduate studies in the United States at Kent State University and the University of California, Los Angeles. In 2008, he moved to UTS where he has been involved in both the adult and teacher education programs as well as other areas of the university including Jumbunna Indigenous House of Learning. Gregory has published widely on critical pedagogy, community, and do-it-yourself pedagogies and is on the editorial boards of the *Journal for Critical Education Policy Studies*, *Australian Journal of Adult Learning*, *Education Policy Futures*, and the *International Journal for Critical Pedagogy*.

Baden Offord holds the Dr Haruhisa Handa Chair of Human Rights Education and is Professor of Cultural Studies and Human Rights and Director of the Centre for Human Rights Education at Curtin University. His research is focused on dissenting knowledge(s) through attention to questions of identity, belonging, power, place, and everyday culture. Baden's books include *Homosexual Rights as Human Rights* (2003), *Landscapes of Exile* (2008) and, *Inside Australian Culture* (2015). He is a contributing editor for *The Review of Education, Pedagogy and Cultural Studies* and serves on the editorial boards of *Cultural Studies Review* and *The International Journal of Human Rights*.

Rebecca Olive is a Postdoctoral Research Fellow at The University of Waikato. With interests in recreational sport and physical activities, gender, social media, ethnographic research methods, and theories of power, ethics, and pedagogies, she has published in journals including *International Journal of Cultural Studies*, *Continuum*, *Media International Australia*, and *Sport, Education and Society*. In addition she continues to write a blog, *Making Friends With the Neighbours*, and contributes to surf media, festivals, and exhibitions.

Kim Satchell is a mid-north coast of New South Wales surfer, poet, performer, writer, and academic based at Southern Cross University and an educator/trainer for the North Coast Institute of TAFE. His research interests are in cultural studies and the ecological humanities particularly concerning the literature of place. He has written extensively on these areas and has future projects currently in planning exploring the cultural heritage of the Solitary Island Marine Reserve and its adjacent communities.

Katrina Schlunke is Associate Professor of Cultural Studies and Director of the Transforming Cultures group at the University of Technology Sydney. She is the author of *Bluff Rock: Autobiography of a Massacre*, coauthor of *Cultural Theory in Everyday Practice*, and coeditor of the *Cultural Studies Review*. She has undertaken research exploring the intersections of Indigenous knowledges and representations of the past along with an Australian Research Council funded project looking at Captain Cook in the popular imagination.

Lisa Slater is Senior Lecturer in Cultural Studies at the University of Wollongong. Her research seeks to understand the intercultural formation of settler and Indigenous Australia. Her current projects include an examination of contemporary Indigenous cultural practices, with a particular focus on the ways cultural production—most recently cultural festivals—provide insight into the expression of Indigenous sovereignty and interventions in settler colonial authority. She is currently writing a monograph that analyzes "good" white women, anxiety, and Indigeneity, with recent projects taking a strong focus on remote and rural Australia.

Amanda Third is Principal Research Fellow in Digital Social and Cultural Research in the Institute for Culture and Society at Western Sydney University and Research Program Leader in the Young and Well

Cooperative Research Centre. Her current research investigates the sociocultural dimensions of young people's technology practices, with an emphasis on the practices of marginalized young people. She currently leads an Australian Research Council project that investigates contemporary knowledge brokering practices in the context of the Technology and Wellbeing Roundtable. She has published widely on a range of cultural studies topics, and is author of *Gender and the Political: Deconstructing the Female Terrorist* (Palgrave 2014).

Graeme Turner is Emeritus Professor of Cultural Studies at the University of Queensland, and was founding Director for the Centre of Critical and Cultural Studies (2000–2012). His research has covered a wide range of forms and media – literature, film, television, radio, new media, journalism, and popular culture. He has published 23 books with national and international academic presses; including (with Anna Cristina Pertierra) *Locating Television: Zones of Consumption* (Routledge, 2013), *What's Become of Cultural Studies?* (Sage, 2012) and *Ordinary People and the Media: The Demotic Turn* (Sage, 2010). A past president of the Australian Academy of the Humanities (2004–2007), an ARC Federation Fellow (2006–2011) and Convenor of the ARC-funded Cultural Research Network (2006–2010), Graeme Turner has had considerable engagement with federal research and higher education policy. He is only the second humanities scholar to serve on the Prime Minister's Science, Engineering and Innovation Council.

Megan Watkins is Associate Professor in the School of Education and member of the Institute for Culture and Society, Western Sydney University. Her research interests lie in the cultural analysis of education and the formation of human subjectivities. In particular, her work engages with issues of pedagogy, embodiment, discipline, and affect and the interrelation of these to human agency. These interests mesh with her exploration of the impact of cultural diversity on education and the ways in which different cultural practices can engender divergent habits and dispositions to learning. Megan also has extensive experience as a literacy educator, conducting pioneering work in the field of genre-based approaches to teaching writing and postprogressivist pedagogies. She is a recipient of two Australian Research Council (ARC) Linkages grants: *Rethinking Multiculturalism/Reassessing Multicultural Education* and *Discipline and Diversity: Cultural Practices and Dispositions of Learning*.

Linda Wight is Lecturer in Literature and Screen Studies at Federation University Australia. Her PhD dissertation examined the depiction of masculinities in recent science fiction texts recognized by the James Tiptree, Jr. Award for doing something new with gender. She is currently continuing her research into masculinities in science fiction and has published several papers on this topic. Linda is also currently working on a series of papers exploring the construction of gender in the most recent trilogy of James Bond films.

Index

Action Research 133, 134–39, 143, 147
Activation 18, 51–65, 201, 206
Ahmed, S. 98, 120
Allen, J. 27–31
Ang, I. 93–4, 153–54, cultural intelligence 93–4
Aquarian Archive 24, 30
Aquarius and Beyond community conference 24, 26, 30–6
Aquarius Festival of University Arts 27
Australian Government *Collaborative Research Network* xiii, 3
Australian Professional Standards for Teachers 136
Australian Research Council 134, 146

Barcan, R. 12, 13, 166, being "good enough" 12
Beachcombing 84–8
Belonging in the Rainbow Region 26, 65
Bennett, T. 202, 205
Birmingham Centre for Critical Cultural Studies 25, 54, 149, 176
Blue Mountains, Australia 168, 171
Bringing Them Home report 119
Bushfire: see *natural disaster*
Butler, J. 96–8, 112, 120
Byron Bay 53, 181, 185, 188–89, 192

Cantonese 141
Care 19, 123–27, 208, 211, care as interest 19, 20, 116–21, 123, 208–9, care of the self 87–8, 118, 121, "care package" 172
Catastrophe capitalism 172
Child Migrant Education Program 133
Clifford, J. 169
Community engagement 18, 35–6, 94, 105, 134, 207

Context: contexts of possibility 202, as disciplinary 7, 9, 12, 17, 25, 53, 55–6, 58, 64, 154–55, 160, 166, 197, 206, 213, as institutional xv–xvi, 12, 17, 25, 35, 52, 167–68, 197, 208, 213, as object of study 25, 35, 48, 83–4, 155, 168, 171–72, 176–77, 185–86, 202, as personal 5–6, 8, 10, 18, 39, 43, 62, 188–93, 197, 208, 211
Couldry, N. 54
Critical pedagogy: *see* pedagogy
Cultural Studies on the Divide xiii, xiv, 3–4, 9–12, 15, 18, 22
Cultural studies: and human rights 58–60, as intervention 32, 149–50, as practice 17, 21, 25, 33, 155, 165, 177, 196, 212, crisis narratives in 16, decline xvi, 6, 15–17, 196–99, doing cultural studies xvi, 3–7, 9–11, 14–15, 39, 52, 58–60, 64, 156, 159, 165, 199–201, 211–12, epistemologies of xvii, 9, 126, 151, 199, 201, hope for xvii, 153, life lessons from 166, methodological irreverence in 204

Dasein 14–15, 122, 200
Deaths in Custody report 119
deCerteau, M. 104–8, 111, 114, tactics 104, 106
Deleuze, G. 73–85, 87–8, 208
DIY pedagogy 20, 149–52, 156–160
Dunstan, G. 27–31

Ellsworth, E. 201
Engaged research: as engagement 94–9, and knowledge 108–11, and performativity 97, *see also* Pedagogy
English as a second language (ESL) 133, 137, 146
Evers, C. 186, 191

Index

Foucault, M. 76, 77, 80, 118–19, 167, 173, 179–81, 184, "Discipline and Punish" 167, history of the present 167
Freire, P. 25, 62, 202
French (language) 141

Giroux, H. xvi, 5, 20, 25, 40–1, 46–7, 53, 56, 153, 159, border pedagogy 20, 153, public intellectuals 159
Giroux, S. 55
Grossberg, L. xvi, 14, 45, 58, 65, 159, 198, 212
Guattari, F. 74–6

Hall, S. xvi, 17, 25, 55, 57, 64, 93, 138, 160
Haraway, D. 116, 127
Hebdige, D. 149, 160
Heidegger, M. 14–15, 122–23
Hickey–Moody, A. 151

Ivory tower, see the university

Japanese (language) 141

Kantorowicz, E. 102–13
Kellner, D. 4, 62, 211
Knowledge ecologies 19, 20

Language background other than English (LBOTE) 133–35, 139–42
Little publics 151, 157

Mandarin 141
Marcus, G. 112, 169
Masculinities 18, 39–49, hegemonic masculinity 40, 41, 43, 47
Ministerial Council on Education, Employment, Training and Youth Affairs (MCEETYA) 134
Muecke, S. 74, 83,
Mulan 142
Multicultural cafes 142
Multicultural education 20, 133–37, 143–45, 154

Natural disaster 20, 168, as crisis 21, as state of emergency 171, destruction 174–75, disaster assistance 171–74
New South Wales 20, 25, 27, 52, 53, 133, 169, 181, 210, Board of Studies, Teaching and Educational Standards (BOSTES) 134, Department of Education and Communities (DEC) 134, 146
Nimbin 26–9
Nimbin Aquarius Softlick 24
Nimbun Hemp Embassy 33
Nimbuns 28

O'Connor, J. 203
Offord, B. 24, 30
Other 135, 151, alterity 18–19, 191
Other-than-human 19

Pedagogies of self 5–9, 10, 12–15, 18–20, 151, 158, 197–201, 208, 211
Pedagogies of the field 3–4, 6, 12, 55, 84, 156–58, 197, 200
Pedagogies of the institution 6, 12, 57–8, 197, 208, 213
Pedagogy: and subjectivity 5–7, 10, 39–41, 165–68, 185–87, 201, as activation 3, 8, 54, 64, 150, 198, as diagnosis 4–5, as disciplinary terrain 4–5, 8–12, 21–2, as engagement xvii, 24–37, 52, 96, 111, conscientisation (*conscientização*) 211, counter-pedagogies 156–60, creative practice as 71–88, 176–78, critical pedagogy 47, 72–3, 152–56, 202, 209, critical performative pedagogy 46–9, 84, 151, 157, 176–78, definition 4, 10, 13–15, 73, 76, 80, 123, decline in cultural studies xv–xvi, 15–18, 57, of place 86–8, 168–69, 176–77, teaching xvi, 3, 42–5, 55–8, 60–5, 133–37, 138–39, 143, 176–77, see also signature pedagogy
Penrith City Council 172
Probyn, E. 190, 191

Racism: pedagogy of 119–123, 141–42
Rainbow Power Company 27
Reverend Billy: see Talen, B.
Rodman, G. 16–17, "the sigh" 17, 199

Salvation Army 171–72
Scholar-activism 155–58
Schooling 134–37, 147
Schulman, L. 199, see also signature pedagogies
Science fiction 18, 39, 41–9, definitions 41, teaching science fiction 45–9
Self: Self-as-scholar 6–9, 13–15, 39, 197, 200–1, vulnerabilities 11
Serres, M. 74, 79–82, 86, 207, 208

Shacking-up 84–8
Signature pedagogies 10–11, 13, 17, 21, 199–204, deep structure 200–1, 209–12, habits of mind 10, 200, implicit structure 11, 199–201, 205, surface structure 200–1, 211–12
Sini, M. 6
Southern Cross University 29, 30, 34, 36, 51–5
Stone-Mediatore, S. 159
Storytelling 28, 31, 32, 156–60
Surfing 20–1, 75, 88, 179–93, and the body 79, 180, 182–83, 192, gender and 179–84, 188–92
Sydney University 28

Talen, B. 206–07
The Dream 29
The School of Life 165–66
The University: as enterprise 156, as site of cultural studies practice 3, 10, 12, 22, 24–6, 30–2, 39–41, 52–54, 96–101, 151–55, 165, 197, as Ivory Tower 96, 101–4, 111, 113, 152, legitimacy within 15–16, 58, 61, 64–5, 155–56, 197, precarious employment in xv
Trend, D. 10, 13
Turner, G. 25, 52, 55, 113, 149, 199, "Cultural Studies 101" 25, "What's Become of Cultural Studies" 51, 64

University of Southern Queensland xiii, xiv, 3
University of Western Sydney 137, 146
University of Wollongong 116
Unruly Subjects: Citizenship 55, 60–2

Walt Disney 142
Wenger, E. 95
Williams, R. 25, 54, 153, 209, culture as ordinary 199, 202, whole way of life 54–5, 202
Witnessing 119–120